# UNIVERSITY OF CALIFORNIA PRESS

Berkeley • New York • Los Angeles • London

TITLE:          JAPAN'S HIGH SCHOOLS

AUTHOR:       Thomas P. Rohlen

PRICE:                    $35.00 cloth; $10.95 paperback
NO. OF PAGES:          363 pages with 18 halftones, 16 tables,
PUBLICATION DATE:    27 September 1983                    3 figures

---

*This review copy is sent to you with our compliments.*
*We request that two copies of your review be mailed to us.*

For further information contact:

2223 FULTON STREET      or    50 EAST 42nd ST. Rm. 513
BERKELEY, CA 94720             NEW YORK, N.Y. 10017
(415) 642-4562                      (212) 687-8340

# Japan's High Schools

Published under the auspices of
The Center for Japanese Studies
University of California, Berkeley

# JAPAN'S HIGH SCHOOLS

## Thomas P. Rohlen

UNIVERSITY OF CALIFORNIA PRESS

Berkeley • Los Angeles • London

University of California Press
Berkeley and Los Angeles, California

University of California Press, Ltd.
London, England

*Library of Congress Cataloging in Publication Data*

Rohlen, Thomas P.
Japan's high schools.

Bibliography: p.
Includes index.
1. High schools—Japan.   2. Education, Secondary—
Japan.   3. Educational sociology—Japan.
4. Educational anthropology—Japan.   I. Title.
LZ1316.R63   1983        373.52        82-16118
            ISBN 0-520-04801-6

Printed in the United States of America

1  2  3  4  5  6  7  8  9

*For Ginger, Katie, Duke, Brooks*
*Alison, Michael, and Chris,*
*with the wish that your school years*
*be rich in challenge and joy*

# Contents

# Preface

S IMPLE CURIOSITY initially led me to the study of Japanese high
schools. My own four years in a midwestern suburban high
school had been a poignant and formative time, and I still recall viv-
idly the excitement, the pain and the wonderment of beginning to
shape my own destiny. Looking back as an anthropologist I also
came to see that many fundamental qualities of American culture
were epitomized in the high school experience, and I found myself
wanting to find out what the equivalent experiences were in Japan. I
had also just completed a study of a Japanese bank, and I hoped to
learn about a different kind of Japanese organization, one reshaped
by the American occupation and strongly influenced by a radical
teachers' union.

When I went to Japan for thirteen months of fieldwork in 1974,
the country was not the hotly debated topic that it is in the world
today. I had no expectation that what I was about to study would
prove to be of instructive interest to American educators, or that Japanese education would begin to impress me as a significant element
in American understanding of Japan's economic success. Yet during
the last two years, as this book has taken shape, Japan's industrial
prowess and social order have captured the attention of much of the
world. Japan, whether perceived as a competitive threat or as a
model of efficiency, now merits careful study.

During the late 1970s, furthermore, secondary education in the United States came under fundamental review. We have witnessed an extended period of decline in the basic skills taught and a growing confusion around priorities and approaches to the universal instruction of our adolescents. Rather than just exporting our educational ideas to the rest of the world, we have come to a point where we want to learn what others are doing. Japan's educational system is indeed impressive, and knowledge of it is important to any larger understanding of that nation; but it has many faults, and a certain price is paid for its achievements. I have sought to present both the strengths and weakness of Japanese education in a balanced manner. With Japan's recent notoriety have come facile generalizations and dangerous oversimplifications. If this book serves to correct some of these, I will be amply rewarded.

My original intention was to write an ethnographic account of a particular institution, but the times called for a broader approach, one that would place high schools in the larger Japanese social, economic, and cultural context. An expanded focus has led to levels of comparison and generalization quite beyond the careful anchoring in observational data typical of the ethnographic approach. I have no regrets about working on a broader plain, but it has entailed certain problems. For example, in places I refer to "we Americans" or "the Japanese" when describing cultural inclinations as if there is unanimity of opinion in each country, and yet I am perfectly aware that variation and disagreements exist. Comparative statements involving whole nations often require such language, and a certain nimbleness of thought on the part of readers is almost a prerequisite.

I should also like to point out that my comparisons are made almost entirely between Japan and the United States. I know no other country nearly as well, and for this I apologize to readers with other backgrounds.

My research in Japan was entirely dependent on the goodwill and hospitality of teachers and administrators who gave me their trust and friendship as they patiently guided my learning. I came to admire them for their dedication and to feel deep appreciation to them for sharing their work and their lives with me. To the several hundred teachers in Kobe who cannot be listed by name, I want to express my heartfelt gratitude. I only wish that this book could repay them for their kindness.

Financial assistance was received from the Japan Foundation and from the Committee for Faculty Research at the University of California, Santa Cruz. I gratefully acknowledge this support. Professors Yoshida Teigo and Ueda Hitoshi provided me with my first introductions and were always ready to give further help. I am also indebted to many people for encouragement, and for the special insights gained in discussions of my work, including Ed Beauchamp, Harumi Befu, Keith Brown, William Cummings, Ronald Dore, Sue Hanley, Victor Kobayashi, Hugh Patrick, Dan Okimoto, Henry Rosovsky, Ezra Vogel, and Kozo Yamamura. My former students, Nancy Ukai, Sharon Traweek, Syoko Saito, and Sharon Noguchi, have provided me with valuable information over many years, always with a warm note of interest. Chiyoko Ishibashi helped me with some difficult translation work. To my friend Richard Pascale I owe a special debt for his regular support and his insistence that I continue in pursuit of the larger issues involved in Japanese education.

Marilyn Rose helped with the typing, and I received excellent editorial assistance and encouragement from Margo Paddock and Meryl Lanning. Phyllis Killen at the University of California Press was, as always, of great help.

Most of all I want to thank my wife and children for sharing with me the long months of fieldwork and the often exasperating years of analysis and writing. They patiently put up with the moods, mysteries and dislocations of this kind of work and offered the affectionate support without which I could not have proceeded.

# Introduction

Education is the cheap defense of nations.
EDMUND BURKE

THE ULTIMATE foundation of a nation is the quality of its people. Over the long haul, their diligence and thrift, their creativity and cooperation, and their skill and orderliness compound to shape a nation's level of achievement. Certainly such things as natural resources, great leaders, a talented elite, and astute policies also have a significant influence on the general performance of societies. We regularly study these more apparent considerations, but too often we fail to come to grips with the fundamental issue of the quality of average daily behavior in national populations. International differences in average behavior are indeed difficult to measure and assess. Often they are relegated to the residual category of culture and then essentially ignored. Nevertheless, how well a population performs the basic tasks of social existence when multiplied out day after day, year after year, is the underlying basis and sense of dynamic for key institutions that in turn shape a nation's place among all nations. The historical rise and fall of civilizations, in other words, rests heavily on such assumed matters as socialization, fundamental skills, and general morality. In our modern sophistication, we are prone to discount the significance of these basic issues in analyzing long-term national developments.

Japan is a case in point. A nation pitiably poor in natural resources,

I

Japan has the highest population density per acre of arable land in the world; nearly all her energy and raw materials must be imported. In this century, she has rarely enjoyed the leadership of strong or brilliant individuals, suffering great destruction in World War II as a result. Japan's bureaucratic elite has established highly effective industrial policies in the postwar period, and her managers have shown great skill in creating efficient economic institutions, but these would have amounted to very little without the crucial ingredient of superb human capital. Crediting Japan's bureaucrats and managers with Japan's success—a success so in fashion today—misses a crucial point. These men could not have produced what has been accomplished only by millions of Japanese working together.

This book is about how that population is being educated and developed, and the results are assessed in comparison with the United States. The quality of a citizenry is the product of a number of basic institutions, most notably the family, religion, and schools. Of these, schools are the most accessible, the most comparable across cultures, and the most responsive to public policy. High schools occupy a particular place in the socialization process. Their students stand at the threshold of adulthood, reflecting the work of parents, teachers, and schools. At the same time, the final steps in shaping a national citizenry are clearly evident in high school education. High schools illustrate the manner and the intensity of the educational effort, and the outcome of that effort is reflected in the conduct of high school students.

In studying high schools, we not only learn what socialization occurs there, but we have an opportunity to gauge its results. Further, as the end point of mass education, high schools reveal the disparity in skills and habits achieved by members of the same generation, thus allowing us to assess the matter of equality. Finally, because adolescent minds present few barriers to difficult ideas, high school is an excellent point along the educational path to take a close look at the meaning of what is taught—the cultural, political, and intellectual implications of the process.

Japan has surpassed the United States in popular education. The two nations lead the industrial world in percentage of young people entering high school (both above 95 percent), yet in Japan high school is not compulsory. Fewer than 75 percent of American youths took high school diplomas in 1980, whereas the Japanese now gradu-

**Table 1**

Educational Outcome, United States and Japan, for Persons Aged Seventeen in 1974 (in percentages)

|  | Japan* | | United States† | |
|---|---|---|---|---|
|  | *Boys* | *Girls* | *Boys* | *Girls* |
| Graduated from high school | 90 | 91 | 73 | 77 |
| Attended college or junior college | 44 | 32 | 47 | 44 |
| Graduated with B.A. or equivalent | 39 | 12 | 25 | 24 |

SOURCES: Data from United States Department of Health, Education and Welfare, Education Division, *Digest of Education Statistics* (Washington, D.C.: Government Printing Office, 1975); and Mombushō, *Waga Kuni Kyōiku Suijun: 1975* (Tokyo: Okurashō Insatsu Kyoku, 1976).

* Figures represent expected outcomes based on 1973 pattern.

† Excludes persons who may attend college or gain degrees more than one year after their age group.

ate 89 percent from high school (Table 1). And, contrary to American experience, the Japanese have not had to seriously sacrifice quality in their extension of a secondary education to nearly everyone. On international tests of both science and math, Japanese mean scores are higher than those of any other country. The degree of variation in ability among Japanese students is also shown to be very low (Tables 2 and 3), meaning that equality of achievement is notable. Such accomplishments must have something to do with the prowess of Japan's workers and the success of her economy. In fact, although the average level of Japanese intellectual skill and knowledge is high, equally noteworthy is the high level of orderliness and diligence in the general population. Education has something to do with the fact that social problems in Japan are small by Western standards. We must understand how Japanese are taught and how they are socialized if we are to gain insight into the underlying strengths of the country.

American secondary education seems to be in perpetual crisis. Test scores have declined and private school enrollments have risen. Demoralization has spread and increasing school violence seems to follow. The goals and institutional will of secondary schools have come into serious question. From decade to decade our priorities

**Table 2**

Achievement in Mathematics by Thirteen-Year-Olds, 1960–1964

| Nation | Mean | Coefficient of Variation |
|--------|------|--------------------------|
| Japan | 31.2 | .542 |
| Belgium | 27.2 | .542 |
| Finland | 24.1 | .411 |
| The Netherlands | 23.9 | .665 |
| Australia | 20.2 | .693 |
| England | 19.3 | .881 |
| Scotland | 19.1 | .764 |
| France | 18.3 | .678 |
| United States | 16.2 | .821 |
| Sweden | 15.7 | .689 |

SOURCE: Torstein Husen, ed., *International Study of Achievement in Mathematics: A Comparison of Twelve Countries*, vol. 2 (New York: John Wiley and Sons, 1967), p. 22.

shift radically, and the result is a sense of profound contradiction among the many goals of our population.

Rather than making persistent efforts to raise the average level of our human resources, we seem to have resigned ourselves to compensatory technology and other techniques of "foolproofing" our basic production systems by building in the assumption of a low, even declining common denominator. We have become a society with a low expectation of the average citizen. Coping with the human factor in this way creates a vicious circle of declining standards leading to declining expectations. Now a new national administration proposes, in the name of states' rights and budgetary constraint, to relinquish responsibility for improving the situation. But this is not actually a very significant change. We have, in fact, been liquidating our human capital base for some time.

Given the erosion of the American family and the declining commitment to parenting among the young, the troubles of our schools are all the more alarming. The reader will find the contrast with Japan sobering. I say this not because I intend to hold up Japanese education as an example to be emulated, but because once we are aware of its approach and its achievements, we cannot avoid seeing

**Table 3**

Achievement in Science by Persons Aged About Fourteen, 1970

| Nation | Middle School Sample | Mean Coefficient of Variation |
|---|---|---|
| Japan | 31.2 | .474 |
| Hungary | 29.1 | .436 |
| Australia | 24.6 | .545 |
| New Zealand | 24.2 | .533 |
| Federal Republic of Germany | 23.7 | .485 |
| Sweden | 21.7 | .539 |
| United States | 21.6 | .537 |
| Scotland | 21.4 | .664 |
| England | 21.3 | .662 |
| Belgium (Flemish) | 21.2 | .434 |
| Finland | 20.5 | .517 |
| Italy | 18.5 | .551 |
| The Netherlands | 17.8 | .562 |

SOURCE: Data from L. C. Comber and John P. Keeves, *Science Achievement in Nineteen Countries* (New York: John Wiley and Sons, 1973), pp. 159, 108.

ourselves and our problems more clearly. Japanese high schools are a mirror for Americans, but not a model.

Ironically, what the Japanese have accomplished is not much appreciated in Japan. Perhaps public education is a universal scapegoat because expectations are unattainably high, but the fact remains that most Japanese find strong reasons to complain. A powerful leftist teachers' union sees education as creating inequality and serving the interests of the establishment. Parents complain that their children work too hard and worry too much about passing entrance exams. Traditionalists see postwar education as undermining basic Japanese culture and values. There is ample evidence for each of these criticisms.

Foreign observers of Japanese society and education have reflected the Japanese criticisms, especially those centering on the entrance exam competition. Many have echoed the litany of complaints about how exam pressures are responsible for high youth suicide rates, nervous disorders, and even delinquency. As a result, foreign readers have generally held the opinion that Japanese education is notable for its excesses rather than its accomplishments. Recently, however, a fresh and much more substantial perspective has been introduced by William K. Cummings, a sociologist who has examined elementary education in Kyoto in considerable detail.[1] He concludes that Japanese education is praiseworthy on many accounts, including the high standards achieved in basic education, the quality of instruction offered in the arts and music, the success in teaching orderly behavior and social sensitivity, and the broad equality of opportunity established by the compulsory school system.

I am much impressed by Cummings' arguments, and this book supports his perspective in some key respects. I seriously disagree with him about the overall character of Japanese education through twelfth grade, however. The addition of the secondary school level to the picture Cummings draws greatly alters some of the qualities he finds so appealing. This book argues against his judgments of the overall Japanese accomplishment in terms of both equality and the quality of instruction. It also evaluates the role of the teachers' union from a different perspective. I have aimed at putting the admirable and the objectionable into the same framework, in recognition that they are systematically related in Japanese education.

To capture this complexity and to portray the life within Japanese high schools, I conducted a year's fieldwork (1974–75) in five distinctly different high schools, representing a spectrum from the best to the most troubled schools, in the industrial port city of Kobe. During six to eight weeks at each school, I sat in on classes, interviewed teachers, studied records, and gave out questionnaires. Comparisons of the schools reveal much about the structure of social differences in Japan. And, in turn, the underlying categories, activities, values, and procedures common to all five schools reveal much about Japanese public and educational culture.

Seven years have passed since this period of fieldwork, and I have been back to Kobe several times to check details and follow subsequent developments. The ethnographic present remains 1974–75 so far as my observations are concerned, but I have attempted to update the national statistics to make this book as current as possible.

1. See Cummings (1980).

There have been changes in each of the five schools since 1975, but none has affected significantly the character of Japanese education as described in these pages.

No books or articles in English exist on Japanese high schools, and in Japanese nothing has been published of an observational nature. Documentation is minimal. Japanese scholars take their high schools for granted, and they have not studied the variety. My first objective in these pages must therefore be to describe in some detail what Japanese urban high schools are like. Beside being a necessary and legitimate end in itself, this is the first step in discussing the place of education in Japanese society and contemporary culture.

The plan of this book, then, is to move between the specifics of high schools and the relation of high schools to larger matters. After introducing the five particular high schools in Chapter One, the historical context (Chapter Two) and the social context (Chapters Three and Four) of high school education are considered. The goal is to identify the influences that have shaped high schools. The succeeding four chapters return to examining fundamental patterns of high schooling. Chapters Five through Eight constitute an ethnographic account of the Japanese high school organized around the standard topics of space and time, social organization, politics, and instruction. The goal is to consider general questions about the experience of high school as it shapes Japanese character. Finally, in Chapter Nine, the overall pattern of Japanese adolescence is considered as it is molded by education and as it compares with the American experience. The issues of efficiency, social structural variation, and contemporary culture begin to converge here. In the final chapter, some conclusions are drawn.

The structure of the book can be visualized as resembling two concentric wheels, one large and one small. The patterns of organization and practices that mark high schools are the inner wheel, from which a set of issues and questions is drawn out in separate directions like spokes to the larger wheel of more general sociological and cultural questions. The influence along each spoke is two-directional. Schools are shaped by their social environment and they contribute to it, both. No single thesis governs the arrangement. I view institutions as integral wholes and prefer to view them from many perspectives rather than to shine a single theoretical light on them. This is a matter of taste. My preference is to begin somewhat naïvely as an anthropologist set down in the midst of institutional life; from there I work back to professional concerns. The largest issues around which I have organized this study are the classic ones of social structure, culture, and national efficiency. Together they allow us to explore the broadest implications of the interrelations between education and society.

Several cautionary remarks are in order about comparisons of Japan and the United States. Whenever possible I have supplied data on American education to sharpen the sense of differences. But the two societies *are* different in some fundamental respects. For example, Japan is not ethnically or racially pluralistic. Pulling isolated statistics out of the two social worlds can be misleading if we forget that any single comparison involves many basic societal differences. My intention is to clarify, not to distort. To achieve this I must ask the reader's alert cooperation in avoiding the pitfalls of jumping to unwarranted conclusions. Statistical comparisons from different countries, moreover, rarely stand on precisely the same definitional and data collection base. Only when the statistical differences are sizable have I felt justified in presenting them and interpreting their significance.

In reading about another society, our interest is stimulated largely by contrasts with our own. This is perfectly natural and legitimate. Yet when we seek answers for our problems, we are likely to oversimplify the foreign situation and draw lessons before the many complicating factors are fully appreciated. We know that cause and effect are rarely a simple calculation in our own society, but the same level of sophisticated understanding is rarely established about other societies. This is a point worth remembering.

# I

# THE SOCIAL AND HISTORICAL CONTEXT

# 1

# Five High Schools

It is easy to grow older, but difficult to become learned.
A JAPANESE PROVERB

THE TANGIBLE stuff of education is classes, recess periods, extra-curricular activities, school regulations, homework, teachers meeting, students socializing, and all the other minutiae of daily events that occur in thousands of schools throughout the school year. Each of us has been through long years of school. If we do not regularly go back to keep in touch, however, we quickly forget details and soon succumb to the abstractions of the public dialogue about education. The daily flow of classroom life seems remote from debates about budgets and pedagogical theories. The will and con-sciousness of citizens, bureaucrats, and politicians dwell on larger questions and choices, whereas the reality of what goes on in schools seems almost immutable in its regularity.

Events in schools, that is, have a momentum of their own beyond the reach of administrative intent. What occurs in the flow of educa-tion does not always fit the abstract categories and distinctions used to shape general dialogues about the subject. We will start on the inside, with the concrete, by considering the differences in five care-fully selected Japanese high schools.

These schools are distinguished by their place in a hierarchy that is constructed by a high school entrance system that allocates each student to a secondary school on the basis of ability. Our concern here is simply to familiarize ourselves with the variety of schools such an approach produces. The five schools chosen for study represent the very top and bottom and three intermediate points in the hierarchy of high schools in Kobe. Each has a distinct orientation and subculture. Three of the five are primarily concerned with preparing their students for Japan's highly competitive university entrance exams, yet each occupies a separate niche in the competition. The two vocational schools have the official task of teaching practical skills, a job made difficult by the fact that they enroll the less able and less well-adjusted portion of each generation. The five schools thus represent five cross-sections of the educational order. In combination, they reveal much about the inner dynamics of Japanese society.

## Otani

A bell rings in the hall, the chatting dies down, and students begin to move to their seats. Shortly the sliding door opens with an irritating rattle, and the teacher steps into a nearly quiet room. The students rise, some with a studied nonchalance. Once at the lectern, the teacher nods briefly, and in haphazard fashion the students bow in return. A few boys make no pretense of following this courtesy and simply stand a bit hunched over, but here and there other students bow formally. With few exceptions, these are well-scrubbed, clean-cut teenagers who come to school with carefully prepared lunch boxes. They carry their materials neatly in almost identical book bags; Snoopy insignia are popular with the girls and "Madison Square Garden—Boxing" bags with the boys.

The subject is social studies, and for the next fifty minutes the lecturer drones on about the relation of geography to economic development in Japanese history. Those with their textbooks open can see that he seldom diverges from the day's reading assignment. He has prepared thoroughly, and his delivery is persistently serious. He is a pro, but not an entertainer. He uses no visual aids, not even a map. His delivery marches on, punctuated with a few rhetorical questions that he answers without even looking up. Anecdotal materials creep in briefly, but he assiduously avoids diversions. During the lecture the "important points" and "things to remember" are regularly pointed out as the teacher moves over the day's material. Several times an approaching test is mentioned.

The students are trying to be attentive, but it is difficult for a seventeen-year-old to sit through a full day of such lectures. Some students, mostly boys, take notes seriously. Some unobtrusively pass neatly folded messages. Several have magazines tucked inside their books out of the teacher's view. Those lucky enough to be sitting by the window bask in the warm autumn sunshine and periodically crane their necks to see what is going on outside. This is a quiet class, and almost no disciplinary action has been required all day. Just how much is being learned is another question. Only the results of the regular tests reveal the answer, as other forms of feedback from the students rarely occur.

Sitting at the back of this classroom all day causes me considerable discomfort. The lectures have generally been boring, and even the rare spitball prank offers little relief. After lunch, time seems to move especially slowly. Even I—a thirty-five-year-old possessed of a less youthful physiology than that of a student, and with all manner of lively research questions to investigate here—find the monotony almost insufferable at times. This is what my high school was like twenty years ago, I remind myself. Maybe it was not quite so dull. At least my American teachers expected answers to their questions, and they seemed to take pride in setting the textbook aside. Clearly, I am no longer used to this form of disguised imprisonment, and, knowing now that I have a choice, I am no longer ready to acquiesce.

I spent two months in Otani High School. Despite my best intentions, I was rarely able to force myself to sit through entire days with the students. Most often I sallied forth from the teachers' room to attend a few classes, breaking the routine with interviews, readings of the files, and walking observations through the halls. I waited for classes to end just as much as the students did.

During the class breaks, at lunchtime, and after school Otani abounds with high-spirited activity. Take this particular day. When the bell announces the end of the hour and the teacher leaves, pandemonium breaks loose. Some girls scurry for the door to meet their girlfriends in the hall. Some head for the washroom. A boy in a stairwell begins practicing his trumpet. A Japanese chess game is brought out from under a desk and two students pick up their match where they left off after the last period. Several others look on. A small group gathers at another desk to study a car magazine. Two boys are at the blackboard working out a physics assignment. The hallways are full of smiling, noisy kids. Then suddenly it's all over. Ten minutes have passed. The bell rings, and a great scurry begins to get back into the classrooms, to straighten desks, and to stow away gear before the next lecture begins. As the next teacher enters, all becomes quiet once more.

In the late 1960s Otani experienced a brief moment of political drama. Several students, under the leadership of a handful of college radicals, occupied the school for several weeks. Students stayed home, parents fumed, and the faculty debated what to do. The occupying students were finally expelled (and later readmitted), and a set of minor reforms was instituted, including one that made school uniforms optional. In 1975, the majority of Otani students still wore their school uniforms or elements of them. Black pants and white shirts, tennis shoes, and black jackets in winter (patterned on nineteenth-century German student uniforms) is the traditional outfit for boys, and it is still much in evidence; but one does see an occasional pair of blue jeans, and many boys skip their coats. The girls' uniform of white blouse, navy blue pleated skirt, white bobby socks, and navy blazer is often varied slightly with the substitution of a checkered blouse or the addition of a colorful sweater. However clothes-conscious the Otani girls may secretly be, they have not made much of the opportunity created by the dress code reform to move toward fashion or diversity. Modesty and conformity still prevail.

Otani teachers regularly noted that their students were "average" or "typical." Expanding on such observations, they commented: "Our students are neither very smart nor particularly slow." Most come from "stable middle-class families." Many teachers said, in effect, "They are good kids." There may be no such thing as an average high school in Japan when we take into consideration how many ways a school can be judged, but its teachers were making a generalization about Otani High School that is useful as a rough guideline in our effort to compare high schools in Kobe. Otani is an "academic" high school (futsū kōkō, literally, regular high school) belonging to the city-administered school system. Its students, about half boys and half girls, are studying a general curriculum geared to entering college. Sixty-five percent of Kobe's high school students are attending academic high schools, and in terms of ability the Otani students rank about in the middle of this group. Thus, considering the full range of high schools in the city (including vocational and night schools), Otani is above average, but not markedly so.

*Students and teacher bowing*

Otani students and teacher bow to one another at the start of a class period. The bowing is particularly formal because they are being photographed. Otani students do not wear identical uniforms.

Academic high schools like Otani are the single most numerous kind of school in Japan today. Sixty-eight percent of all secondary students are in schools with this kind of curriculum, both public and private. The public variety is somewhat more numerous and generally more highly regarded. Most of Japan's university students are produced by public academic high schools. Nationwide, about 40 percent of all graduates are now advancing to higher education, but from the public academic high schools the rate is about 70 percent. Otani is typical of this kind of school.

Otani's reputation as representative of Kobe's high schools is reinforced by the teachers' general observations about family background. Shopkeepers' children mix with those from families of white-collar workers. There are some students from blue-collar families, but not many. Only one-quarter of the mothers work. An image of respectable, stable middle-class families also results from a reading of the hundreds of family information cards in the school office. There are exceptions, but such students blend in with the others.

Otani has few discipline problems. What worries teachers, parents, and students most is the gap between student ability and educational aspirations. As children of the urban middle class, the expectation is that they will go to college. Virtually all the boys are or should be striving to enter a four-year institution. Parental pressure on most girls is notably less. Should their daughters enter a junior college or go straight into a good job, many parents will be pleased. School statistics indicate clearly just such differences of aspiration. Of the 399 students who graduated in 1974, 63 percent went directly to some form of higher education—a figure well above the national average but just about average for academic high schools across the country. The number of Otani girls matriculating to higher education upon graduation was actually slightly higher than that of boys, but most (75 percent) of the girls entered junior colleges, for which the competition is not intense. Less than 5 percent of the boys entered a junior college.

The figures concerning those who did not immediately enter higher education are also revealing. Twenty-five percent of all the girls graduating from Otani took jobs, but only 2 percent of the boys did. On the other hand, 39 percent of the boys and 8 percent of the girls chose to do a year of postgraduate study in hopes of passing some entrance exam on a second try. Typically, they were aiming at good private universities. If it is assumed that everyone in this group eventually succeeded in entering a four-year university, the final disposition of the Otani class of 1974 would be:

|  | University | Junior College | Employment |
|---|---|---|---|
| Total | 62% | 25% | 13% |
| Male | 96% | 2% | 2% |
| Female | 26% | 49% | 25% |

The above estimate fits closely with the results of a questionnaire I gave to over one hundred juniors at Otani in 1975. Ninety-nine percent of the boys and 78 percent of the girls planned to go on to higher education. The same questionnaire revealed that 18 percent of the boys, but only 4 percent of the girls, were attending a private cram school (yobikō) in the late afternoons to supplement their entrance exam preparations.

This general pattern is typical of urban academic high schools in the public school system. It reveals among other things the special burdens for university preparation that fall on boys' shoulders. If boys are of average ability, as in the Otani case, this burden can be heavy. Entrance exams are the major focus of school and parental concern. Teachers know that much of their school's reputation hinges on the record their graduates achieve on entrance exams. Most tailor their teaching to exam preparation and regularly judge one another by this standard. Inevitably, the students, the parents, and the world at large will judge academic high schools primarily on the basis of these results. As in American private secondary schooling, the most revealing information is where the graduates go to college.

Otani, however, seeks to be more than a machine for university preparation. About half the students are enrolled in some sort of after-school club activity. About one-third of the teachers are actively involved in supporting such activities. I have many warm memories of the noisy enthusiasm of Otani students on sports fields. During lectures they are rarely excited or even very interested. When three o'clock arrives, their faces light up and they find new energy. Within a few minutes tennis practice has begun, the volley-ball team is making diving saves of the coach's smashes, a rock band is warming up in the science room, and the English Speaking Society is memorizing the lyrics of a Joan Baez song. The last hours of the day are an enormous relief for those who stay in school. The Otani students actually enjoy school, or so it seemed to me, because they find ways of expressing their energy and enthusiasm at breaks and after school. Despite the tedium of lectures, students prefer school to home or work.

On one occasion when I was at Otani, a class could not turn off its break-time excitement at the bell and locked a history teacher out for fifteen minutes. Faced with his ultimatum that all would have to stay after school for an hour, the class sent a delegation to the teachers' room to apologize. This had not happened before, and my presence in the class that day may have provoked the excitement; all the same, the incident revealed a few characteristics of this particular school. The students neither fear their teachers nor do the teachers take such pranks very seriously as a threat to their authority or to the order of the school. Occasional outbursts and little jokes are not viewed as part of a discipline problem. The students' normal good conduct and regular study habits have established a basis for faculty tolerance. Compared with other schools that fall in the middle range, I found the students at Otani more playful and naïve, less burdened by the weight of their studies; yet the essential point is that in average Japanese high schools the level of order is high without undue exercise of authority. Students comply with the basic rules, written and unwritten, that protect classroom instruction.

The fun can go too far, however, as happened with one of the senior skits during Otani's *bunkasai*, or Culture Festival. The scene was a cowtown bar, complete with gunslingers at a poker table and dancing girls wearing red garters. The bad guys had started to push the girls around when in walked a version of Bruce Lee in black kung fu pants, swinging a pair of *nun chaku* sticks (Chinese traditional weapons; two blocks of hardwood connected by a chain). Using exaggerated Kabuki gestures, the skit was played out in hilarious fashion to its classic conclusion. The jokes were slightly risqué in several cases, and the cavorting of the bad guys and the dancing girls was a bit more authentic perhaps than is proper for young Japanese to effect, but to my American sensibilities the skit was a high point of creative exuberance. Rarely during my year in Japanese high schools did I witness events witty and imaginative, or as much fun as this. But most of the teachers were shaking their heads in disapproval as they talked about it later, and the principal scolded the third-year homeroom advisors for failing to closely supervise the students' production. The jokes and latent sexuality had crossed the boundaries of Japanese good taste (boundaries I had not perceived), and the teachers were responsible.

This was a line that small-town Americans might have drawn before World War II. Otani, perhaps because it is a solid middle-class institution, must keep moral standards high. What struck me as quite old-fashioned behavior on the principal's part seemed perfectly proper to the teachers and I am sure to any parents who heard of the matter. The atmosphere of relaxed student playfulness outside of class occurs within a framework of firm expectations about proper conduct that would seem highly puritanical by present American standards. This is the case in the majority of Japanese high schools.

## Nada

Nada is the most famous high school in Japan. A private boys' school, it is located in the eastern part of Kobe, several miles from

Otani. Since the mid-sixties, Nada has succeeded almost every year in placing more students in Tokyo University than any other school in the nation despite the small size of its graduating classes. Of its 220 to 225 annual graduates, the number gaining admittance to Tokyo, the nation's top university, has averaged over a hundred from 1966 to 1976. Nada's other graduates almost all take highly prized places in medical departments at lesser universities, or gain entrance to one of the other first-rank schools in Japan. The average high school student's statistical chances of eventually entering Tokyo University are about 1 in 440, but for a Nada student they are almost 1 in 2.

A history class has been in progress for a few minutes. The subject is the Meiji Restoration, the coup d'etat that opened the floodgates of change in 1868 and set Japan careening toward a modern existence. The teacher, a frail older man whose head is just visible from the back of the room, finishes his succinct review of the chronology and dramatis personae and begins firing questions at the class. What stages can we discern in the relationship between Satsuma and Choshū? What was the key internal problem within the Tokugawa house in the year 1866?

The majority of students are sitting up pretty straight now. A few continue to lounge with legs stretched out in front, somehow appearing comfortable on their hard wooden school seats—which are reminiscent of the kind now sold in antique shops in the United States. At the front is a group of boys whose hands shoot up in response to virtually every question, their faces ever alert and serious—caricatures of classroom virtue. The classroom itself is old, but hardly genteel. A nineteenth-century one-room schoolhouse with raised lectern, large blackboard, and a bank of windows on one side.

Class size is large in Japanese public high schools by American standards. Forty-four students is average, yet in private schools the average is larger still, at fifty-four. This Nada class has fifty-five boys. Some have long hair and casual dress, and others wear school uniforms and crew cuts. They fill every bit of space, leaving hardly enough room for the taller students to angle their legs out in the aisle.

The answers to the teacher's questions are notable. Sometimes someone gets one wrong, and there is jovial snickering from friends nearby, but most of the time the students' replies are crisp, detailed, and on the mark. Even those who assume a disinterested pose are alert to the proceedings and quick to note others' mistakes. No agonizing pauses follow questions as happened when, on rare occasions, questions were asked of the students at Otani and other high schools. Nada students obviously know their material backward and forward and feel little hesitancy in displaying their accomplishments.

This is a senior class, and at Nada the national curriculum has been completed by senior year. At Nada (and almost nowhere else) the last year is devoted to intense review and exam preparation. Most academic high schools find the national high school curriculum too intensive to complete adequately by graduation, yet these Nada students are studying the Meiji Restoration for the second time. Now the teacher is going over the key details with them, the kind of details that just might make the difference on the entrance examination to Tokyo University. His questions are meticulously prepared with this in mind. In fact, he regularly reviews his substantial collection of past questions on the subject given by the top universities, and he knows those that have been particularly difficult for his students.

Toward the end of the hour something else occurred that was unique in my experience of Japanese education. The students actually debated in class the merits of several different interpretations of the history of the restoration. A few teachers in other schools I visited solicited student opinions on matters of interpretation, but never did I witness students ready and able to engage in a discussion of the relative merits of one argument over another. Only at Nada and other top schools are students far enough along the way to self-confidence and independence of thought to venture publicly into the murky realms of interpretive relativity. This skill, by the way, is not of real help in passing examinations to Tokyo and other top universities. The point is that Nada students are not only exceptionally well versed in the facts; they are notably articulate and poised for their age. Having heard the school criticized by the media as preoccupied with cramming for exams,[1] I expected the students to be somewhat anemic and compulsive bookworms, but that is not what I found. The boys are about as diverse, as healthy, and as athletic as those at Otani.

What makes Nada distinctive above all else is that it is an exceptionally well-oiled machine for producing successful candidates for

1. See, e.g., Konaka (1974).

the most cherished university places in Japan.[2] It is like the Etons, the Harrows, and the Grotons in the significant role it plays in producing a nation's future elite. Nada epitomizes Japan's version of the elite school.[3] Unfettered by public educational policies, it is one in a species of educational institution that in the last two decades has been progressively replacing the older elite public high schools at the top of the ladder of secondary education.[4] There are not many such schools, but they have enjoyed spectacular success, and none more than Nada. Nada is famous in Japan today, and hardly a week goes by during the six months prior to the entrance exams in February and March when it is not mentioned in some national magazine. A novel about the school was recently serialized in one weekly news magazine, and a book by the school's principal, full of study hints for aspiring university applicants, quickly became a commercial success.[5]

Unlike Eton or Groton, however, Nada is neither ancient nor rich, neither aristocratic nor magnificently endowed. Founded in 1928 with the patronage of three leading sake brewers, Nada initially enrolled students of upper-middle-class families who had failed to gain acceptance to the few public academic high schools, which at that time were the focus of aspiration for all bright boys. Nada's graduates typically went on to Japan's second-ranking universities. The school was famous in prewar days for its judo teams, not its scholar-

2. On this subject see also Takasugi (1979).

3. The species, elite school, includes several varieties that should be distinguished. One is the "lab" schools belonging to the education departments of a number of national universities. Though publicly funded, they are administered independently and can therefore gear up for exam preparation as Nada does. Among top private schools, the crucial distinction is between those like Nada that run from grades seven to twelve and those that run from grades one to twelve. Naturally, they differ because of the degree of pressure to study that their students have experienced in the elementary years: those entering a grades seven-to-twelve private school have had to prepare intensively to enter, whereas those in a one-to-twelve arrangement pass the entrance barrier when they are still in kindergarten. The notorious scramble to get into good kindergartens is largely a phenomenon of Tokyo because most top one-to-twelve private schools are located there.

4. The percentage of entering Tokyo University students from private and national "lab" schools has risen steadily from less than 10 percent in 1960 to over 30 percent in 1975—and to 48 percent in 1982. Equally dramatic has been a shift in the ranking of top secondary schools by the criterion of how many students are placed in Tokyo University. In 1955 the top ten were mostly public high schools; by 1975, the private and "lab" schools had taken over nearly all of the top ten; by 1982, nearly the top fifteen places. Forty-eight percent of the 1982 freshman class at Tokyo University came from private schools.

5. Konaka (1974) and Katsuyama (1974).

ship, and even in 1960, when its star began to rise, it was largely un-known outside of the Kobe-Osaka region.

What caused the change? Not private wealth, but public policy. During the 1950s, public school redistricting had cut off some very able students in nearby suburbs from access to Kobe's best public high schools. They went to Nada, and as they did well in college en-trance exams, the school's reputation slowly climbed.[6] The caliber of students Nada could attract improved progressively, and by the mid-sixties the school was climbing the charts of the nation's top ten secondary schools as measured by success in entering Tokyo University. It dominated that list as the country's top high school during most of the seventies.

Unlike public high schools, which have just three grades, many private schools in Japan embrace a larger segment of education. Some of the most established offer classes at all levels, from primary through university. Nada has a middle school, where three-quarters of its students spend three years, entering directly from elementary school. Only fifty-five students are accepted at the beginning of ninth grade, and this entrance exam is highly competitive. Because of its reputation, the school has the choice of the best young stu-dents in the heavily populated area that includes both Kobe and Osaka. Elementary school teachers advise parents that only those boys in the top 1 percent of the prefectural aptitude exams should bother to apply to Nada, and even then only one in three is accepted. Applicants for the few slots that open for ninth-grade entrance come from as far away as Hokkaido and Okinawa. Much of Nada's suc-cess, of course, lies in the fact that it receives exceptionally talented students.

Compared with its reputation, the school itself is hardly impos-ing. Occupying the equivalent of one city block in a relatively quiet neighborhood, it consists of several classroom buildings, a gymna-sium, and two or three smaller buildings. There are no dormitories or dining halls, and the music room and the library are small by the standards of Japanese public high schools. The classroom buildings, which date from before the war, are ugly and need repair. Redeeming the whole environment are lovely, large pine trees that shade the area.

6. I am indebted to Robert Ozaki, who grew up in Ashiya, next to Kobe, during this time, for pointing this out to me.

But the school's playing fields boast no grass, and the two clay tennis courts are maintained rather casually by the tennis team itself.

The teachers—the majority of whom are quite old—make little or no effort to supervise or involve themselves in extracurricular activities. They are expert at helping students prepare for examinations, and they neither emphasize nor exemplify a renaissance ideal of well-roundedness. Unlike public school teachers, they are not expected to stay after school as advisers to sport teams or hobby groups. Some do, but many more do not.

Nada is run on a shoestring budget.[7] The principal, assisted by an office staff of two, handles all administrative matters and yet continues to teach math regularly. Such frugality helps explain why the tuition is within reach of the average family. In 1974, entering students paid about $400 in entrance fees and about $500 annual tuition (based on the rate 250 yen = $1).[8] This level of expense was about average for private schools in the area; and parents considering Nada for their children are likely to feel that they will get considerably more for their money from Nada and that acceptance to a national university—the likely outcome of a Nada education—means low tuition costs at the university level. Nada is in all respects a good investment. The school offers no scholarships and receives little in alumni contributions except for its infrequent capital improvement campaigns. The only criterion for acceptance is aptitude; family background or parental willingness to make a large contribution to the school are of no consequence. The principal confided to me when we first met that school finances are a headache, and that he is always hoping for sizable donations from the alumni.

Nada students do come from families that are clearly above average in both education and income, however. A particular formula apparently generates a Nada student: take 1) a very bright boy with 2) well-educated parents who are 3) enthusiastic about educational achievement, add 4) a small, stable, well-off family in which 5) study conditions are excellent, give this student 6) a good public elementary education supplemented by 7) intense tutoring, and you

7. Per capita administrative costs for private high schools in Japan run about 20 percent lower than for public schools. *Shingaku Shimbun* (Tokyo), October 21, 1973.

8. Nada and all other private high schools receive government subsidies to help defray the costs of teachers' salaries. Hyōgo prefecture pays 50 percent of private teachers' salaries. Tuition and other costs to parents amount to 62 percent of total costs in the prefecture's private high schools.

*The front gate to Nada High School*

The building in back is the gym, which was built before the war when the school was famous for its judo teams. The trees and plants inside the gate are all identified by tags in Japanese and English so that students will learn their names.

have a good chance of producing someone who can stand for the school's entrance examination with reasonable confidence.

Family conditions must be nearly ideal to produce boys able to enter Nada, and the school continues this pattern by maintaining optimal conditions for preparing strong candidates for university entrance examinations. Unlike public schools, where numerous goals and educational priorities are at cross-purposes, Nada and other elite private schools enjoy the luxury of pursuing a single major goal: entrance to the top universities. In fact, a construct of the ideal educational machine for this particular purpose looks very much like Nada:

1. students, faculty, and administration all committed to the same goals and priorities;
2. homogeneity of ability among students;

3. latitude to move forward in the curriculum as rapidly as possible;
4. no extraneous interference from educational requirements or philosophies or pedagogical practices that do not contribute to the central goal of preparation for entrance exams;
5. a conception of teachers as experts in their subjects as defined by university entrance examinations;
6. no limits on the school's ability to attract the most capable, well-prepared students;
7. a track record and reputation that draw the best applicants.

Nada comes close to fitting all these criteria, certainly much closer than even the public high schools, and only its lack of scholarship monies and its large class size are notable limitations.

Consider the fact that the senior year is spent in review. This acceleration is not achieved by some gargantuan labor but follows rather naturally the facts of the situation. Entering Nada students are exceptionally well prepared. Most are already a year ahead of others their age. The school has them for six years, and over that time it can accumulate its gain over the national curriculum in small annual increments. Fast tracking in other countries would have such students advancing into university-level work and engaging in independent research projects. In Japan, however, the magnitude of entrance exams has made independent research of virtually no consequence at the secondary level.

The faculty is made up of outstanding teachers largely selected from the public high schools. Nada recruits by offering no obligatory extracurricular work, better students, higher status, and no requirement to retire at age sixty. The school has no union problems, and this appeals to the teacher who wants to concentrate solely on an academic subject.

Obviously, Nada attracts excellent students; but it is worth noting that despite having entered the inside track in Japanese education, most of them continue to study hard. Many attend summer cram schools during vacations. They know that Nada alone does not guarantee admission to Tokyo University, that ultimately they will face the exams on their own. In each class there are students who lose interest or motivation and fall behind during the six years. Typically, they enter top-ranked private universities.

Nada's basic approach certainly challenges the ideals of liberal education and the well-rounded individual. Yet the school does in fact encourage participation in extracurricular activities, so long as this does not seriously interfere with exam preparation. Notwithstanding the single-mindedness of the faculty and the school's inherent efficiency as an exam preparation machine, Nada is a notably relaxed and lively place. Even without faculty supervision, after-school sports and other activities are popular, with more than half of the boys participating. And if student independence and self-government is the issue, Nada meets the test better than the four public schools I studied simply because the teachers give students so much discretion. As in all organizations, the delegation of authority must fit the capacity of those given the responsibility. Nada students are capable of carrying on club activities without teacher guidance. The question of the faculty's role in personal guidance, in school discipline and morale, and in extracurricular activities—all crucial matters in public high schools—is of little consequence at Nada. Bright and self-confident students make a big difference. Everything about the school's extracurricular life, from an active use of the library to broad participation in the student literary magazine, reflects Nada's rich environment for education. The other high schools in Kobe that I studied placed greater emphasis on creating a full educational environment; but without almost constant faculty encouragement and support, all extracurricular activities would quickly flounder.

But there are clear limits to this educational atmosphere. Take the case of a Nada junior who had been selected to spend a year in the United States as an American Field Service exchange student. His spoken English was already far superior to that of his English teacher, and a year living with a family in rural California would make him virtually bilingual. The Nada teachers saw the matter differently. Spoken English, to begin with, is not on the university entrance examinations, and nothing the boy would learn during a year in an American high school would be of any help, either. During that year the student would begin to forget the exam-relevant material he had learned at Nada. In their estimation he would slip from being a strong candidate for Tokyo University to one whose chances were slim. A compromise was finally reached, since the boy was adamant. He would do an extra year at Nada after his return, making up the the time "wasted" abroad. For Nada and for Japanese society in general, gaining special skills and experience means little if a student does not get into Tokyo University first.

Often in Japan one hears the lament that the examination system has caused sports to become the specialty of high schools and of students lacking academic aspirations. Indeed, the best national teams are generally produced by schools of low academic standing, schools that concentrate on sports just as Nada does on exams. College-bound students often avoid sports or quit them a year early, to focus exclusively on taking the entrance examinations. Nada no longer turns out strong sports teams, but it keeps quite a number in the field considering the constraints of exam preparation. The explanation I was given for this is that the school's accelerated approach leaves more leeway for extracurricular activities than is available to top students in public schools.

Teachers long associated with the school note a change in student character since Nada has become academically exceptional. Until the 1960s, they say, the school produced its share of writers, entertainers, and artists, but recently students with such inclinations are rare. A number of well-known comedians and actors and the novelist Endo Shusaku are graduates of the old Nada, but famous alumni from the next generation are likely to emerge in areas such as medical research, law, and government. Between one-quarter and one-third of each class chooses to study medicine today. One teacher observed that as university humanities departments attract more and more female applicants they appear less competitive and challenging to the ablest boys. In fact, it is easier to get into the literature and education departments at Tokyo, so naturally their prestige is lower.

For Nada students, this can be important. The elite-consciousness of the students is remarkable. In interviews with prowling journalists (not an uncommon phenomenon) there is always someone who, in answer to the inevitable question of what he wants to become, answers "prime minister." The sense of self-importance and stature shown by these students is not based on family, but on their own accomplishments. Their fathers are usually upper middle class but not prominent or powerful. During elementary school these boys were at the top, and they have already succeeded in entering Japan's best secondary school. Japanese parents do not fret about having a "brain" in the family, and no peer pressure descends on them for excelling at their studies. Most high school boys are simply worried about getting into some university, or whether to go to college at all; many Nada students have begun to worry about how they will use their elite education to serve the nation. In their precocious responsibility as future leaders, they may even decry their own elite status and protest, in a reverse form of self-congratulation, the exam-oriented popular obsession that underwrites their self-importance. The world over, elite education seems closely associated with a peculiar moral critique of social structure that in the abstract is egalitarian. Does making it to the top through education create a form of guilt and righteousness that the self-made do not experience? Whatever the answer, social criticism is clearly a habit that Nada students develop earlier than most.

## *Sakura*

When Nada's students are heading home or already sitting around the family dinner table, a group of their peers are just beginning their classes at Sakura, a technical night high school located just a few blocks away. If the boys at Nada have exceptionally bright futures, the prospects of Sakura's students are exceptionally bleak.

On a January evening, at 5:30 p.m., the sun has set an hour ago, and it is very cold. The building lacks central heating, as almost all older Japanese buildings do, and the only warm place when school begins is the teachers' room with its two gas stoves. Students begin collecting there. The older ones standing around are allowed to smoke, something strongly forbidden in most schools. As classrooms start being used, stoves are lit, but only by sitting near them can one feel really warm. Most of the classrooms and hallways remain vacant because the night school has few students in comparison with the technical high school that occupies the same building in the daytime. The classrooms inhabited tonight are like tiny ships in a dark, cold sea. Most students remain bundled in their coats. The school does not require uniforms, and school attire is varied. The majority of students work at manual jobs, many in factories; many ride motorcycles to work. The blue-collar group tends to dress somewhere between Bob Dylan, the Hell's Angels, and Ringo Starr. Others, who come from offices or shops, tend toward Ivy League styles. The jumble of appearances seems almost impossible to an American used to the symbolic hostilities and segregating aspects associated with this range of dress styles in the United States.

A new term is beginning, and the young literature teacher tells me on the way to class that he will discuss with the students what textbook selections they should read during the weeks ahead. "It's all very difficult for them, but if they choose, it helps." The class has an official enrollment of only seventeen students, but tonight just four are present when class begins. A few straggle in as the hour progresses. Sakura experiences about a 50-percent absentee rate.

> **Teacher:** "All right, quiet down. It's a new term and not a very long one. What should we read before your class trip next month?"
> *(Three of the four have brought their textbooks, and they silently thumb through them for some time before one, the student council president and a self-confident character, raises his hand.)*
> **Student:** "How about the selection from the X novel? It looks interesting."
> **Teacher:** "Which one?"
> **Student:** "The one that starts on page 135."
> **Teacher:** "Oh, that one. We did it last term. Don't you remember?"
> *(All look sheepishly through the text for a few more minutes, until the teacher breaks the silence once more.)*
> **Teacher:** "There are two selections we might do, the essay by Z or the piece of criticism by Y. Which looks better? We'd better do something. It's a short term."
> *(More silence.)*
> **Teacher:** "All right, we'll do the essay by Z."

The "discussion" comes to an end. Everyone opens his book to the appropriate page, and the teacher appoints a student to read aloud. His progress is slow as he stumbles over three or four characters per sentence. I am shocked to find that I know some characters the students are regularly missing. And so it goes for the remaining class time: seven lines of text covered in thirty minutes. The almost constant corrections of pronunciation make the lesson unbearably tiresome and boring. There is no time to discuss the meaning of the essay, its style, or its charm. The fact is that the students simply cannot read it.

This particular textbook is the easiest available among those approved by the Ministry of Education for this level of high school; still, it is over the heads of these students. By law, the teacher must proceed, ignoring this fact. Special remedial courses or programs are not available except to the mentally handicapped. For many of the students, the passage being read is more like a foreign language than something written in their native tongue. One is reminded of the stereotypical Latin class in which not very bright students are dragged sentence by sentence through the translation of some piece of reputedly great literature. When with great relief they finish, they have understood nothing.

Most Sakura classes are like this—night after night. Those students who make it to school, presumably the more interested and ambitious, brazenly maintain a running commentary on their problems. "It's too difficult." "Teacher, we can't do this." "Let's do a different part." "Let's stop early." They tease one another a lot. "How did you know that one? You can't even read a comic book!" Classes are often three-ring circuses of side comments and disruptions that the teachers generally tolerate in good humor. Despite their efforts at discipline, they share the frustrations of such a gross mismatch between ability and curriculum. When the interference continues too long, order is reestablished by the teacher, who yells a variety of Japanese equivalents of "Shut up!" The friendly, jovial teacher of one art class opens almost every paragraph of his lecture with some such exclamation.

It is apparent that few students are actually paying much attention. Some take notes, do the assignments, and are engaged intellectually in the subject; yet the large majority cannot or will not do this. Talking, looking out the windows, arriving at class late, openly passing magazines around, and even roughhousing during lectures are common. It surprised me to witness discourteous behavior toward teachers. But experienced instructors dismiss this, saying that their students have had great difficulty in school for so long that just coming to school is quite an accomplishment and a sign of positive involvement. "They do not mean to be discourteous. Their future will be spent working in a factory somewhere, and the chance they will need English, or will want to read a classic of Japanese literature, or spend any time thinking about European history is remote." Knowing this full well, the teachers, in good soldier fashion, go on instructing them in these subjects.

Sakura teaches electronics, and this vocational side of the curriculum does not constitute a marked exception to the description above. Behavior in vocational classes is not much better, and teachers complain as often about the quality of student work. Even though the future success of many students will probably center on the technical skills they are learning, they do not take their vocational courses very seriously either. As a vocational teacher remarked, "Just how well they master these skills will not affect their immediate job prospects greatly because high school graduates with technical training are in short supply." The very diligent student receives strong recommendations from teachers and special help in securing a particularly attractive job, but few find such favor worth the extra effort.

Even in the night school, going to college is the status goal. Despite accumulated disadvantages, nearly one-third of the second-year students at Sakura say they hope to go to college. They are not expecting to enter by passing exams, however, but by being accepted into one of the private colleges with such low standards that being able to read, write, and pay tuition are all that is required for admission. The percentage who aspire to higher education drops considerably over the time before graduation, but the remarkable fact remains that some actually do go on to junior colleges and low-ranking private universities.

This makes sense only if we realize the popularity of education in Japan and the effects of mass education on schools at the bottom of the system. The declining level of educational attainment in night schools is a direct product of the growth in new public high schools. Only the weakest students are left for schools like Sakura. Even among this group, however, the desire to go to college and thus escape the onerous social identity of being just a high school graduate is powerful. Mass education carries such consequences.

Nowhere in Japanese education are there more problems than in night high schools. In an era of nearly universal high school attendance, they have become something like the catch below the kitchen sink.[9] Students failing to enter any daytime high school now gather in the night schools. This means that night schools generally enroll students from the lowest two percentiles (in terms of academic ability) of any ninth-grade graduating class. In the highly ranked world of urban high schools, Sakura represents the bottom rung.

When first instituted in pre–World War II years, night schools were very different. They were established to serve the needs of poor but ambitious and able students who had to work to support themselves

9. About 3 percent of the nation's high school students were enrolled in night schools in 1980. Total enrollment in night schools declined by nearly 60 percent between 1965 and 1975, as more schools were built and more families decided to pay for private high schooling.

while achieving a high school education. Until the late fifties, it must be remembered, a minority of Japanese obtained a high school diploma. Many night school students then were country boys who had taken urban jobs following graduation from junior high school. They hoped to move up in the world despite the disadvantages they faced, and night high schools offered them the opportunity. Working all day and going to school until ten or eleven at night taxed their endurance, to be sure, but they were ambitious and fairly able, inspiring hope. To their teachers and employers they often epitomized the especially popular image of the country boy making good in the big city. Their hardships were joined to a sturdy optimism.

At Sakura, such students can still be found, but they are now few. The majority today come from city backgrounds, and about one-quarter do not even work during the day to support themselves. This is not to say that night school students are largely middle-class, for that is not true. Rather, most would have preferred to go to a day-time high school (public or private) but, failing acceptance, they turned to the night school as a last resort. The majority of Sakura students in 1975 applied for admission only after being rejected by several daytime high schools. Rarely are there more applications than openings to Sakura, and to fill its official quota of eighty freshmen the school has a late application period and has been willing to accept students clearly incapable of high school work.

Dropout rates from high school in Japan as a whole average only 3 percent, but at Sakura less than half of those who enter stay to graduate.[10] No one flunks out. The faculty is willing to ignore poor attendance and examination results. Diplomas are awarded to those who simply stick it out for four years. (Night schools require an extra year because there are fewer daily class hours.) Study itself may not be difficult, but simply finding the willpower to go night after night, including Saturdays, proves too much for half the students.

The teachers at Sakura were among the most devoted and skilled I met in Japan. Their students' problems were large enough and intrusive enough to push aside the more usual preoccupations of Japa-

10. In Tokyo the annual dropout rate for night schools is 18 percent of the total enrolled. It is 5.5 for public vocational schools and a mere 0.4 for public academic high schools. Tōkyō-tō-Toritsu Kyōiku Kenkyusho, *Kyōiku Jihō* (Tokyo), no. 1 (1977), p. 16.

nese high school teachers with narrow subject matter and academic achievement. Most wish to teach better students, but once they accept the Sakura reality, many learn to cope and to find fulfillment by relating to the individual needs of students—just the reverse emphasis from those at Nada. Yet to the competent and experienced core of Sakura teachers are added many young newcomers to the profession who must begin at the bottom of the professional pecking order. And in the night schools, there are some painfully inadequate older teachers nearing retirement. What keeps the able teachers in this kind of teaching? Many stay at Sakura because it allows them to pursue a second occupation or avocation during the day. Among the best Sakura teachers are an artist, a small businessman, a Christian minister, and a teacher who is studying English literature full-time in a university. Most newcomers, however, take their jobs at Sakura with the understanding that it is a first step up the ladder. They are impatient to move up to a daytime high school where what they learned in college has some relevance to their classroom performance. Turnover among young teachers is thus high. Sakura is a hardship post, and as such its leadership must cope with morale problems among teachers who wish for greener pastures.

There are also many things to praise about Sakura and reasons to take heart. Under such difficult conditions, the good teaching that does take place, the learning that is accomplished, and the warm human relationships that do develop seem especially notable. During class breaks, many students gather in the teachers' room to talk and joke in a pleasant, informal manner with the teachers. When it is time to leave for the next class, both students and teachers linger too long and are often late. In no other school I visited is there as close and friendly an atmosphere. There is more humanity and more candidness all around. The proverbial Japanese propriety and restraint are not much in evidence here.

## Okada

Perhaps because it is winter, everything in this school seems a bit muted and under wraps. At Okada student uniforms are required, and the dress code is followed with greater scrupulousness than in the other schools I have visited. The halls are relatively quiet, and more students nod politely to teachers as they pass. The formal bow before each class hour seems more comfortable to these students. In fact, several younger teachers with breezy manners appear to resent the ritual more than do their wards.

Classes are very much like those at Otani: hour-long, well-prepared lectures, interrupted by neither student disturbances nor discussions. More students are paying close attention here than at Otani, it seems, but the difference is slight, and it is quite possible that it was the sunny autumn weather rather than some intrinsic difference that made the Otani students seem brighter, more cheerful, and less soberly diligent.

Like Otani, Okada is a good high school in the minds of teachers and parents. Disciplinary problems are minimal, and nearly all of its 650 girls and 545 boys are headed for higher education. The school's atmosphere is decidedly serious. Unlike Otani, Okada belongs to the prefectural high school system. It possesses greater resources, a longer history, and a higher average level of student exam performance. The great majority of good academic high schools within Kobe actually belong to the prefectural administration; I selected Okada for my study to represent this general stratum within urban Japanese education. There are prefectural schools in Kobe superior to Okada, schools that until the mid-1960s occupied the local pinnacle of education where Nada now stands. There are also prefectural academic high schools below Okada on the ladder of status and performance. They look very much like Otani in their college entrance record.

Nearly all of Okada's graduates go to college, and about 10 percent attend some national or public university. (By contrast, more of Otani's graduates take jobs, and less than 5 percent attain places in national or public universities.) Very rarely does an Okada student succeed in entering Tokyo, Kyoto, or one of the other top-ranked schools. Only the three elite private schools and the three best prefectural high schools in the city can claim the distinction of turning out such students; Nada, of course, is far ahead of the rest. Still, Okada does better than most of Kobe's academic high schools in several respects. Few girls take jobs upon graduation, and more than 60 percent of them go on to four-year colleges. Recall that only 25 percent of Otani's female graduates advance to a four-year school. A

*A biology class at Okada*

Uniforms are required. Note the undecorated classroom and the loud-speaker above the blackboard.

solid group of Okada students also attends the better private four-year colleges each year,[11] and fewer of them than of Otani students require a year of post-graduate study to gain acceptance. Clearly, the difference between the records of Okada's and Otani's students is not great in light of the much more striking contrasts that exist within the total Kobe school system. But to ambitious and concerned parents the nuance is universally noted and appreciated. Given the choice, very few indeed would fail to select Okada over Otani for their children, and even the teachers at Otani recognize the difference. When I told them that I was going next to do research at Okada, several said jokingly, "Find out what their methods are and tell us the secrets of their success."

Academic high schools all focus on the goal of college entrance, yet prefectural schools have the reputation of concentrating on this

11. For example, Doshisha, Ritsumeikan, and Kansai Universities.

goal more intensely than city-run schools.[12] Okada, in many ways nearly imperceptible to the untrained eye, confirms this stereotype. During the third and final years, for example, class schedules are arranged so that those planning to take the entrance exams to science-oriented departments get a heavier dose of science and math, and those aiming at the liberal arts take more history. The school forbids its students from taking part-time work for several reasons, including the need to concentrate on studies.[13] Teachers are candid about the "facts of life" regarding entrance exams, and elective activities during school time have an academic flavor. Unlike Otani, Okada's library is crowded at lunch with browsers, and when teachers were ordered by the Ministry of Education to organize a weekly leisure-oriented elective hour (the rather pathetic result of official concern that Japanese schools were too single-mindedly oriented toward work), some Okada teachers persisted in offering foreign languages, science, and other subjects in the guise of hobbies. At both Okada and Otani one can find many teachers who view themselves as experts in their subjects, especially in the kinds of minutiae that can be objectively tested as on university entrance examinations. It is noteworthy in this regard that Nada recruits the most experienced and professional teachers out of the prefectural high schools. One teacher moved there from Okada during my study.

Physically, the main school building is old, poorly lighted, and in general need of repairs. No other school I visited was as run-down. I was told that the broken windows were the work of neighborhood youth, not Okada students, and the explanation seemed plausible because the school is surrounded on two sides by clusters of slum-condition shacks. But the essence of the problem is the school's age.

Okada celebrated its fiftieth anniversary in the early seventies. Before the war it had been a prefectural girls' high school, a publicly funded institution created on the lines of an upper-class finishing school. It had a special Western-style room where the fine points of foreign etiquette were practiced; and during the war its students dug air raid trenches in their bloomers and middy blouses. Coeducation arrived with the occupation, but teachers still claim that the stu-

12. In Kobe there are nineteen prefectural high schools and thirteen city high schools.
13. For these reasons, see Chapter Nine.

dents retain a "well-mannered passivity" from the school's previous incarnation.

In doing field research, a wealth of local history inevitably emerges that, to those working daily amid these memories and legacies, can be thoroughly absorbing, causing them to see the historical uniqueness of their school as the primary reality. I felt the magnetic charm of just such a perspective as the weeks went by in each of the five high schools I visited, and each move from one to the next came as a shock. Gradually I learned to balance the nature of the very different schools with the emerging picture of a system that ties them together into a single institution of secondary education. The perspective and actions of students and teachers cannot be understood unless their preoccupation with their own schools is acknowledged, yet an interest in sociological analysis and generalization demand that one grasp the larger structural whole.

### *Yama*

One spur of the Kobe Electric Railroad runs up Rokko mountain above the older and most heavily industrialized part of the city into a small plateau recently opened as a suburban area of modest family residences. Each morning it is filled with student commuters, many headed for Yama Commercial High School. As the train winds slowly up the mountain, it passes trains headed down, packed with office workers and their commuting children. To look down past the lush green of the mountainside to the ugly, grime-covered neighborhoods tucked in among the factories below leaves an indelible impression. The physical contrasts involved reflect basic dimensions of the sociology of Kobe society. This railway line, as it bisects the city's working-class neighborhoods near the harbor and the middle-class neighborhoods located on the higher ground, serves as a conduit between residential and educational elements that have been jumbled by history. The oldest and most prestigious public high schools are located below in the older neighborhoods, now lower-class, and the newer schools like Yama Commercial, low in prestige, have been built among the recently developed and more desirable residential areas.

Only a very naïve visitor would mistake the quiet, clean surroundings and Yama's relatively new buildings as indicative of its character. Japanese would notice that Yama students on the train rarely carry books, and they could not ignore the number of girls with "mature" hairdos and the number of boys sporting Elvis haircuts and foppish, strangely cut uniforms. Upon entering the school they would also notice a large sign publicizing the school's problem with tardiness. Because Yama is a vocational high school, such blatant indications that it has problems would confirm what Japanese already expect: vocational schools are known to collect the less able and the more troubled.

Yama draws its students from the lower third of Kobe's graduating ninth graders; and over 80 percent of Yama's students say that given a choice they would choose an academic high school.[14] Few are proud or happy about being at Yama. Because they fall below the entrance requirements to public academic high schools and because typically they cannot afford private schools, they enter Yama by default. Under these conditions, faculty and students find it difficult to be enthusaistic about their common tasks. This is a poor foundation on which to run a school, but other problems of a critical nature also plague Yama.

The character of the vocational curriculum holds no particular interest or future advantage for many students.[15] They see it as blocking the way of preparing for higher education, a dream that more than one-third of the students still harbor, regardless of their previously poor performance. Yama, furthermore, has more than four girls for every boy, and this, too, is the source of problems. The reason is that commercial high schools are preferred by girls and technical ones by boys in what is in effect a voluntary sex role bifurcation, despite the official policy of coeducation. In the United States the same bifurcation occurs at the course level in such subjects as technical drawing, auto mechanics, and art, but in Kobe this means separate schooling.

If Yama itself is at a disadvantage, compared with academic schools like Otani and Okada, many of its students also have problems at home. Teachers say poverty and broken homes hang like a dark shadow over student life. In some of the worst cases, school seems like an opportunity and a blessing in comparison with conditions at home.

14. Kobe-shi Kōtōgakko Kyōshokuin Kumiai (1973), p. 36.
15. See ibid., p. 39.

There has been considerable talk in Kobe of closing the vocational schools, due to their unpopularity and the particular difficulties of educating students uninterested in the vocational curriculum. Twenty years ago, when nearly half of all young people were not even going to high school, vocational schools were hard to enter, and the diploma meant better pay and employment. But as academic high schools became more available, vocational schools began to decline. The general quality of vocational school graduates has dropped notably, and as a result companies view vocational training with little respect. Vocational schools now carry a stigma, and parents worry about bad peer influences.

The presence of large numbers of tenured teachers of vocational subjects, firmly supported by the teachers' union, and unresolved policy questions about educational opportunity, deadlocks the issue of closing the vocational schools. Viewed objectively, the needs of Japanese society are for more, not less, vocational training and for less, not more, university graduates. The bachelor's degree is devalued as more and more receive it, yet demand grows for many technical skills. But Japan, like the United States, has entered an age of mass higher education, and the trend is difficult to reverse. Vocational high schools are caught in the middle of this historical disjuncture.

We might begin by asking what actually happens to the graduates of Yama Commercial High School. The class of 1974, which lost ten members along the way, had 302 girls and 95 boys at graduation. Seventy-eight percent of the girls and 61 percent of the boys took jobs, mostly in large firms, where they began working in clerical positions. Another 40 students (10 percent) are listed as working at home or attending special schools, such as those for beauticians or auto mechanics. Fifty-seven seniors (14 percent) went on to higher education:

|       | University | Junior College |
|-------|------------|----------------|
| Total | 17         | 40             |
| Girls | 5          | 39             |
| Boys  | 12         | 1              |

As at Otani, more Yama boys than girls go to universities. The opposite is true of junior colleges. But the caliber of the schools involved is very different from those to which Otani or Okada students are heading. Yama students enter universities and junior colleges that have very low admissions standards. Often a teacher's recommendation suffices, and there is merely a perfunctory entrance examination. Four or five Yama students, invariably boys, do a year of exam study hoping to gain acceptance to a university of somewhat higher status. Yama clearly stands above Sakura, the night school, as far as future prospects are concerned, but a great gap exists between Yama and academic Otani in the scholastic achievements of graduates.

Although many talk of wishing to go to university, most Yama students still view high school as the last stage of their education. They have no strong reason to study. They are pressured neither by the prospect of entrance examinations nor by employment worries. Companies rarely look closely at grades, and the demand for high school graduates has remained high in Japan even during recent recessions. Yama students who do no homework and pay no attention in class are about as likely to get a reasonable job as their more studious peers.

During my first day at Yama, one of the teachers took me on a tour of the school. Walking around outside, we found several girls sitting behind a building drinking coffee. My escort asked them firmly where they belonged, and they explained that their class was doing "self-study" (jishū)—meaning that the teacher for that hour had not shown up. They got up quickly and hurried back to their room. As we passed their classroom later, two boys suddenly climbed out a window and walked out the school gate.

Other scenes come to mind. A young male teacher is trying to explain English grammar to a class of largely inattentive students. One girl is brushing a friend's hair; several students are staring out the window; others are passing around movie magazines; and a handful of boys in the back talk incessantly. The teacher tries to make jokes, but they are too witty for the students, and he laughs alone. In fact, it seems he is lecturing to himself. Clearly, he has not yet learned to control his class. More experienced Yama teachers use thoroughly planned exercises that force all students to pay attention. They do not hesitate to play the role of drill sergeant when disturbances arise. This teacher complains that the students have no interest in his subject and that the text is over their heads. He wishes he could be transferred. Perhaps the students wish the same.

At noon, many students leave the grounds to eat in one of the small restaurants in the neighborhood. Not only does this add to the eternal tardiness problem, other temptations are involved, and a few students skip afternoon classes. Once several came back acting rather silly and could not settle down in class. Going to speak to them, the teacher noticed the smell of alcohol. "We ate some whiskey bonbons" was the explanation. Unsatisfied with the answer, the teacher pursued the matter after class and discovered that a group of students had in fact wandered into a candy store at lunchtime and bought small (decorative) bottles of whiskey that they naïvely quaffed on the way back to school. They were almost as surprised as the teacher at the result.

Such innocent developments occur along with less easily dismissed problems. During my time at Yama the wall between the boys' and girls' lavatories was attacked with what must have been a sledgehammer. The floor was strewn with cigarette butts, a symbolic expression of defiance as well as a sign that the vandals were nervously trying to act tough. But such destruction is rare at Yama. The school is in a good neighborhood, and it shows no signs of external vandalism. The culprits in this case were never caught, but everyone speculated that Yama boys were involved.

About twice a year Yama boys get into a fight with a group from some other school. Schools known for being tough tend to maintain rivalries, though Yama has too many girls to be high on the list. Such fights are not part of the academic high school student's world. According to the teacher in charge of Yama discipline, only about 10 percent of the students are involved in trouble during their high school careers, so it is unfair to portray the entire school in terms of delinquency. But in comparison with the academic high schools I have described, the proclivity for delinquency and the discipline problems this creates for teachers is a hallmark of Yama and other schools in the lower third of Japanese urban education.[16]

As with most schools, Yama prohibits smoking off as well as on campus, but a school survey shows that about 20 percent of the older students smoke. Another school rule prohibits motorcycle riding. Accidents and arrests reveal that many boys break this rule. It is worth noting that the teachers have remained firm in their insis-

16. The issue of delinquency as it correlates with school types is taken up in Chapter Nine.

tence on these prohibitions despite the knowledge that they are contrary to student custom and difficult to enforce. "Teachers should know what is best" and "There is a right and wrong way in these matters" are their explanations for taking responsibility over what in the United States would be considered private matters.

To Americans accustomed to much more serious conditions in urban high schools, Yama may seem tame; but to Japanese, the school's problems are deeply disturbing. With 96 percent of Kobe's young people now in high school, teachers in schools like Yama and in low-status private schools find themselves facing problems that high schools even ten years ago did not have to face. They are not well equipped to handle delinquency or lack of motivation. Ten years ago most vocational school students were going directly to work after ninth grade. A work environment created very different pressures, under which no peer subculture supported delinquency.

To my surprise, Yama students participate in extracurricular activites at about the same rate as students in academic high schools. Several of the girls' teams, in fact, are among the strongest in the city. The boys' sports teams suffer, however, and sometimes do not even have enough members to practice properly. Only on the sports fields does Yama have much life in the afternoons; many clubs are dormant. A few girls meet eagerly once a week with the art teacher to draw. "He's been to Paris," they remark in awe, and "he doesn't think like a Japanese." And a music club is busy, too, thanks to another dedicated teacher. But not enough teachers stay around to help. Those that do tell of enthusiasm but little leadership or organizational ability among the students. They say teacher guidance is crucial to the maintenance of extracurricular activities.

Yama's annual Culture Festival is an illustration. A teacher who had been staying past six o'clock most nights for several weeks, helping her homeroom prepare its musical presentation, noted, "In most things they learn slowly; they don't concentrate well. There are disturbances, and many do not show up regularly. All the same, they want to do a good job and feel great pride in their performance." Some of the girls want to see their boyfriends downtown after school, and some students work at part-time jobs. Teachers have to work hard to shape a satisfactory presentation for an event like the festival.

Participation is a general problem. Many Yama students do not want to participate in school events. Large or small extracurricular efforts are thus more problematic than in academic high schools. At vocational schools such as Yama, organizational skills, free time, and self-confidence among students are in as short supply as academic interest, preparation, and ability.

## Summary

Obviously, the spectrum of differences among high schools in urban Japan is large, though perhaps not as large as in nations with greater ethnic and social diversity. Key questions arise: To what extent does the school ranking reflect differences of family background? Does sorting by entrance examination calibrate socioeconomic factors with the structure of educational outcomes? The answers help measure mobility and social hierarchy in Japan.

A spectrum of school subcultures apparently exists that correlates academic achievement, orderly behavior, high morale, and a preoccupation with university entrance exams, on the one hand, and, on the other, academic difficulties, delinquent tendencies, and low morale. Each of the five schools has its own balance of these two sets of qualities (see Table 4 for a simple comparison). Here is evidence that Japan, like the United States, has great problems extending secondary education to an entire population. The growing power and prestige of private education at the elite end and the many frustrations of vocational and night schools at the other give witness to fundamental problems with the public policy of universal education. That quality and equality are counterpoint ambitions is no surprise, but the role of high school and university entrance exams in shaping both seems unusual, at least to Americans.

The differences among high schools in Kobe should warn us against making facile generalizations. Clearly, neither Japanese society nor its high schools are monolithic, a point too regularly ignored in foreign treatments of Japan. The basic observational grounding of this book is these five schools. The challenge is to retain a focus on diversity while considering Japanese high school education as a whole. Both levels of generalization are crucial.

Indeed, many common threads run through all five schools. They share the same cultural heritage and general history. They are differentiated, positioned, and defined largely by the same system of high school and university entrance examinations. Their admin-

**Table 4**

Enrollment and Educational Outcome in Five Schools in Kobe, 1974

| School | Type | Approximate Enrollment | Percentage of Students Advancing to University | Percentage of Students Advancing to Junior College |
|--------|------|------------------------|-----------------------------------------------|---------------------------------------------------|
| Nada | Private, academic | 675 boys | 100 | |
| Okada | Prefectural, academic | 650 girls 575 boys | 72 | 14 |
| Otani | City, academic | 610 girls 610 boys | 62 | 25 |
| Yama | City, commercial | 900 girls 300 boys | 6 | 10 |
| Sakura | City, night technical | 210 boys | 2 | 6 |

istrative structures, schedules, textbooks, and curricular designs are largely generated by the same Ministry of Education formulas. Their subcultural differences constitute a single evaluative set for parents, students, and the teacher corps. Finally, teachers circulate among a city's public schools, and their union's perspective and political activities embrace nearly the entire spectrum.

# 2

# History

The greatest innovation in the world is the demand for education as a right of man; it is a disguised demand for comfort.

JAKOB BURCKHARDT

UNIVERSAL compulsory education encompassing the youth of whole nations is a recent development. Schools have existed for a much longer time than school systems, and learning and teaching presumably have been part of human society since its origins. Ancient Rome and Greece had schools, as did China and India. Plato and Confucius were schoolteachers. But their schools were not part of large public bureaucracies. Only after the creation of nation states, the assumption of power by secular authorities, and the rise of industrial production did compulsory education gain acceptance in Europe. Publicly run and financed schools open to all children were then defined as necessary to the realization of many cherished social ambitions. It was a short step from that point to an education based on merit, certification, testing, and all the rest. What in 1860 was a revolutionary notion, widely resisted in the most advanced nations, within a century became an institution that is taken for granted as much as are taxes and public welfare.

Japan did not begin to establish the machinery of a modern nation state until 1868, and yet her leaders accomplished the process of institution building in a relatively short time.[1] By the turn of the cen-

---

1. General histories in English of Japanese education include Passin (1965), Kaigo (1968), Anderson (1975), and Kobayashi (1978).

tury, most children were enrolled in elementary schools, giving Japan the distinction of having quickly equaled the West in the spread of public education. This distinction was of dubious merit at first, however, because the rapid creation of public elementary schools, at a rate of over three thousand per year from 1870 to 1880, was not accompanied by extensive teacher training.[2] Fewer than 20 percent of the teachers in 1880 had any formal training in the use of the radically new textbooks and methods that the Ministry of Education hurriedly produced. The institutional apparatus of a modern system of education was established quickly, but the content of education developed slowly. In terms of devotion to education, degree of popular involvement, and importance of learning to adult success, traditional Japan was at least traditional Europe's equal. But the cultures were different. Before 1868, Japanese educational practice was very different from that in the West, and in the course of its development during the past century some of its distinctive character has remained.

A system of education can be profoundly modern in its public mandate and its embrace of an entire population, yet the echoes of legacy can be heard daily in schools and classrooms. The lower in the institution one goes, the more likely it is that one will encounter the flow of cultural continuity.

Japan's alternate seclusion from and warm embrace of foreign influence is a basic element of her cultural history, and it helps explain why her educational legacy is remarkably rich and varied. No other modern system has experienced more outside influence or undergone more radical transformations. Consider the following synopsis: 1) Before 1870, the influence of Confucian models of schooling, largely imported from China, prevailed;[3] 2) with the creation of compulsory public schooling in 1872, European influence came to dominate the newly established national system; 3) frequent shifts in the use of Western nations as models led to a surprising eclecticism within the pattern of borrowing;[4] 4) sponsored by a surging nationalism and by reaction to foreign influence, a prolonged search for a more Japanese kind of education based on tradition and Jap-

2. Kaigo (1968).
3. See J. W. Hall (1959) and Dore (1965).
4. I. P. Hall (1973) offers a lucid account of this era.

anese uniqueness began in the 1880s.[5] This culminated in the late 1930s, with the ascension of nativism and militarism.[6] 5) All of this was abruptly reversed in 1945, when the victorious Americans "democratized" Japanese education using the American model;[7] 6) the Americans left in 1952, and a prolonged shaking out of and adjustment to the American-imposed system began.[8] 7) The astounding economic growth and social change that marked the postwar period transformed education once more.[9] As industrial output grew at a rate faster than any country had ever experienced, higher education became the ambition of most Japanese families, and the percentage of persons graduating from high school jumped from under 40 percent in 1950 to 90 percent by 1975. The five high schools considered herein have emerged from this history.

The term "traditional" can easily be misleading if it implies an undifferentiated past, and yet from history must be gleaned and condensed that which is significant to the present. Japan has a long history, and almost from the beginning of recorded events there are references to schooling and education. It should be no surprise that, over the course of twelve hundred years, numerous approaches and various types of schools emphasizing distinct educational ambitions and values have developed. The focus here will be on the three most immediate legacies: education in the Tokugawa, the prewar, and the occupation eras. None of these approaches totally replaced its predecessor as time progressed; rather, the transformations involved much mixing and accumulation. Today's high schools mirror elements of all three legacies.

## The Tokugawa Pattern

From 1600 until 1868, when Japan was opened to the West, a particular prosperous kind of feudal society developed. Throughout this

5. Dore (1964), I. P. Hall (1973), and Roden (1980).
6. See Murthy (1973) and R. K. Hall (1949, 1949a).
7. General Headquarters for the Supreme Commander, Allied Powers (hereafter, GHQ) (1948), Gayn (1948), R. K. Hall (1949), Kawai (1960), Anderson (1975), and Lee (1974).
8. Passin (1965), Nagai (1971), Duke (1973), Thurston (1973), Lee (1974), Anderson (1975), Kobayashi (1978), Kaigo (1968), and Friedman (1977).
9. Lee (1974), Yamamura and Hanley (1975), Rohlen (1977), Kobayashi (1978), and Cummings (1980).

Tokugawa period, the country was at peace. The rulers were samurai warriors turned bureaucrats. Cities prospered, and their populations of tradesmen and merchants grew. Agriculture and trade flourished, and Japanese culture experienced a rich development and diversification. Many schools—more than in any previous period—were established, some to serve the needs of the warrior class, others for the urban merchant class, and some even for farmers' children. It is estimated that by 1850, at least one-quarter of the population was literate, a sign of the extent of educational development and, incidentally, an accomplishment that put Japan on a par with the leading countries of Europe at the time.[10]

Governments—that is, the many separate feudal authorities (daimyo) that ruled sections of the country—set up fief (han) schools to educate the sons of samurai families for more effective service in their administrations. The military arts were an important part of the curriculum, but following the lead of the Tokugawa shogun's own official school, Confucian studies were the centerpiece.

Because these official schools for samurai were the most influential of the period, they must be considered in some detail.[11] Their basic rationale lay in the notion that education would produce virtuous and ethical administrators who by their proper conduct and example would order society and cause it to flourish. This is an idea at the very heart of Confucian thought, and it appealed strongly to the Tokugawa shogun and feudal lords seeking effective government. Confucian studies achieved a number of needed changes simultaneously. The samurai were made more civilized and skilled as administrators. The new political order was provided with an overarching ideology that supported the established order and authority. Proper behavior in the key feudal relations and between classes and within fundamental institutions was codified following Confucian prescriptions.

The basic metaphor of the Confucian moral system is the proper family: correctly ordered by differences of function and authority, with filial piety the central virtue, the family is the model for society as a whole. Translated into the feudal arrangements of the time, this meant that loyalty and obedience of subordinate to su-

10. Ono (1979).
11. This section draws substantially on J. W. Hall (1959), Dore (1965), Passin (1965), Kaigo (1968), and I. P. Hall (1973).

perior was made the highest moral virtue. Relations throughout society were described by a rigorous application of hierarchical distinctions, and the lord-retainer relationship had both real and symbolic prominence.[12]

How was this realized in educational practice? Fief schools, by their very existence, expressed the connection between study and service to the lord and domain. Study was an important duty. Daimyo had Confucian tutors and ceremonially paid their humble respects to the reigning ideology. In the Confucian approach to education, correctly ordered conduct was emphasized as it expressed and embodied the correct relations and attitudes at the foundation of a harmonious society. Formality and hierarchy were thus stressed, and ceremonies and school etiquette were attended to in detail. At school, reading and writing were mastered in the process of memorizing the Confucian classics. Teachers lectured on the implications of the classics for proper conduct as a samurai. The crucial emphasis was thus on moral education, with the classics as guides and daily conduct in the school as the mirror. Accordingly, authority was properly strict, and elaborate sets of rules were created to help translate moral ideas into practice. Given the Confucian idea of government, moral education was vocational training for young samurai.

We are not considering a philosophy so much as an orthodoxy in speaking of the Confucian learning in these schools. Learning was the process of submitting to and mastering the wisdom of the sages. Early in the Tokugawa period, a sharp and intellectually profound debate had developed between Confucian scholars over the meaning and relative weight of the classics; heterodoxy was banned by official decree, and only one correct way of understanding the Confucian heritage was permitted. Thus, learning was not built on the assumption that knowledge awaits discovery. Truth was known and was contained in the classic tradition. Scholars still discreetly debated their interpretations, but for students there was only right or wrong in learning the meaning and significance of the classics. Debate focused on the applications of classical wisdom to specific issues of policy, but this debate was for teachers and administrators, and it was conducted across domains rather than within them. The correct attitude for students was serious humility. Respect was a key

12. On Japanese Confucianism, see esp. Maruyama (1974), Najita (1974), and Najita and Scheiner (1978).

symbol of Confucian virtue. Diligence and good attendance were recognized as often as intellectual brilliance. Independence of thought was not regularly rewarded or encouraged.

For Japan, the study of the Chinese language has been much like the study of Latin in Europe. During early periods of Japan's history, in a pattern remarkably similar to her more recent borrowing from the West, Chinese culture received great prominence, and its mastery became a source of authority. Formal schools centered largely on Chinese learning, and teaching the classics could become excessively formal and antiquarian. Teachers were often stiff, and their subjects were far from practical, yet Chinese learning remained a basic ingredient of Japanese education for a millennium. "The more difficult and agonizing a subject, the greater its mystique and authority": this adage still seems to fit the Japanese approach to formal education. With its eternal enthusiasm for form and correctness, the complex rules of Chinese composition and the vast corpus of its literature to be memorized constituted a particular challenge to mental discipline that set a pattern still in practice.

Yet reactions to the excesses of sinophilism also highlighted such "Japanese" qualities as unadorned simplicity, spontaneity of emotions, and a primordial closeness to nature.

Mornings spent with the books were generally followed by afternoons spent practicing military skills. A balance between the two was considered ideal. Fencing and other martial arts relied on action and were viewed as corrective to the pedantic tendencies of Confucian book learning. The martial arts were also seen as essentially Japanese, in contrast to scholarship, which tended to worship Chinese examples. A self-satisfied reliance on scholarly abilities, it was feared, could lead to dissoluteness of character, which physical training would remedy. The formalism and cerebral qualities of scholarship have always had their detractors in Japan, especially when foreign learning is in the ascendency.

But Chinese and native thinking did merge in one crucial area of education: the development of individual character. Both took human nature to be inherently good and perfectible. The source of personal development was "spiritual," that is, the individual's spirit (his will and fortitude, for example) could be strengthened and made more mature (in wisdom, patience, and so on) through rigorous training and difficult experiences.[13] The child, weak and ignorant because of blind preoccupation with itself and its needs, could learn to become the perfected adult capable of fulfilling social obligations with selfless spontaneity, and capable of comprehending the true interdependent nature of the universe with objective clarity. Strict training would produce this spiritual maturity, a key ingredient of the ideal Confucian governor. Ultimately, spiritual development was thought to lead to mystical realms of enlightenment. Both book learning and the martial arts were understood to contribute to spiritual growth, especially when they involved hard work, challenge, and rigorous discipline. Pleasure, however natural it is for humans to seek, could not contribute to spiritual growth.

The influence of the teacher's example and guidance in this process of character building was important. Between outstanding teachers and their students, a master-disciple relationship developed that was often lifelong. Good teachers showed the way through their own conduct; and knowing from experience the path to maturity, they could calibrate the right balance between forcing their students forward and offering consolation and understanding. Because character development was so central, many saw actions as more important than words. Anecdotes about a teacher's life were often more revered than his remarks in class, and much teaching centered on the examination or discussion of concrete examples of behavior. In this manner external formalism was linked to internal mysticism.

The formal and scholarly mode of orthodox Confucian learning and the bureaucracy of the larger fief schools caused many of the more independent teachers to establish their own small private schools (shijuku).[14] Teachers and students shared a simple, pure existence—eating, studying, training, and bathing together. Often the students were boarders in their teacher's home, sharing his entire life. The teacher was like a parent and the senior students like elder brothers, creating a discipleship with a close-knit group of followers. As in actual families, the true character of the teacher radiated throughout the life of the school.[15] All experience was part of education, and the whole person was engaged in the educational pro-

13. The classic statement of this attitude in English is Nitobe (1905).
14. See Jansen (1961), Dore (1965), Bellah (1957), Passin (1965), and Kaigo (1968).
15. Jansen (1961) is particularly useful as a description of this pattern.

cess. This intimate setting for rigorous learning defines a primitive ideal that is still quite alive.

Schools for townsmen and farmers also grew rapidly in the Tokugawa period. Small, private, and focused on the practical skills of reading, writing, and arithmetic, these schools enjoyed such popularity in the cities that there and in the more prosperous regions of the country some half of all children attended them. The children were sent for practical reasons—for the added status that literacy brought and for the moral lessons offered. The virtues of persistence, equanimity, frugality, and meticulousness were emphasized as of both moral and practical worth.[16]

It is true that nineteenth-century Western educational values were in some respects close to the Confucian approach. Restraint, moral rectitude, and character development were of great concern to many European and American educators, and only with the secularization of education in recent times have these matters faded in significance. In this regard, Japanese and Western schooling may well have diverged rather than converged in character between 1870 and 1945, for secularization in Japan did not undermine Confucian morality as greatly as it did the Christian approach. Because Confucianism was not a religion of faith, but of governmental orthodoxy, it was not as vulnerable to the rise of science and other trends that eliminated religion from the public domain. Secularization, the victory of utilitarianism in social thought, carried the West along a new tangent at an especially swift pace.

## The Prewar Pattern

In 1868, the feudal system was overthrown and a national government was established in the name of the Meiji emperor. This government set out to modernize Japanese society so it could withstand the threat of foreign imperialism. The principle of universal compulsory education was established in 1872, at a time when class distinctions were being abolished and a new nation's young leadership was forcing the entire population toward national development. Education was to produce loyal subjects capable of generating industrial and military strength.

16. Bellah (1957).

The shadows of Perry's black ships hung over the birth of the new school system, which was based on the two hundred fifty or so fief schools and many of the existing forty thousand commoner schools. But ambitions ran far ahead of resources, and the development of secondary and vocational schools proceeded much more slowly. By 1907 the length of compulsory education had been extended from its original four years to six years, and by 1935 all students were attending school for at least eight years. Japan had already caught up with the West in this respect.[17]

The extension of education within the population was inexorable, but up until World War II several major shifts of direction occurred in basic policy. During the 1870s, foreign influence was extraordinarily powerful. Foreign advisors and teachers were employed in large numbers; the new official textbooks were largely mindless translations of borrowed Western texts; and the official curriculum and pedagogy were modeled on foreign practice. Japan's leaders, admiring Western technology and learning, made a radical effort to create national strength and a modern society through universal education.[18]

But most Japanese teachers understood little of what they were to teach, and many parents reacted against the sudden imposition of a foreign and often incomprehensible system of education. Such ludicrous developments as elementary school pupils intoning a Japanese translation of McGuffey's reader as if it were a Buddhist sutra were not unheard of in the first years. No wonder schools were often targets of popular riots against the government in the 1870s.

Reaction to the extremes of foreign influence surfaced in the 1880s, and a search was begun to recapture valuable elements of the Tokugawa legacy.[19] The content of education progressively became more nationalistic and focused on national needs. The reaction did not undo the institutional foundations laid in the 1870s, but it refocused attention on moral issues. The Ministry of Education set out to clearly establish: 1) Japanese morality and values as equally significant to Western science and technology, and 2) Japanese social loyalties and practices as basic to the new system of education. Both

17. Passin (1965), Kaigo (1968), Kobayashi (1978), and Anderson (1975).
18. I. P. Hall (1973) is the best source in English on this period.
19. See Shively (1959), I. P. Hall (1973), Pyle (1969), and Roden (1980) for details.

were encapsulated in the Imperial Rescript of Education (1890), which became the guiding inspiration for public schools until 1945:

> Our Imperial Ancestors have founded Our Empire on a basis broad and everlasting, and have deeply and firmly implanted virtue; Our subjects ever united in loyalty and filial piety have from generation to generation illustrated the beauty thereof. This is the glory of the fundamental character of Our Empire, and herein also lies the source of our education. Yet, Our subjects, be filial to your parents, affectionate to your brothers and sisters; as husbands and wives be harmonious, as friends be true; bear yourselves in modesty and moderation; extend your benevolence to all; pursue learning and cultivate arts, and thereby develop intellectual faculties and perfect moral powers; furthermore, advance public good and promote common interests; always respect the Constitution and observe the laws; should emergency arise, offer yourselves courageously to the State; and thus guard and maintain the prosperity of Our Imperial Throne coeval with heaven and earth. So shall ye not only be our good and faithful subjects but render illustrious the best traditions of your forefathers.[20]

In essence, the Confucian teachings of the Tokugawa period, briefly abandoned, were thus emphatically reinstated as a means of anchoring the new education culturally and making it an instrument of legitimation and support for the political institutions of the state. Because the Meiji emperor was the official source of this new direction in his role as provider of moral guidance for the country, both intentions were reinforced. He was Japan's crucial link to the past and the center of all legitimacy and authority. Schools thus enshrined the state's highest values, old and new. Reverence for both Western learning and Eastern morality were combined around the ultimate concerns of ordering and strengthening the young nation.

Japan's leaders, trained in fief schools themselves, traveled abroad and discovered in France, Germany, England, and the United States which educational ideas would suit their purposes.[21] From France they borrowed the system of centralized national authority and a strong emphasis on state-run normal schools; from Germany was drawn a system of higher education built around a few elite public universities; England provided a foreign example (in schools like Rugby) of Spartan character building through athletics and moral

20. Passin (1965) contains various other important documents in Japanese educational history.

21. I. P. Hall (1973) contains fascinating details.

discipline; and from the United States they borrowed many practical pedgagogical techniques and an interest in vocational training. Student uniforms, Western art and music, science and mathematics curricula, considerations of school architecture, the use of desks and blackboards, and hundreds of other details were imported and retained. All of this was combined with an essentially Confucian outlook and a nationalistic set of goals.

Morality was put symbolically at the top of the curriculum. The essential character of teaching retained many similarities with Tokugawa practice. It was one thing to import textbooks, altogether another to import the intangibles of teacher attitudes and behavior. Initially, teachers were largely from the samurai class, and they set down a pattern of behavior that centered on devotion to duty, exemplary personal conduct, considerable independence of style, firm authority, and personal involvement with their students. They were employees of the emperor's national government and in the vanguard of the effort to modernize Japan, and their status thus remained high despite the bureaucratization of education. Teachers trained in the new subjects were considered among the most enlightened in comprehending the nature of the modern Western world. Isolation had ended abruptly for Japan, and the cadre of newly trained teachers were often viewed as shepherds guiding the population from one world to the next. Self-righteous, misguided, and pompous activities like those to which zealous missionaries are liable were also part of the image of the teacher.

The government's new normal schools sought to preserve and standardize traditional and modern ideals. By 1890, normal school training was quite demanding, and the students attracted to these schools were of high quality. The imprint of the national government's will was clear, both in the development of a standard approach to curriculum and in the intensity with which these colleges tried to develop teachers of character and moral leadership. A critical instrument in the second effort was the establishment of a military mode in the extracurricular affairs of the normal schools. Regular army officers were assigned to put into place physical education programs that included military drills, and they established rigorous discipline in the life of the schools. Army officers came to exemplify loyal patriotism for future teachers. Mori Arinori, the minister of education who sponsored this development in 1885, explained:

The things we hope to achieve by means of this training are three: first to instill—with the sense of urgency possessed by actual soldiers—those habits of obedience which are appropriate in the classroom. Secondly, as you know, soldiers are always formed into squads, each squad possessing its own leader who devotes himself, heart and mind and soul, to the welfare of his group. And thirdly, every company has its commanding officer who controls and supervises it, and who must comport himself with dignity. By the same token our students, by trading off the roles of common soldier, squad leader and commanding officer, will build up the traits of character appropriate to each of these three roles.[22]

A subtle shift from Tokugawa practice, but one of great consequence, must be noted here. The modern school system was on a new scale and required extensive bureaucratic regulation. Previously, a teacher's authority had rested largely on the respect and affection of his students, but under the new system it became a matter of training and decree. Intimacy was less certain, and the respect for a largely foreign subject matter was less reliable. Mori's intentions were to rectify these problems by providing admirable teachers who knew how to create a rule-governed order, and he set in motion a trend that by the 1930s had led to the assignment of military officers not just to normal schools but to all public schools. Military attitudes and practices were thus extended from the drill fields to the classrooms and into the very heart of many schools.

Such extreme developments had not been planned, and their major causes lay outside the Ministry of Education in the general political climate. All the same, the creation of a national system of education and the introduction of a largely foreign curriculum were too much for a population to swallow within a decade or two. Meiji Japan as a whole was quite unstable because of the rapid changes taking place, and reaction to the foreign direction of cultural change was to be expected. That foreign ideas were seen as destabilizing, and that stability was sought in traditional values, was to be expected. Yet the Tokugawa educational emphases on character, duty, and social harmony were no longer as readily tempered by the humanism of student-teacher intimacy once mass education had been instituted. A manipulative bureaucracy clearly had unlimited opportunities under conditions of rising nationalism to nudge public edu-

22. Ibid., p. 427.

cation toward authoritarian and militaristic practices in the name of strengthening the nation and preserving its heritage.

Today all of this is much-regretted history, of course, but the basic political issues have hardly disappeared. The ambiguity felt about the contradictions between Western and Japanese culture remains. So does the issue of the role of public education in the social order. The two issues intertwine, because in emphasizing Western (utilitarian) or Confucian ethical values, schools are in fact teaching political behavior. This is true of schools in every nation, of course, but acutely so in Japan, where the Tokugawa heritage and Western thought have been pushed close together in education. Other Japanese institutions clearly favor one or the other.

Between the broad national ambitions of compulsory education and the advanced, specialized work of universities lay the less clearly defined territory of secondary schooling. The Meiji government in 1872 proposed a plan for creating secondary or middle schools that would bridge the considerable gap between elementary and higher education. These schools were to be neither compulsory nor directed to a large segment of the populace. They were explicitly designed to offer a general preparation for entering elite universities. Thus, at their inception, Japan's secondary schools were subordinated to the goal of university entrance.[23]

Numerous early shifts occurred in the details of middle school design, but it was finally settled that each prefecture would have one "ordinary" boys' middle school, and the nation would initially have five "higher" middle schools. Most graduates of the latter would step directly into the imperial universities. The ordinary middle schools were the precursors of today's high schools. They offered five years of courses and followed six years of compulsory schooling and two years of upper elementary education, making them equivalent to grades nine to fourteen.

Being few in number, the ordinary middle schools were viewed as elite institutions. This impression was reinforced by the inclination of school authorities to facilitate entry for the children of the upper classes. Because the new prefectures followed the lines of Tokugawa feudal domains, the new middle schools were readily equated with the former domain schools. At the prefectural level, the points of

23. Kaigo (1968), and I. P. Hall (1973).

continuity from Tokugawa into Meiji also included many faculty members, the expectation of public service from the best graduates, and the general close ties to government.

The five higher middle schools, equivalent to modern universities in most respects, were oriented to the national level. They were the epitome of the elite track, as only the most outstanding graduates of the ordinary middle schools gained admission. Only higher middle school graduates advanced to the imperial universities, whose graduates were virtually assured positions of national authority and prestige later in life. Naturally, the greatest competition to advance upward focused on entrance examinations to the ordinary and higher middle schools. From the beginning, entrance exams and career ambitions were closely tied together.[24]

The curricula of the middle schools were broad and academically rigorous: they included ethics, language, Chinese classics, a first and second foreign language, agriculture, geography, history, mathematics, natural science, physics, chemistry, calligraphy, art, poetry, and physical education. Initially, foreign instructors were employed to teach some of these subjects. Lafcadio Hearn and a number of other Westerners known for their deep involvement with Japan formed their initial acquaintance with the country as teachers in these middle schools.

Vocational subjects, both technical and commercial, were added as electives by late in the century, but middle schools did not evolve in a pragmatic direction. There was no need to do so. Although most graduates of ordinary middle schools (80 percent, in fact) did not advance to universities in the nineteenth century, most nevertheless aimed at higher education. Failing entrance, they still found excellent employment. Government and business organizations sought general managerial talent from the ordinary middle schools, for their graduates represented the top 10 percent of the nation's young men.

A simple but powerful formula that has dominated Japanese secondary education ever since was thus established: the difficulty of a school's entrance exams is the crucial measure of its students' talent. Employers chose to let this criterion of school reputation, rather than an individual's grades or subjects studied, guide their selection

24. Spaulding (1967).

of personnel for managerial jobs. Entrance exams thus became the route to success. For the upper and middle classes, it was the practical way to the best jobs, whether the subjects studied ever proved practical or not. The formula has not changed in a hundred years.

Middle schools were only for boys, an assumption that came very easily to the Meiji mind. It was consistent with tradition and with the deeply rooted notion that, beyond the basis of elementary school, the educational needs of boys and girls were different. Girls were destined to be homemakers. From the very beginning, a separate form of secondary education was planned for girls of the upper class, one that did not lead to higher education. Ethics for women, etiquette, home economics, child care, sewing, and handcrafts were to be taught in addition to a general academic curriculum. The number of "girls' high schools" increased greatly after the turn of the century.

Public vocational schools joined the secondary school ranks late. Vocational subjects in the ordinary middle schools had not gained acceptance, and as the needs of Japanese industry advanced, separate vocational schools (technical, commercial, agricultural, and merchant marine) were developed in response. Vocational education was respected, but clearly it was a side track from the elite path, and one of considerably lower status.

Despite the rapid expansion of education, elitism persisted. By 1895, three distinct forms of public secondary education were in existence, yet their combined enrollment numbered under forty thousand; of this number, thirty thousand were boys attending ordinary middle schools. Furthermore, only one in five of the boys in ordinary middle schools was able to advance to a higher middle school. The path upward from the elementary level was narrow indeed.

Following completion of the six compulsory years, the majority of students followed a different track created at the turn of the century, advancing to upper elementary schools (two years), and then taking employment. On a part-time basis they would continue in "youth schools" (five years), where they received some vocational training, further basic education, and some military training. The students who received this much less intensive education were at that time largely farm children, for whom full secondary education seemed irrelevant. Youth schools were not recognized as part of secondary education. They did not offer credentials, nor did they open possibilities for further advancement. All the same, it is worth noting that by 1941 most Japanese youth were actually staying in school on a part-time basis until age seventeen.

The considerable expansion of secondary school enrollments from 1900 to 1935 did not significantly alter this pattern because the population of elementary school students also grew rapidly. Boys' middle schools grew at a slower pace than girls' high schools and vocational schools. Thus, in 1935 roughly one in twenty fifteen-year-old boys was attending an ordinary middle school, and a somewhat larger proportion were in vocational schools. Similarly, about one in ten girls was able to enter a girls' high school.

Over time, university enrollments increased as the government progressively allowed private colleges to become universities. There were about nine thousand places in the five imperial universities in 1918. By 1945, the number of university students had increased to one hundred thousand and the total enrollments in all institutions of higher education had reached approximately four hundred thousand. Higher education expanded greatly, but the proportion of all youth going to universities was in fact rising slowly, because the total population was also growing rapidly.

Throughout the seventy-five years between its foundation and its demise, the prewar system grew in a manner that enhanced the elite status of these secondary schools and universities that had been established first. Boys' middle schools retained their superior status over vocational schools and girls' high schools. Older middle schools and universities retained prestige and attracted the best applicants. Maintaining the rankings were the entrance exams.

Competition to enter universities remained severe. Universities (public and private) had places for only one-third of all middle school graduates in 1935. Half of those who were not accepted took jobs, but the other half chose to study another year and try again. The competition to enter the top higher middle schools and then the imperial universities was particularly stiff, with less than one in six applicants accepted at the higher schools and one of two at an imperial university. But this preoccupation with higher education and entrance exams existed only among a small proportion of the total population: even in 1935, less than 3 percent of all elementary school graduates were going to a university.

Given the great rewards that followed a university degree, it was natural that considerable pressure for private secondary education would develop among the urban middle class. Wealthy parents whose children failed to enter public middle schools sought private options. The same tendency occurred at the university level. Government policy limited the growth of private universities, but by 1935 two-thirds of all university students were in private institutions, and about one-fifth of all middle school boys were in private school. Yet the prestige of private institutions, as "second best," remained lower than public middle schools and universities.

Despite an unconvincing start, the education system contained the seeds of a meritocratic order. The key was the objectivity of the entrance exam system. Soon the ordinary middle schools were admitting a larger proportion of boys who did not come from the former samurai class, boys of notable talents who had studied hard and passed the entrance exams. Gradually a greater proportion of such commoners succeeded in entering the higher middle schools and ultimately the imperial universities. The extension and standardization of elementary education also laid the foundation for a growing equal opportunity, for it meant an equal start for all children. And, at the other end of the educational system, access to the best positions in government, academia, and business were open to university graduates regardless of family background. By the turn of the century, graduates of the imperial universities were rising to positions of influence throughout society. Most were, by then, from commoner stock. The private universities, notably Keio and Waseda, also came to emphasize entrance examinations as the number of applicants surpassed the number of openings. They, too, became part of the meritocratic machinery as their graduates joined the business, media, and cultural elites.

It is interesting to speculate on the reasons for the relative ease with which this quite revolutionary development occurred. Certainly examinations are a noteworthy part of the Confucian heritage, but in ancient Japan and throughout the Tokugawa period they were less important than class, lineage, and particularistic ties. The *han* schools were not dominated by examinations or by other objective judgments of individual merit. All the same, merit was recognized and rewarded informally in the administrations of many

Tokugawa domains. The crucial historical point is that the new Meiji government was created and led largely by ranking samurai—men who had themselves risen due to merit, and who as reformers knew the frustrations and inefficiencies of allocating authority by particularistic criteria. These men cut themselves off from their own class and from *han* loyalties to support the development of an educational system that drew commoner talent into the imperial universities and into the bureaucracy. Once established, and this took thirty years, the meritocracy became self-perpetuating, each generation of leaders committed by their own careers to its basic values.

A social/cultural explanation is more speculative. There is no doubt about the centrality of personal bonds of loyalty and group membership during the Tokugawa period. Universalistic aspects of social relations hardly existed. Lord and retainer, master and apprentice, elder and junior, members of X village, followers of Y teacher, loyalists of Z lord—these were the categories of social thought. Nor did the new cultural ferment and the import of Western thinking during the Meiji era significantly alter the character of social relations or the preferences of individuals for particularistic ties. Japan, as has been noted so often, is a group-oriented society—neither individualistic nor socialistic. Such a society can choke on its own narrow particularism if it does not have well-entrenched mechanisms that counterbalance its powerful tendencies to allocate rewards and favors on the basis of personal affiliation. What can happen all too easily is that those responsible for selecting people for universities, jobs, and so forth cannot resist personal pressure from relatives, friends, and colleagues. The weight of personal obligations requires a powerful counter-mechanism.[25] An impersonal exam system that adjudicates the selection process is just the solution. Once established, this system in Japan created its own constituency and provided the great majority with the promise of opportunity. Probably no Meiji leader thought about matters in quite this way, but the fact remains that outside of education, particularism retained its extraordinary power, and the Meiji leadership was anxious to assure that the nation would benefit from a secure flow of talent to the top. The sacredness of exams in Japan, even today, seems proportional to the power of the particularistic forces it holds at bay.

25. I am indebted to Ronald Dore for his suggestion of this idea.

## *The Occupation*

By the end of the war, Japan was a nation economically prostrate and socially disorganized. Defeat and then occupation would shake the very foundation of Japanese national identity. Cities lay in ruins, people were hungry, the emperor had announced the first surrender in Japan's long history, and the Americans were going to run the country. What Japan had represented during the long and very costly struggle—the proud virtues of an independent nation—was discredited by defeat and condemned by the flamboyant democracy and individualism of the victors. Values, at least official ones, were largely turned upside down during the period immediately following the signing of the peace. While the great majority of Japanese, their sense of the past and future paralyzed, simply tried to survive and avoid trouble, the basis for a new society was laid.

The Americans were sent to demilitarize and democratize Japan. Fresh from a global defeat of fascism, they were a naïvely confident group that neither questioned the superiority of the American system nor understood much about Japan. The success of this vast social engineering project using American ideals as the model probably depended on such naïvete. The scope of the occupation made the New Deal, from which many occupation authorities had come, look modest. Yet, because implementation was left to Japanese government officials, the Americans avoided many of the perplexing realities that would have impeded momentum. A new constitution, a new set of civil rights, and a new political system were established. Land reform, the end of large financial combinations (the *zaibatsu*), "emancipation" of women, unionization and organization of leftist parties, freedom of religion, and freedom of the press were among the major changes initiated within the first year. The Americans also set out to transform Japanese education, which they saw as a key to democratizing Japan.

How did the Americans view the prewar system? The political objections were stated by William J. Sebald, an assistant to MacArthur:

The former Japanese system of education, through centralized control, and with the assistance of a well-knit bureaucracy, had been used by the country's leaders as part of a policy of developing an obedient and subservient population. Schools had been transformed, primarily into agencies for indoctrination in militarism and ultranationalism. For many years, teachers and students had drawn their inspiration from the Imperial Rescript on Education promulgated in 1890, with the result that the importance and integrity of the individual were dwarfed into significance by the growing power of the state.[26]

American educators added other criticisms:

The Japanese system of education in its organization and curricular provisions would have been due for reform in accordance with modern theories of education even if there had not been injected into it ultra-nationalism and militarism. The system was based on a nineteenth-century pattern which was highly centralized, providing one type of education for the masses and another for the privileged few. It held that at each level of instruction there is a fixed quantum of knowledge to be absorbed, and tended to disregard differences in the ability and interests of pupils. Through prescription, textbooks, examinations and inspection, the system lessened the opportunities of teachers to exercise professional freedom. The measure of efficiency was the degree to which standardization and uniformity were secured.[27]

And the teaching profession was not democratic:

Teachers were followers rather than leaders. They were poorly paid and received far less compensation than other government officials of comparable rank . . . As members of the national civil service, teachers were responsible to the national government in Tokyo rather than to the local community in which they served. The right of teachers to organize associations was severely limited by the government; teachers' associations were government-sponsored, subsidized, and controlled.[28]

In essence, wherever the prewar system differed from the American ideal, it was undemocratic and unprogressive.

The Americans intended to reconstruct the entire system in a reform no less revolutionary in scope than that which had established public schools eighty years before. A new and powerful authority, a pliant population, and a discredited past combined as they rarely do in history to make sweeping change possible. Unbeknownst to the American authorities, many school officials, dressed in formal mourning clothes, had already reverently burned their schools' pic-

26. GHQ (1948), p. 8.
27. *Report of the U.S. Education Mission to Japan, 1946.* Tokyo: General Headquarters, Supreme Commander, Allied Powers. Civil Information and Education Section, p. 6.
28. Ibid.

tures of the emperor in secret midnight ceremonies, preparing for the new era.[29]

There were, however, serious limits to reform. Most important was the lack of physical resources. The bombings had ruined about one-third of all existing schools. Classes were being held even in streetcars and public bathhouses. Government coffers were empty, and merely finding enough money to pay teachers was difficult. Leadership and staffing were also problems. During the war, the training of new teachers had fallen behind, and many potential teachers had been drafted. Young women had entered the profession in large numbers. The Americans, furthermore, initiated a purge of right-wing teachers, causing the mass resignation of those military officers who had been assigned to school duties. A sizable number of principals and senior teachers had resigned in 1945, some in atonement for the war deaths of students whom they had taught to accept militarism, others because they saw themselves as unable to adjust to the new democratic era in education. In Hyōgo Prefecture, at least, the official purge found few other identifiable rightists to remove.[30]

What offended the Americans in Japanese textbooks was immediately announced, and the teaching of many aspects of ethics, history, and geography was suspended while new textbooks were written.[31] Major reform awaited the arrival in March 1946 of a study mission of education experts from the United States. Within a month the mission had studied the situation, deliberated, and written and issued its report. It was no surprise that their suggestions for sweeping change were based entirely on the American system, and especially on those policies that academic experts were urging on their colleagues in the United States.[32] Their plan called for a three-year extension of compulsory education to ninth grade and the elimination of different kinds of secondary schools in favor of comprehensive high schools. A uniform 6−3−3−4 system (six elementary, three middle, three high school, and four university years) replaced the differentiated complex of prewar schools. Coeducation was rec-

29. Kobe-shi Kyōiku-shi Henshū Iinkai (1966).
30. Ibid.
31. This account depends heavily on Kawai (1960), Passin (1965), and Anderson (1975), as well as GHQ (1948) and Kaigo (1975).
32. Kawai (1960).

ommended for all levels, and an expansion of opportunities for higher education was urged. The regulatory control of private education was criticized. The report also condemned the centralized nature of administration and called for greater community and teacher initiative. The formation of school boards and parent-teacher organizations was suggested. Social studies, which had not received much attention in the prewar system, was encouraged as fundamental to the training of a well-informed, independent citizenry. Vocational subjects were promoted and the narrow preparation for university entrance roundly condemned. The report even raised the issue of the Japanese language, suggesting that the roman alphabet replace the thousands of Chinese characters as the official system of writing.

The most central theme of all, however, was individualism. In contrast to the authoritarian dominance of a standard curriculum, the differing developmental needs of individual personalities was set forth as the major theme of the new education. The refrains were those so familiar to American ears:

> A system of education should be so organized as to encourage the fullest development of which each individual—boy or girl, man or woman—is capable as an intelligent, responsible and cooperating member of society . . . Freedom of inquiry, rather than exclusive memorization of factual knowledge for examination purposes, should be emphasized.[33]

Further:

> Education shall aim at the full development of personality, striving for the rearing of the people, sound in mind and body, who shall love truth and justice, esteem individual value, respect labour, and have a deep sense of responsibility, and be imbued with an independent spirit, as builders of a peaceful state and society.[34]

"Citizens, not subjects," was the goal. Teachers were to exercise their "professional freedom" to tailor their teaching to foster the growth of independent, productive community members. The goal of equal opportunity pointed to a system of mass education, one in which abilities were not tracked and the sexes were not separated; and the ideals of individualism and democracy required a

33. *Report of the U.S. Education Mission to Japan, 1946*, p. 18.
34. Japan's Fundamental Law of Education, 1947, GHQ (1948), p. 109.

flexibility and independence at the classroom level that was equally challenging.

The Japanese were to decide their own future educational system, intoned the Americans. In keeping with the American preference for grass roots development, the Japanese were to adjust policies locally as implementation progressed. The Americans assigned young officers, one to each prefecture, to supervise the progess but not to actually administer the system, and these men bounced around the countryside in their jeeps supervising reform in schools and communities without in fact directing action. In Kobe, I heard stories of principals in middle schools ordering their students to begin square dancing upon the approach of an American jeep.

The concrete problems of creating enough new classrooms to realize the goal of compulsory education through ninth grade were tackled by local Japanese officials. Elementary and middle school classes often shared the same buildings; even temples were commandeered, and a capital financing campaign that depended heavily on "voluntary contributions" from parents and leading citizens was undertaken. By early 1950, enough classrooms had been created to substantiate the new compulsory education law, but a by-product of this effort was a continuing acute shortage of facilities for the secondary level.

Other structural changes met a similar mixed fate. Almost all institutions of higher education were allowed to call themselves universities after 1947, and the number of universities jumped from forty-nine in 1942 to 245 in 1955.[35] Enrollment levels did not rise much in the national universities, but private universities expanded rapidly. As a result, the university student population began to mushroom, growing by 450 percent between 1950 and 1970. The opportunities for higher education were expanded by the reforms, but not without a price: in those private universities that grew most rapidly, student-teacher ratios, institutional facilities, and the level of instruction deteriorated significantly, and the gap in quality between the elite national universities and most private universities increased.[36] The move to mass higher education not only preserved

35. A thorough treatment of the statistical changes in postwar education is offered by Lee (1974).
36. Mombushō (1976).

but actually enhanced and elaborated the hierarchical structure of higher education.[37] University entrance exams remained critical to career success; the major difference after reform was that more and more young Japanese were drawn into the competition.

National universities were finally opened to women, and female enrollments in these top schools slowly rose, but never approached parity with male levels. Progress toward full equality of participation for women in higher education has not fulfilled American expectations. The occupation did, however, end all legal and structural barriers faced by women, and today as many high school girls as boys are preparing for higher education.

The Americans also attempted to rearrange the political control of education.[38] The central authority of the national Ministry of Education was pinpointed as the source of prewar political problems. Regimentation and nationalistic indoctrination were attributed to the ministry's dominance. The Americans wanted decision-making power shifted to local school boards. As a result, laws were passed that set aside the ministry's authority to write textbooks, and teachers were encouraged to select or create their own. Normal schools, reestablished as university departments of education, were encouraged to formulate democratic approaches to schooling. School boards, teachers, officials, and professors of education began earnestly—and, some recall, endlessly—discussing the issue of democratizing teaching and school administration. Accustomed as they were to highly detailed and professional direction from the authorities in Tokyo, localities typically found their new independence disconcerting. Ironically, initiative in creating grass roots democracy remained largely with the Ministry of Education and the Americans in Tokyo.

A new political force also entered the scene. Teachers' unions, encouraged by American policy and led largely by committed leftists, grew in membership and power at a rapid rate.[39] It is undoubtedly true that before the war many teachers had resented official policies, but rarely did they organize to protest. Those few that did were of a leftist persuasion, and many of them were jailed or lost their jobs.

---

37. Nagai (1971).
38. Brett (1954), Hidaka (1956), Kawai (1960), Steiner (1965), and Duke (1973).
39. Duke (1973) offers a valuable history of the teachers' union movement in Japan.

After the war, they were the first to seize the organizational opportunity. American educational policy was close to their initial aims, and unionization was being encouraged. To young teachers, their union embodied many of the new ideals for an independent, progressive education. Even most older teachers saw unionization as the wave of the future. In an atmosphere of radical change, the great majority of teachers joined one of the several unions that rose in Tokyo and spread across the nation.

Although there seems to have been little contact between the new unions and the American authorities, the actions of one group reinforced the other until around 1950. Both sought to weaken central authority. The unions had little immediate power, but once well organized and consolidated, they assumed an increasingly active role in the politics of education. Unlike American unions, they were totally outside the governmental framework, and as public employees' unions their right to strike was not even recognized. Once the occupation had ended, the largest and dominant union, the Japan Teachers Union, assumed a posture of staunch opposition to the Ministry of Education. When the Americans departed in 1952, Japanese education was politically polarized. At issue was the control of schools and the continuation of the occupation-sponsored reforms. The polarization was also highly charged ideologically, as the union leadership was strongly leftist and the government firmly conservative.

As the ministry and the union began to clash over numerous issues, it became clear that control of public education was to be a major issue in postwar Japanese politics. The issues of traditional versus foreign ethics, of order versus freedom, of school and teacher independence versus administrative authority became entangled with political ideologies and the general power struggle between the ruling conservative party and the leftist opposition. Even the most minute detail of school administration was a potential cause for political conflict.

The occupation's reforms were least effective at the high school level. The ideal was derived, of course, from the comprehensive public high school as it had developed in rural and suburban America. Its three organizing principles—1) coeducation, 2) a mix of college preparatory, vocational, and general education tracks, and 3) universal admission based on local residence—expressed the spirit of

American democracy. All three were foreign to Japan at the time of the occupation.

The American model for the conduct of high school education is one so familiar that we take it for granted. It rests on the notion of the school as a microcosm of the small community: high schools are properly rooted in whole communities and should reflect their diversity. Thus residence and only residence, not ability or vocational goals or any other segregating criteria, should determine admission. This establishes a foundation for equality of educational opportunity. We know all too well that there are great problems with this approach when the pattern of residence is not that of a small (relatively homogeneous) community, but that knowledge is not part of the ideal. In theory, a mixing of students of all ability levels will nurture an egalitarian spirit of community and mutual respect.

The second basic principle of American high school education is choice. This follows logically from the fact of student diversity, from the ideals of freedom and individualism, and even from the tradition of local school autonomy. We assume that schools, teachers, and students are different, want to be different, and should be different. We therefore build in choice at every opportunity. The comprehensive school has many curricular offerings. Arguments for larger high schools were made on the grounds of greater diversity of courses. Electives multiply as far as budgets permit. Teachers select their own textbooks. The faculty plans the curriculum, the schedules, and most requirements. State requirements are typically limited to civics, driver education, and physical education. Graduation requirements, until recently, have been statements of the minimum, as are the new state competency tests. In all cases, we try to preserve choice despite the demand for standards. Of course, being Americans, we typically complain that not enough choice is provided, that high schools are too bureaucratic, and that they produce mindless conformity. Indeed, along with all forms of mass processing, our schools do have these inclinations. The point is that our cultural and educational heritage has made choice a central value and has put it in an adversarial position to many critical considerations of organizational efficiency and educational standards. Each step up the school ladder brings greater choice, for it is our hallmark of adulthood and citizenship.

A corollary is the notion of personality. The educational ideals of the occupation included emphasis on adjusting education to differences of personality, tailoring programs and teaching to individuals. Americans eschew school uniforms, favor individualized study programs, and in a myriad of other ways encourage individual expression. The goal was and is to foster the development of distinct personalities and talents, and at no point in the educational process is this more important than in high school. In America at least, students are understood to be both rapidly gaining independence from parents and family and searching for their own identities. Clearly, our cultural preoccupation with individualism underlies this emphasis. The Americans encountered a very different situation in Japan, a society that elevates the group and the nation as the moral priorities of education.

Yet citizenship was also a crucial ingredient of the American proposals. In the American model, high schools teach the attitudes and behavior that make for strong grass roots democracy. Civics courses are a start, but student government, classroom discussions of current events, and teacher encouragement of student self-expression (even criticism of authority) are pedagogically important. Student clubs and extracurricular activities are valued for education in self-governance and initiative. In high school, students should have the chance to play at being citizens of democracy. The high school, in effect, should be a microcosm of the ideal small town in its political processes as in its sociological composition. Citizenship in Japanese prewar education had meant loyalty and duty.

Indeed, the American model was a radical departure from the educational goals, ideals, and practices of previous Japanese secondary education. The Japanese not only heard about the American approach, they were encouraged to visit schools in the United States; and in fact, they became quite familiar with our institutions firsthand. The influence of such exposure is not easy to assess. Clearly, many American practices seemed impressive to the visitors in the light of democratic ideals, but often what worked in America struck them as impractical for Japan. American parents were not preoccupied with university entrance exams. There was no tradition of a highly structured national curriculum established by a Ministry of Education. The American teachers' tolerance for variety, uncertainty, and disorder was clearly greater. And American students, perhaps because of a different upbringing or elementary education, were

far more independent and outspoken than their Japanese counterparts. Such comparisons are behind the general reluctance of Japanese school officials to adopt in toto the American model. One high
school in Kobe, for example, offered comprehensive (academic and
vocational) curricula under the same roof. It still exists, but the experiment was unsuccessful because the two types of students and
the two faculties could not resolve their status and other differences.

There is no question that throughout the postwar period a goal of
Japanese secondary educational policy has been the extension of
equal opportunity. But just after the war the situation was far from
favorable for establishment of the American high school pattern.
The most critical problem was the insufficiency of high school classrooms. The old ordinary middle schools had been relatively few in
number, and even stretched to their seams after the war they had
room for less than half of the ninth-grade graduates. In the reformed
6–3–3–4 system, the new compulsory middle schools (grades seven
to nine) took priority over the high schools in the allocation of
space. The meager financial resources available had to be devoted to
the task of completing enough classrooms to support the compulsory system. It is estimated that over one-quarter of all schools
had to be rebuilt in 1945 just to restore Japanese education to prewar
conditions.[40]

The construction of new high schools and the expansion of existing ones began in earnest only in the mid-fifties. Yet, by 1975
nearly every Japanese was able to advance to high school. This great
achievement, however, came after a pattern of high school organization that was quite contrary to the American model had been established in Japan's cities. In the late forties and early fifties the
high school shortage was acute, and it was certain to remain so for
quite some time. Local governments in charge of such decisions re-
sponded by retaining entrance exams as the most appropriate means
of allocating the scarce space in public high schools. With private
schools also retaining their entrance exams, the postwar high school
system did not move toward the American pattern of attendance
based on residence. Rather, whole cities and prefectures (or large divisions within them) became school districts containing numerous
vertically ranked high schools. Officially there has never been any

40. Kobe-shi Kyōiku-shi Henshū Iinkai (1966).

ranking; but in fact, the hierarchy of preference, academic excellence, and prestige of the prewar system remains unaltered.

Under the American directive to reopen schools and operate normally as soon as possible, local officials had no option initially except to stay with the prewar faculties and programs. When the American plan for comprehensive high schools was suggested, the old divisions (boys' academic, girls', and vocational) still remained. Integrating the sexes into coeducational high school was not difficult. All it required was opening all entrance exams to boys and girls. Few teachers had to change jobs. Throughout most of Japan, girls' public high schools disappeared from the map.

Integrating vocational and university-oriented academic programs was more difficult. School faculties adamantly resisted the idea of dispersion, and the costs and confusion of reequipping schools to handle vocational subjects seemed forbidding. Alumni protested the threatened ending of school (especially elite) traditions. And everyone worried that the subsequent turmoil in secondary education would put the local students at a disadvantage in preparing for university entrance exams.

As a result, with some exceptions (mostly in rural areas), comprehensive high schools American-style were not created. Rather, the hierarchical order in each locality was reinforced by the retention of the academic-vocational distinction; and the orientation of high school education continued to be primarily to university or job preparation rather than to the experience of citizenship in an engineered social context. Japanese high schools did not become representative of social diversity. Rather, they continued to reflect the stratification and segregation of academic ability.

The opportunity for thorough reform came and went roughly between 1946 and 1950. After that, only the goal of universal high school education was vigorously pursued. More and more students were poured into the existing structure of high schools. New schools (academic or vocational, but not comprehensive) were also built, and applicants assigned them to a rung on the existing school status ladder. Invariably, the new schools ended up at the bottom. They were untried, with no track record. To Japanese students and parents, with their aversion to risk, being new meant being undesirable. As high school enrollments reached near universal levels, officials could congratulate themselves on having achieved equality of educational opportunity through the twelfth grade; but this claim only measured the most surface kind of equality.

More crucial, however, was the rapid growth in university openings. High school students doing university preparatory work expanded proportionally. In the prewar period about 10 percent of Japan's youth were studying for higher education, laboring over subjects like English and physics. Today over 50 percent attend academic high schools and are cramming for entrance exams. The change has been particularly notable for secondary-school-age girls, who not only began attending coeducational high schools after the war, but who, for the first time, were able to compete for university places on an equal footing with boys. The proportion of females attending academic high schools is now the same as for males.

What did the extension of high school attendance to nearly the entire population of youth aged seventeen, eighteen, and nineteen mean in the light of Japanese educational history? First, what had once been a rare honor and privilege became commonplace. A high school education at present carries little distinction. One has to go to a university, a good one at that, to accomplish anything. It is unfortunate but true that increasing attendance has the effect of diminishing the social worth of education at any level. Second, the postwar popularity of higher education established the college preparatory model of high schooling as dominant. Thus, the intense and heavily academic curriculum and style of the prewar elite secondary schools became the pattern for a high school education that extended down through the middle class and into the working class. Ironically, this trend was developing momentum at a time when the occupation's theme of democratizing education was still quite influential. The magnetism of university prestige attracted parents and students to the traditional elite model of secondary schooling.

The American proposals for comprehensive high schools attended by a diversity of students and focused on citizenship and expressive activities never captured the popular imagination. Just as average Japanese, now that they can afford it, seek the most prestigious French labels when buying clothes, so they have demanded academic high schools for their children. The American comprehensive high school is still talked about in educational circles, but it would take an extraordinary social revolution before social and cultural conditions would favor it as the answer to Japan's educational problems.

## *Summary*

There is a temptation when reviewing the present in light of the past to use such labels as modern or traditional and thereby to bifurcate institutional reality simplistically. In 1875, the new state-run and Western-influenced system certainly stood in stark contrast to the previous Confucian-based system of fief and commoner schools. But during the intervening hundred years the original dichotomy was transformed 1) as traditional elements were revived, 2) as borrowing continued from evolving Western systems, 3) as education became a larger and more integral part of society, and 4) as Japan became industrialized and urbanized. At times official policy led the way; at other times the dynamic came from society. Postwar changes, once the occupation's reforms were in place, have been largely the result of social change.

Three distinct traditions of secondary education in Japan have been identified here: the Confucian, the prewar elite, and the American. All three contribute to the character of contemporary high school education, yet what has developed since 1945 is not dominated strictly by any one of these models. The Confucian emphasis on familial order and morality contrasts with both the pragmatic intentions of elite secondary schooling and the American emphasis on individualism and democracy. The Confucian ideal remains particularly influential in the realm of interpersonal relations, where it provides standards (rarely met) for teacher and student conduct within the school context. The school by this perspective is a family-like community, and teachers and their students have familial roles to play. The prewar legacy of rigorous preparation for university remains most influential in the academic realm. Hard work and efficiency in meeting competition is its guiding inspiration. The rewards and punishments that are its ultimate concern stem from the hierarchical facts of life so much appreciated in Japan. But the ultranationalist aspect of the prewar approach that legitimated hard study as preparation for national service has largely disappeared. Now exam preparation appears quite egoistic.

The American model remains the source of political rhetoric and the guiding principle for reform of high school education. The extracurricular side of school affairs gains legitimacy as part of democratic education. When the teachers' union pushes against authority and the weight of entrance exams, it often uses the American model. To the Japanese, American high schools are less oppressively serious, uniform, and competitive, and as such they represent a dream of individual freedom. Of course, having seen the problems of our high schools or having heard stories about them, most Japanese teachers see that reality does not match the dream. They know that to institute diversity and choice in high schools is to challenge both the Confucian emphasis on social order and the principles of efficient preparation inherent in the prewar legacy. These issues are more sharply drawn in education than in any other Japanese institution, because time has compounded rather than simplified the value choices involved.

The overwhelming facts that face high schools today are that nearly all young Japanese are enrolled and that the majority of them intend to go on to college. If history has provided a set of contrasting ideals and legacies, contemporary Japanese society has come to constitute an environment for education that establishes entrance examinations as the key to understanding its dynamic.

# 3

# University Entrance Exams: A National Obsession

> As long as learning is connected with earning, as long as certain jobs can only be reached through exams, so long must we take the examination system seriously. If another ladder to employment was contrived, much so-called education would disappear, and no one be a penny the stupider.
>
> E. M. FORSTER
> *Aspects of the Novel*

PICK UP any of Japan's national news magazines in February and March and you will find university examinations to be lead stories, surpassing in popular interest for the moment even political scandals, economic problems, and gossip about movie stars. From the end of New Year festivities to the beginning of the new school year in April, an inordinate amount of attention is given to the trials and tribulations of the three-quarters of a million adolescents hoping to enter university. What makes this 1 percent of the population so fascinating is that their individual destinies are being shaped to a remarkable extent by just a few hours of test taking. The competition is severe and the preparations are grueling. Ominous labels have been coined to express this concern. It is the time of the "examination hell" (*juken jigoku*). Students are enlistees in an "examination war" (*juken sensō*). Twelve years of schooling culminate in this moment, which is a crucial turning point in the life cycle of most Japanese. Like other such moments, the whole nation undergoes the experience vicariously each year.

It is midnight. Families, friends, and even interested observers stand shivering in the cold on some campus waiting for university officials to post the names of the successful candidates for admission on large, floodlit bulletin boards. There is much nervous chatter, and the sense of excitement is heightened by the fact so many are braving the cold just to learn the results as soon as possible. The lists begin to go up. Flash bulbs pop, journalists scurry around, and people stand on tiptoe to search for names they know. Shouts of happy surprise are heard. Others remain intently searching, and some turn and silently disappear from the scene. The weekly magazines almost invariably put such a scene on their covers each spring.

Most candidates do not go themselves to see if they have passed, but ask a relative to look for them or pay a small sum to an undergraduate-run business to send the results by telegram. Yet the anticipation, ecstasy, and disappointment written on the faces of the crowd when the names go up epitomize the drama of what in effect is a great annual event equivalent to the baseball championships and the blooming of the cherry trees. Even television crews cover the top university announcements.

The magazine cover photographs deserve closer attention. Almost invariably they are of successful candidates just at the moment of discovery and celebration. Some leap for joy; others display a smile of deep satisfaction; others embrace parents or friends. For them a long preparation is over. Typically, the celebrant portrayed is attractive and well-dressed. Four years of glamorous freedom and a life of achieved high status are before the lucky person. Lurking in the background and a bit out of focus, one can almost inevitably find those who are not celebrating. For them, the struggle to enter a good school goes on. The two figures, one ecstatic and the other crestfallen, belong together. They symbolize in the popular imagination the rewards and suffering Japanese must face in the pursuit of educational distinction, which is followed by a good job, economic security, respect, and status in a technocratic world.

Not every student can attend university—not by any means—and yet the popular dream of almost all parents is for their children to do so. Democratic ideology supports this and makes politicians and educators most reluctant to acknowledge any institutional and individual limits to their dream. The magazines are both reflecting popular interest and sustaining the dream.

Can we in America imagine *Time* or *Newsweek* publishing week after week as many as fifteen pages of statistics on the application levels and results of university entrance exams? These are accompanied by lead articles on the exams and the techniques of prepara-

*Student jumping for joy at being accepted
to Tokyo University*

The cover of a national news weekly shows a student jumping for joy at being accepted—presumably to Tokyo University, for the building in the rear looks like that campus. By the apparent age of the celebrant, he has finally succeeded in passing the entrance examination after a number of tries.

tion that in the United States would be relegated to scholarly journals of education.[1] The statistics reveal the competition rates for
universities and departments, and then, when the exam results are
in, they document the success rates high schools achieve in applying
to virtually all the universities and departments in the nation. However tedious, it is precious information to ambitious parents and, I
might add, to the foreign interloper trying to understand Japanese
high schools.

The ten or twenty most successful high schools, Nada among
them, are regularly highlighted, shrewdly evaluated, and gossiped
about. The magazines also discuss the noteworthy characteristics of
each year's examinations: Which universities and departments had a
surprisingly high or low number of candidates? Which high schools
did especially well? What new style of exam questions appeared?
What trends will be important for next year? Parents of future applicants, recent university entrants, and a general population fasci-
nated by the drama avidly consume this kind of journalistic post
mortem.

A psychology of status and rank, so developed in Japan, animates
the discussion. As soon as the University of Tokyo publishes its results, the magazines carry a list of the most successful high schools
with an analysis of their ups and downs in past competition. Changes
in the ranking are subjected to close scrutiny by these publications,
and the principals of leading secondary schools are interviewed by
phone. When Nada dropped from first to second place in the rankings in 1977, the analysts, with remarkable astuteness, concluded
that this was not really a sign of decline because more Nada students
that year were aiming at entering medical departments at other universities. Since medical school competition is generally more difficult than entrance to Tokyo University, they concluded that Nada
had retained its crown as the top secondary school in the country.
In America, few people have even heard of a Groton or an Exeter,
nor do most care about minor details in the performance of these
schools' graduates in getting into Harvard.

Great social competition invariably is built on clear, prominent
goals. Tokyo University, or "Todai," stands as Mount Olympus, and

1. The class (or honors) lists for Oxford and Cambridge Universities are published
in the London Times, but this is merely a shadow of the attention showered on Tokyo
University students.

ranking starts there. Although only a minuscule number of families has a direct interest, the nation's largest newspapers publish the entire list of its successful candidates. Personal distinction is involved, and the list is important sociological data. For sixty years Todai entrants have gone on to run most of Japan's key institutions. Parents of successful candidates are interviewed, and they proudly recount how their son or daughter suffered the grueling work necessary to pass the examination. Did they adopt a special strategy? Did they go to tutoring schools? How many subscribed to magazines designed to help students prepare for the examinations? What time did they usually go to sleep? How did their fathers help? We ask these kinds of questions in the United States of sports heroes and movie stars.

Japanese parents worry terribly about doing the wrong thing when it comes to their children's education, and every scrap of factual information can be useful. This is why articles listing the better nursery schools, for example, attract wide attention; why entrance examinations to some private schools are published verbatim in local newspapers; and why mounds of statistical material on competition ratios regularly appear in popular magazines.

These parents and students who anxiously scan the magazines for information generally suffer enormous tension and an oppressive burden of preparatory work. They stand ready to agree wholeheartedly with any assertion that the "exam hell" must be ended. The same media organizations that sell copy using the annual drama also commission scholars and intellectuals to write essays critical of the system. Like all great obsessions, this one evokes much regret and denial. The media knows how to play both sides of the street. Time and again one reads how examinations are ruining the schools, the young, and Japanese society; how cramming produces warped personalities, crushes enthusiasm, and nips creativity in the bud. One would think education had reached a crisis point, that either the exam system must be scrapped or Japan will lose its humanity and vitality. Yet, ironically, the critics are themselves graduates of the best universities, and their readers are the middle-class parents who will go to extremes to improve their children's performance. Japan's examination hell has been around quite a long time. Hardly a soul in the entire country will say anything publicly in its favor, yet private behavior feeds the competition.

This schizoid quality is a distinguishing mark of most powerful

social syndromes. Calls for reform and desperate effort escalate together. Politicians, educators, and bureaucrats regularly announce
that the stranglehold of exams will be broken, yet changes prove ineffectual. Hypocrisy, confusion, and despair mix with the private
cynicism.

The cast of stereotypical characters reflects this ambiguity. There
is the pushy mother, known as *kyōiku* (educational) *mama*, and the
robot-like student with thick glasses who grinds away at books day
and night. Fathers just work late. The student, in this case, becomes
the hero who through diligence and sacrifice enters a great university and, presumably, goes on to serve the nation with distinction.
There is the idealistic teacher who fights the exam system, publicly
praised by his colleagues but privately condemned as failing the real
needs of his students. And there are athletes who have chosen sports
over studies. Japan has no Renaissance men. The institution attracts
and repels, rewards and punishes in great measure. Exams have been
a major aspect of the Japanese popular imagination since Meiji,
nearly synonymous with social success. They epitomize the excesses
of the world's most advanced meritocracy.

## *The Competition*

In 1980, for example, about 90 percent of all young Japanese were
graduating from high school.[2] Only 6 percent had chosen to end their
schooling at ninth grade, and a mere 4 percent dropped out of high
school. A larger percentage of young Japanese were graduating from
the twelfth grade than in any other country in the world. Over 65
percent of them had taken a college preparatory course, and even
some who finished vocational courses decided on college. You will
recall, for example, that some of the students of Sakura Night Vocational School hoped to go to college.

Polls revealed that 80 percent of all high school freshmen had
aimed at a higher education.[3] Yet by the time for actually applying to
university, grades, teacher discouragement, parental attitudes, and
family resources dissuaded some students from making the attempt.

2. The main source for statistical profiles of Japanese education is the Ministry of
Education (Mombushō). For 1980, the basic publication is *Waga Kuni no Kyōiku Suijun: 1980* (1981).
3. See, e.g., the poll published in Nihon Hōsō Kyōkai (1975).

*Students waiting for a high school
entrance exam to begin*

Middle school students in Tokyo waiting for a private boys' high school entrance examination to begin. (Courtesy of *Asahi Shinbun*.)

It costs about $35 just to submit an application to a private university (this is a significant source of income for the institutions), and the costs of actually attending university are high enough to be a serious drain on family finances. Naturally, parents must consider a child's chance for admission and return on the investment. The result of such considerations in 1980 was that 42 percent of all high school graduates took jobs.

The remaining 58 percent of high school seniors decided to apply to one or more institutions of higher learning. There were 590,000 places in higher education available and about 636,000 seniors applying. The fit between the two would have been close except that about another 200,000 students from the class of 1979 and before, those who had failed to enter a university but who had not taken employment, were back taking entrance exams again after a year or more of extra study. These students are called *rōnin*, "lordless wandering samurai." Thus, over 200,000 students would not find a place—one out of every four taking the exams.[4]

Compounding the sense of competition was the number of seniors who applied to three or four schools. In all, some two and a half million applications were received by universities and junior colleges for those 590,000 places. On the face of it, then, the overall competition ratio for a hypothetical average was four to one: four applicants for each opening.

The situation facing those who aspired to a four-year university was especially bleak. There were 412,000 openings and some 452,000 seniors applying, joined by nearly all of the 200,000 *rōnin* returning to try again. Among the seniors trying for the first time, one in three failed to gain acceptance. Many of them became *rōnin*, and thus the pattern continued for another year.

Actual competition ratios vary a good deal from school to school, department to department, and year to year.[5] Among the four-year universities are some private ones that have only slightly more applicants than openings. These are the very lowest ranked universities. Many junior colleges also take in most applicants. Competition ratios for the very top universities are not necessarily the highest. Many students avoid wasting their efforts on examinations that attract the nation's best prepared and brightest students. Competition actually clusters toward the middle, especially the higher end of the middle. Applicant-to-opening ratios at the lesser national universities, for example, averaged seven to one. At the better private uni-

4. In 1975, e.g., 33 percent of those entering universities had done at least a year of *rōnin* study, according to Fujita (1978). The picture is hardly changed in 1982. The Ministry of Education reports that in 1980 at least 220,000 students, most *rōnin*, were enrolled in *yobikō*. Reported in "Entrance Exams as Tough as Ever (2)," *Mainichi Daily News*, February 11, 1981, p. 3.

5. Competition ratios broken down by university and department are regularly carried in the national student newspapers *Zenkoku Shingaku Shinbun* and *Jūken Jōhō Pāku*.

versities the ratios were similar. More than eight applications for each position were received at Keio and Waseda, the two most distinguished private universities, and more than half of the successful candidates entering these two schools in 1980 had done at least one year of *rōnin* study. Perennially, applicants to medical departments face the most competitive circumstances. Ratios of twenty to one, thirty to one, and even forty to one regularly arise for all but the very best medical schools. Difficulty is not measured by competition ratios alone. The level or quality of competition is most crucial. Some of the best schools have low ratios, but no one doubts the difficulty of succeeding on their exams.

Applications are made with care, and only the most likely schools are selected. One result of the extensive media coverage is that applicants can seek points of slight advantage. The process is considerably more rationalized than in the United States. With reams of statistical material in hand, students, parents, and teachers are able to scan the entire field and make judgments about where the best chances lie.

Are the choices different for males and females? Only slightly more men than women were entering institutions of higher learning in 1980, a change from the previous decade or two, when men predominated. This shift is largely explained, however, by a particularly rapid growth in the number of junior colleges. Approximately 30 percent of those students going on past high school attend junior colleges, yet 90 percent of them are female. The percentage of women in four-year universities also increased from 8 percent in 1960 to 18 percent in 1980, but this is still quite low by American standards. The fact remains that approximately two of every three females are headed for junior colleges, whereas nine of every ten males are aiming at four-year universities. Furthermore, the percentage of women in the total enrollments of Japan's top public and private universities has remained notably low. Only 7 percent of those accepted at Tokyo University in 1980 were women, and most entered only two departments, literature and education. Kyoto University, number two in Japan, accepted a freshman class containing 8 percent women.[6] And Keio University enrolled one woman for every

6. These figures come from 1) profiles of universities in the *Zenkoku Shingaku Shinbun*, a newspaper that carries information for students preparing to apply to universities, and *Shukan Asahi* (April 4, 1980), pp. 22–29.

nine men. None of this stems from overt discrimination in the examination or admissions process. There are no quotas or biases in the mechanism, and the examinations are objective and open. Relatively few women apply. In 1975, for example, 210,000 males, but only 81,000 females, applied to four-year universities. The acceptance rate for the females (71 percent) was actually higher than for males (61 percent).[7]

The roots for these male-female differences lie largely in parental attitudes toward a daughter's education.[8] As our focus narrows to the four-year schools and then to the best universities, we are in fact centering on the institutions that lead to more valuable jobs upon graduation. Men in Japan spend their lives at such jobs; women are not expected to do so and in fact rarely pursue careers. That only male students are intensely supported and pressured to enter a good university, regardless of family finances and the psychic costs, is no surprise. Nothing reflects this better than the fact that about 85 percent of all students doing *rōnin* (a costly burden on parents) are male.

Girls are lucky, people say, because they avoid the exam hell. Only the very best female students allow themselves to consider the best universities as they progress through school. Their parents may even discourage them. Why? Graduation from a top school can hurt a woman's marriage prospects, and most parents see a woman's place as ultimately in the home. It is considered an unwise use of family resources to pay for more than a year of *rōnin* preparation for a girl. Further, over the years of primary and secondary education, parental favoritism and suggestion have widened the academic gap between males and females. Preparation is neither pleasant nor glamorous, and few daughters utter complaints. By the end of high school a significant difference in exam-taking ability has emerged between the sexes.

At Tokyo University in 1980, there were about 13,000 applicants for 3,077 coveted places. This competition ratio of 4.1 is about the national average, but it tells us little. More revealing is that among the successful applicants, 35 percent were taking the test for the second time and 10 percent for the third time or more. The successful

7. Mombushō (1976), pp. 212–213.
8. A poll of 1974 reveals that 99 percent of parents plan for a university education for their sons. For daughters, 13 percent plan only for high school, 30 percent for junior college, and 56 percent for university or beyond. Nihon Hōsō Kyōkai (1975).

candidates came almost entirely from only the several hundred best public and private high schools. Twenty-nine percent came from the perennial top ten and two-thirds from but fifty elite schools. Nada headed the list with 131 entrants. Most successful candidates had attended cram schools and had averaged about five hours a day of homework for at least the three previous years.

Is such effort worth it? Obviously, many Japanese think the answer is an emphatic "yes," at least as far as young males are concerned. The reason is not the quality of education acquired, but the quality of the employment prospects awaiting Tokyo graduates. That is the real prize.

## The Rewards

The precise and elaborate ranking of universities by the measure of exam competitiveness correlates with the ranking of jobs to be gained four years later.[9] Tokyo University is the major gateway to top jobs. It stands at the top of the employment pyramid, and any analysis begins there.

The reader unfamiliar with Japanese employment must keep in mind that in Japan, the university graduate taking a good job hopes and expects that his career will remain with that company or government entity until retirement. There is no developed job market for executive, managerial, or white-collar talent. Some of the well-educated do change around, and there is considerable transfer within any organization, but promotion and career success depend heavily on rising within the organization with which one starts. This fact makes the first job out of school far more important in Japan than in the United States or Europe. Proving one's worth is important for promotion to top positions within any organization, and getting oneself on the first rung of a desirable career ladder is a one-shot matter in Japan that is heavily dependent upon the status of the university one is just leaving. The right organization is defined by its future prospects and reputation, both of which are factors well correlated with material rewards, personal power, social prestige, and

9. Another measure of the value of university entrance is the price paid for copies of the test leaked out before exam day. The incidence of such cheating is rare, but the temptations are great at medical schools and elite universities. In 1979, copies of the Waseda University School of Commerce exam sold for $40,000 each.

work satisfaction as the Japanese see it. Graduates are, in fact, choosing lifelong institutional affiliations, not just specific jobs. To join a top institution one must come out of one of the top universities, and so forth on down the line.

Companies naturally try to hire those they perceive as the most talented individuals. Many of the country's top firms simply do not interview except at the top schools. And because there are no employment-oriented professional schools in Japan to provide a second chance to prove one's academic worth, the university entrance exam is *the* critical point of selection between high school and employment. Positions on the track to high government responsibility go to graduates capable of passing special employment examinations. Some latitude might be expected here, yet graduates of top universities do exceptionally well, and again Tokyo University dominates.

Having entered the top institutions, do the graduates of elite schools continue to rise? News magazines periodically survey the largest firms, ascertaining the educational background of top executives or newly appointed middle managers in order to gauge the ongoing predictive strength of top university affliation. In just two years, in four weekly magazines, fifteen such articles appeared with titles like "The Universities That Produce the New Middle Management," "Top Corporations and the Reality of Educational Background," and "The Top Twenty Universities in Terms of Company Presidents Produced." The material presented is factual and impressive. The results of one poll on the university background of top company presidents, for example, reads:

| | |
|---|---|
| Tokyo University | 357 |
| Keio University | 133 |
| Kyoto University | 125 |
| Waseda University | 92 |
| Hitotsubashi University | 79 |
| Kobe University | 53 |

Tokyo, from which about one in every hundred university students is graduated, can claim one-third of all large company presidents.[10] A survey of one hundred major companies listed on the Tokyo Stock Exchange in 1978 found that one-quarter of all chief ex-

10. *Shukan Yomiuri,* June 24, 1975.

ecutive officers were Tokyo graduates.[11] Invariably, the other schools listed are Keio and Waseda, the top private schools, and a set of the leading national universities. Other surveys produce much the same results regarding middle management positions. Take for instance one focused on the educational background of section chiefs in Japan's largest corporation, Japan Steel:[12]

| | |
|---|---|
| Tokyo University | 98 |
| Kyoto University | 23 |
| Tohoku University | 23 |
| Kyushu University | 23 |
| Waseda University | 19 |

At Sony Electric, famous for its self-proclaimed policy of ignoring educational background for promotions, the list reads:

| | |
|---|---|
| Tokyo University | 20 |
| Osaka University | 9 |
| Yokohama National | 7 |
| Kyoto University | 5 |
| Kyushu University | 5 |
| Tohoku University | 5 |
| Keio University | 4 |

Again, except for Keio and Waseda, all the schools represented are national universities. Together these elite schools account for about 10 percent of Japan's university population. The sad fact is that Tokyo graduates who fail to reach the top or near-top are subjects of much gossip, both empathetic and scornful, so great is the built-in expectation that they will do well after graduation.

Top jobs in the corporate world correlate closely with university background, but the national bureaucracy, including nearly all ministries, is positively dominated by Tokyo University. This has been true for eighty years. Middle management in the bureaucracy also comes largely from Todai, and 50–75 percent of all executive-oriented starting positions in most ministries go to its graduates.

11. *Business Community*, 18 (Spring, 1978), quoted in Beauchamp (manuscript).
12. *Sandei Mainichi*, March 16, 1976. Compare this with the findings of a 1981 Standard and Poor's survey: of 55,834 American executives, 1,827 (3 percent) and 1,494 (2.6 percent) had graduated from Yale and Harvard, respectively. "Executives and the Colleges They Went to." *Christian Science Monitor*, September 8, 1981, p. 19.

Typically, they improve their hold with promotion. A survey of all ministries and agencies in 1978 (Table 5) found that 62 percent of the executive positions were filled by Tokyo graduates.

In the Ministry of Education—explicitly assigned the task of disassembling the elite university influence over exams and jobs— sixteen out of eighteen of the top positions were filled by Tokyo University graduates in the mid-seventies. The national police headquarters, the public corporations, and even some prefectural governments follow the same pattern. Relatively speaking, business is less elitist than government, and small business is less elitist than large business. The pecking order of status among institutions is roughly proportionate to the number of elite university graduates, especially those from Tokyo. And finally, the faculty of Tokyo University is made up almost entirely of its own graduates.

The significance of the educational hierarchy does not end with elite jobs. Employment prospects are allocated by school rank down through the entire spectrum of middle-class positions. All companies, even modest ones, rank universities and high schools when hiring new employees.[13] Differences in the quality of candidates are presumed on the basis of school rank, which of course ultimately affects the entrance competition. For students of Otani and Okada, who have no thought of applying to Tokyo or the other elite national universities, there is still a very clear set of priorities among the middle-level private universities they are considering. Small gradations in their relative difficulty are appreciated, and a decision to do an extra year of *rōnin* study in order to make a try at a higher ranked school is not unusual. Four years later that extra year is likely to pay off in better job opportunities.

Entrance exams thus obviously serve as crucial screening devices for employers. They sort the nineteen-year-old population into an extensively differentiated hierarchy of presumed intellectual ability and dedication.

Not going to college means beginning work with an almost irremediable disadvantage. Going back to school is not an option, and

13. This is documented in a general manner by surveys of the Ministry of Labor [Rōdoshō] contained in its annual, *Rōdō Hakushō*, and specifically by my fieldwork in several Japanese companies and my work with high school career guidance counselors.

**Table 5**

Percentage of Officials Ranked Section Chief or Above in Ministries and Agencies of the National Government Who Are Graduates of Tokyo University

| Office | Percentage of Tokyo University Graduates |
|---|---|
| Ministry of Finance | 88.6 |
| Ministry of Foreign Affairs | 76.0 |
| National Land Agency | 73.5 |
| Autonomy Agency | 70.5 |
| Ministry of Transportation | 68.5 |
| Ministry of Construction | 67.5 |
| Ministry of Agriculture & Forestry * | 64.7 |
| Ministry of International Trade & Industry | 63.7 |
| Ministry of Labor | 61.7 |
| Ministry of Justice | 60.7 |
| Economic Planning Agency | 60.0 |
| Ministry of Education | 60.0 |
| Defense Agency | 57.9 |
| Environment Agency | 55.9 |
| Ministry of Postal Services | 50.8 |
| Ministry of Health & Welfare | 48.6 |
| Prime Minister's Office | 45.9 |
| National Police Agency | 44.9 |
| Science & Technology Agency | 44.9 |
| Administrative Management Agency | 40.5 |
| National Government Average | 62.3 |

SOURCE: Data from "What Does A University Mean to the Japanese," *Business Community* 18 (Spring 1978), p. 56.

* The figure for the Ministry of Agriculture and Forestry includes the Forestry Agency and Food Agency.

rarely will even the most talented high school graduates gain promotion above the university group in any sizable organization. Not long ago many very able high school graduates were attaining high rank in companies, but today, with more than half of all males obtaining some sort of higher education, a high school degree looks very insignificant.

Education and jobs are closely tied in every industrial country, but the Japanese situation has several important characteristics. As already mentioned, the weight of education in determining careers is increased by the one-company, one-career pattern. In management and technical areas, mobility and lateral opportunities are minimal. Movement out and up is rare in the case of most white-collar workers. Second, the rankings of universities in Japan are surprisingly sharp. One standard, entrance exams, makes this possible. By comparison, in the United States, regionalism in choice of schools, the unevenness of student quality, and admissions criteria that include many significant factors other than tested ability all contribute to the inclination to recognize four or five large tiers among universities but to remain vague about the matter and to withhold judgment when it comes to individuals. We acknowledge elite schools and distinguish educational status, but there are so many exceptions and many extenuating circumstances that our rankings do not influence the allocation of jobs in anywhere near as profound a manner. We also look at grades in college, a factor of little significance in Japan, and we have graduate schools where the deck is reshuffled.

Most European school systems, by comparison, involve considerable early tracking. Educational achievement levels and jobs are sorted out for most young people starting much earlier, and the entrance competition for universities involves a much smaller proportion of the total population. Only Japan and the United States take all willing students right up to the point of applying for higher education.

Japan is distinguished among industrialized societies by a system that retains the hierarchy and government-subsidized qualities of an elite higher education originally constructed on the nineteenth-century European pattern while expanding educational opportunities American-style in the postwar period. A hierarchical, ordered mass education has evolved. The expectation of lifetime employment gives entrance exams a weight and a broad currency that is particular to Japan. It must also be recognized that the Japanese are a highly achievement-oriented people who have long been encouraged to view education as a crucial avenue for personal advancement. A potent mixture results when the Japanese national character responds to the sharply drawn system of incentives and penalties presented by postwar education.

## The Questions

The student caught in this crucible must concentrate on just one thing: preparing to answer particular kinds of questions. The examinations given by universities constitute an unintended cryptographic code by which social structure and personal ambition are translated into the imperatives of educational preparation. If entrance exams centered on musical skills, everyone would study music. If they were to measure manual dexterity, hand exercises would become enormously popular. What they do in fact measure is important for us to understand.

The only nationally standardized examinations, comparable to our Scholastic Achievement Tests, are conducted by private companies for the purposes of giving high school students practice in test taking and allowing them to see how they stack up against each other. Each university writes its own examination and offers it once a year on its own campus. Examinations last two days. The national universities have just begun (in 1979) jointly giving a standard screening examination. Those successful in this test can then go on to the examination of a particular national university.[14]

Hundreds of separate entrance examinations are given on campuses all over the country in February and March. A student cannot apply to more than two public universities because their exams are offered on only two occasions. The schedule for private universities is wider, but the fact of separate examinations still greatly constricts

14. The screening test (*kyotsuichi shiken*) serves only to qualify students to take particular university exams; those that pass the screening test must still take the entrance exam of a specific department. This test could be the foundation of a single national entrance exam someday, but it is too soon to assess its impact. In 1979, 341,000 students took the test to qualify to apply for approximately 96,000 places in national and other public universities.

the field of choice. Application to several departments of the same university is generally ruled out. Considerable care and planning is thus required in the application process.

Examinations would not be so singularly critical if other critieria were used in the admissions process. Only a few private universities do this and only in a minority of cases. Neither teachers' recommendations, nor grades in secondary school, nor extracurricular activities, nor personal character, nor special talents contribute to acceptance by Japanese universities. A small percentage of places in some departments of some private universities, are reserved to admit candidates by teachers' recommendations. But no student dares to count on this. In Japan, how one does during two days of answering questions makes all the difference. It is the sole and final measure of academic accomplishment.

Entrance exams have two facets: a compulsory part and an elective part. Each department specifies for its applicants what choice they have. Topics such as math and ancient literature are divided into several degrees of difficulty, with departments requiring a higher degree of difficulty when the subject is particularly relevant. The compulsory subjects are math, English, and Japanese. Science, medicine and engineering students must elect one social science topic for testing and are required to be tested heavily in math and science. About half of their total score will come from these two subjects. Humanities, education, social science, and law applicants are required to take the full battery of tests in social studies and Japanese but are examined in only one science of their choice and are allowed to skip the most difficult math section. In sum, all students must concentrate on math, English, and Japanese, and in addition they must specialize to a degree in either science or social studies, depending on their career inclinations. It is not possible to change departments once accepted by a university. Changing universities means beginning as a freshman all over again.

The exam questions are easily graded, as might be expected. Short-answer and multiple-choice questions prevail. Few, if any, essay or interpretive questions appear. Foreign language composition and oral skills are not tested. Nor are intelligence quotient kinds of questions to be found. Japanese universities have never made a serious effort to judge a candidate's raw aptitude for learning. They want to know how much has actually been learned and how well information and theory can be applied to problem solving. Emphasis is on mastery of facts, control over details, and practiced skill in the application of mathematical and scientific principles. As most anyone with experience in exam taking realizes, some forms of learning and knowledge can be tested with precision and some are measured inadequately by the inherent nature of virtually any question-answer approach. Science and math fit the short-answer mode comfortably, humanities and social sciences do not.

Distortions are produced by any examination process, but in Japan, because of the great competitive pressures to prepare, the distortions are magnified. No matter how difficult or obscure questions become, the enterprising and brilliant students will master them. Such distortions flow back through the whole educational system, as parents and teachers respond to shifts in the nature and focus of exam questions. Of necessity, exams are based on the public school curriculum. Without a nationally standardized curriculum, entrance exams of the Japanese kind would be neither fair nor really possible. Some alpha factor of extra difficulty, reflecting what the faculty feels a well-prepared student should know, is added to the exam questions. The alpha factor is naturally greater the higher one goes up the university ranks. Supposedly, it is the faculty's way of sorting the sheep from the goats. The alpha factor makes a real difference on exams to the elite schools.

The process of making examinations is not subject to public scrutiny. Nor is it monitored by educational specialists. Rather, it seems to result from a mix of traditional practice and conventional academic insight. Secondary teachers are not called in to explain what they have been teaching students, as is done with SATs in the United States. Rather, the standardized high school textbooks are consulted. Most central to the process of making up exams today is last year's examination for the same department. Basically, each year a new set of questions is ground out on the old model.

With so much riding on examinations and with so many years of preparation invested by each candidate, universities recognize a responsibility to make no sudden changes. They announce plans for revision sometimes as far as ten years in advance. If a new economic theory or new questions in microbiology are going to be included, the groundwork for such learning must be laid in junior high school. If the correct answer regarding the causes of World War II changes, then students trained to give the old answer should not be penalized. For reasons like this, the reform of the content of entrance examinations moves with glacial slowness. Each announcement of an intention to change the exams significantly is met with near panic by parents, teachers, and students. All fear that a disadvantage will be created for those who have been diligently preparing for the wrong questions. The content of examinations is, indeed, a sensitive public issue.

Following is a typical question that actually appeared on the Kobe University examination in 1974.[15] Kobe is an excellent national university just a notch or two below Tokyo. The question is from the social studies section.

Select the appropriate answer for each numbered blank space from the list that follows the passage below. Fill in the dates directly.

The philosophy that arose in ancient Greece had an enormous influence on subsequent human thought. The earliest form, (1) _____ philosophy, arose in the (2) _____ century in the (3) _____ region. Liberating itself from the mythological approach to natural phenomena, this philosophy aimed to explain the fundamentals of nature in a rational manner. (4) _____, who explained the origin of things to be water, and (5) _____, who treated the basis of matter mathematically, were representative scholars of the age. Following the war with (6) _____, democratic government was implemented with Athens as its focal point, and a school of teachers, the (7) _____, arose to give instructions to citizens in the arts of public debate. This development began the division of philosophy into component fields. As can be seen in the famous phrase, "Humans have many ways of measuring things," of (8) _____, the existence of absolute causality was denied by the assertion of subjective understanding. (9) _____ offered counter-arguments to this in his teaching. Known for his special questioning of students as a way of teaching them to understand the truth, he was misunderstood by his society and sentenced to death. One of his students, (10) _____, recorded his words and also bequeathed to the world a theory of idealism and a treatise on political utopia, and another student, (11) _____, drew together and synthesized all of existing Greek philosophy, for which he is now regarded as the figure representative of Greek learning at its zenith. In the latter half of the (12) _____ century, Hellenism arose, and, reflecting the decline of the democratic independent city-state, philosophy shifted from being primarily part of the education of a democratic citizenry to being part of the tendency to seek psychologi-

15. Questions are quoted from a book entitled *Kobe Daigaku*, published by Kyōgakusha (1974), one of an extensive annual series on the entrance exams of over 350 universities.

cal solace and contentment. The (13) _____ school, which explained matters in terms of pleasure and pain, and the (14) _____ school, which sought to eliminate appetites, were characteristic of the age. Both subsequently spread to the aristocracy of ancient Rome, where Emperor (15) _____, who wrote his confessions, and the philosopher (16) _____ were representative figures.

| | | |
|---|---|---|
| a. Academia | n. Dorian | aa. Enlightenment |
| b. Aristides | o. Pythagoras | bb. Natural Philosophy |
| c. Aristophanes | p. Plato | cc. Absolutism |
| d. Antoninus Pius | q. Hesiod | dd. Stoic |
| e. Euripides | r. Peloponnesus | ee. Socrates |
| f. Cicero | s. Macedonia | ff. Thales |
| g. Chrysippus | t. Mycenae | gg. Hadrian |
| h. Constantine | u. Attica | hh. Phaedrus |
| i. Natural Law | v. Aristotle | ii. Protagoras |
| j. Existentialism | w. Archimedes | jj. Persia |
| k. Seneca | x. Ionia | kk. Polybius |
| l. Sophists | y. Epicurean | ll. Marcus Aurelius |
| m. Solon | z. Xenophon | mm. Laconian |

Answers:
(1) i, (2) 6th B.C., (3) x, (4) ee, (5) o, (6) ii, (7) l, (8) hh, (9) ee, (10) p, (11) v, (12) 4th B.C., (13) y, (14) dd, (15) kk, (16) k.

I selected this question because it is about a time and place in history supposedly more familiar to Western than to Japanese students. Questions related to Chinese and Japanese history also appear, of course, but for those of us without the necessary background they are more difficult to evaluate. The style of the questions does not show geographical variation.

How many American high school seniors would even want to attempt answering this question—one about their own tradition? Very few, of course. Our education is not geared to this sort of testing, even when it does take up ancient civilization as a subject. The American sense of education rebels at the thought that the way to learn about Greek thought is to master the names, dates, places, eras, schools of philosophy, and philosophical lineages involved. We want to focus on the essence of what we think the Greeks valued—independence of thought and rationality—two items that tests do not reliably measure.

For Japanese such facts are the foundation for further learning and the essential equipment of an educated person. Perhaps more to the point, they can be tested objectively. To the contemporary Western educator, the debates among Greek thinkers and the differences between their approaches are more interesting. We would pursue this angle in class discussions, attempting to show the relevance of such debates to contemporary problems and issues. If there were time, we would also dig into the logic used by various schools to train minds in analytic thought. Precious little of such an approach would help a Japanese student prepare for a question like the one above.

The approach of Japanese high school textbooks is always neatly mirrored in the exam questions. Greek thought, for example, receives an average of ten pages out of 220 in the various texts for the year-long required course "Ethical Thought and Society." These pages read exactly like an encyclopedic entry on the subject. The authors skim from topic to topic at a rapid pace in order to introduce as much as possible in a limited number of pages. The result is a high density of items to memorize, from ten to twenty per page, but no textual material to chew on and no real basis for class discussion or individual speculation. Greek schools of thought, for example, are typically encapsulated in a sentence. The pace of the course, furthermore, precludes exploring in any depth. This course covers all of Western and Eastern philosophy and religion in one year (from Moses to Dewey in the West and from Confucius to Nishida Kitaro in the East). A little bit of time is spent on the place of ethical thought in society and culture. But because speculative issues do not appear on entrance examinations, this section of the textbook receives little attention from students and most teachers.

The encyclopedia quality of social studies examinations is not in itself the heart of the problem. A degree of such information is necessary as the foundation for deeper learning. The problem arises from the excessive amounts of information required to do well on exams. One gets the distinct impression that professors, themselves often masters of the encyclopedic approach, take particular pride in their ability to concoct exams that are notably difficult, for this enhances their school's and their own status. If distortion begins from the fact that university entrance depends solely on objective examinations, it is greatly magnified by the excessive difficulty generated in narrow realms of learning.

Consider a question on European geography from the same examination:

Fill in the blank spaces in the paragraph below.

The Rhine, one of the most important rivers in Europe, rises from the Alps and flows into Lake Boden. From there it runs west, cutting through the Jura mountain range and turns north in Basel, a city in Switzerland. At Basel, the borders of West Germany, (1) _____ and Switzerland meet; the national railroads of these countries extend their roots into this city. There are three major national railroad stations. The Rhine turns north from Basel and the view suddenly opens up before it. This indicates that the Rhine has entered (2) _____, a long and narrow plain 30 km. wide and 300 km. long bounded by (3) _____ on the east and the Vosges mountain range on the west. The surrounding area consists of forests, swamps, and (4) _____.

In the plain, which is made of rich (5) _____ earth, the main crops are wheat and corn.

Along the mountainside, splendid (6) _____ follow the course of the river. Around Mainz, the riverbed starts narrowing and the mountains on both sides form a sheer rise. Along the mountainside, vineyards still continue; on the hills old castles appear. The Rhine cuts across the Rhine Range, which is made of schist, enters a plain around Bonn and finally drains into the (7) _____ in Holland.

The ratio between the maximum and minimum water flow within a year differs in the upper stream and the lower stream. The ratio is large in the upper stream beyond Basel; in Basel it totals fourteen meters; in the lower stream downward from Basel the annual fluctuation gets smaller; and farther down from Cologne (Koln) the flux tends to be almost constant.

The Rhine is also an important river from an economic viewpoint. (8) _____ and steel are transported in flat-bottomed black ships. The Rhine is (9) _____ on which ships flying the flags of many nations pass.

The river is connected with the Mediterranean area through (10) _____ and with the district of Paris through (11) _____. The Rhine is the most important main artery of Western Europe's river transport system, one that connects Switzerland, eastern France, part of West Germany, and Holland. Ships up to two thousand tons can actually go up the river as far as Basel. The major river ports are (12) _____ in Holland; Duisburg, Mannheim, and Ludwigshafen in Germany; Strasbourg in France; and Basel in Switzerland.

Answers:
(1) France, (2) the Rhine Trough or Graben, (3) the Black Forest, (4) riverside terraces, (5) brown, (6) vineyards, (7) North Sea, (8) coal, (9) an international river, (10) Rhone-Rhine Canal, (11) Marne-Rhine Canal, (12) Rotterdam.

Clearly, the realm of practical knowledge has been left behind here.[16] Details are required of the kind that will probably never again be needed once the candidate is safely past the gates of some university. In fact, much of the social studies part of entrance examinations seems like nothing more than a giant trivia contest compiled by scholars instead of popular culture freaks. Is it surprising that many Japanese adults have an almost obsessional interest in and capacity to master facts? But the youthful energy spent in developing this skill is appallingly great.

Compared with social studies, the math and science part of the test is quite straightforward and impressive. The questions are difficult, to be sure, but the objective short-answer approach fits the pursuit of these subjects. Theory, problem solving, and logic are central to most questions, and the exam system buttresses this emphasis in Japanese education. The level of accomplishment expected on science and math questions is probably roughly equivalent to what is taught to second-year science and math students in the best American universities.

The English section of the entrance exams is regularly criticized by Japanese and foreigners, either for the slightly archaic constructions and vocabulary put there by English literature professors whose specialties are not the modern period or for the drawing of a right/wrong distinction between two usages that seem equally correct to native speakers. Although I encountered fewer of these faults than I was led to expect, I found high school teachers at Nada and other top schools preparing their students to handle archaic constructions. It is also remarked that to do well a student should digest a small dictionary of English vocabulary. Words like mediate, midday, folly, portable, bough, spectacle, and wrenched appear on the Kobe University test. Yet, as we would expect of a nation seeking information from the world, the greatest stress is on comprehension. Students are asked to translate sentences of the following sort:

> Stripped to their essentials, man's major problems have always hung on the necessity of making adjustment to the irresistible force of change.

16. It is, however, more sobering to read about a 1974 survey of geography knowledge among American high school seniors undertaken by the Educational Testing Service for the U.S. Office of Education, which found that 41 percent could not locate Egypt on a map and only 54 percent correctly chose the USSR as the country located in both Europe and Asia.

Or,

> With the continuous decrease, during the past few decades, in the length of the working day, recreation, or leisure time activity, has become a social problem of vital importance and one that has engaged the interest of many investigators.

Some attention is also given to colloquial English. Here the level of difficulty matches what might be expected of a moderately educated American high school student:

> Fill in the blanks with the word appropriate to all three sentences under each number.
> 1. His folly has ( ) about his ruin.
>    If children are badly ( ) up, they don't know how to behave.
>    The sad news ( ) tears to her eyes.
> 2. Father ( ) up smoking.
>    The ice ( ) way and they fell in the water.
>    The plants ( ) in to the cold weather.

A most notable point is that neither spoken English nor an ability to express oneself in the written language is tested.[17] The fact that most educated Japanese can read English with amazing skill but hardly speak a word follows from the nature of such exams.

## The Business of Cramming

The source of the questions considered is a 200-page paperback entitled *The Kobe University Examination: Questions and Answers*, published commercially on an annual basis as part of a series that covers the exams of over three hundred fifty universities. In addition to the questions and answers for the preceding three years, these books outline in detail how the types of questions and the emphases have shifted recently and suggest appropriate study strategies for each university. This is but one of many comercially distributed study aids. So rich, in fact, are the products available that 20–40 percent of the floor space of bookstores frequented by students is devoted to exam-oriented materials.

Cramming is big business in Japan, and many firms compete in a large and hungry consumer market. Practice test books, invariably thick, are some of the most rudimentary items offered. Comprised

17. Some universities have added a small foreign-language and comprehension section using tape-recorded spoken English.

of questions borrowed from past exams, they allow candidates to test themselves to their hearts' content in the privacy of their own homes. Books of facts that regularly appear in questions, all kinds of chronologies, vocabulary lists, catalogs of common mistakes, and other guides to short-answer test taking also abound. For sale are flash cards, pocket-sized books of facts that students can pull out and use on buses or while waiting their turns at bat, study hints illustrated with humorous cartoons, and even high-minded books preaching the need for planning and persistence. The commercial prospects inspire great ingenuity. Browsing in bookstores peddling these products is a popular pastime for many high school students. Pursuing the equipment of competitive preparation and glancing through guides to colleges fascinates those caught in the exam obsession.

One small but entertaining illustration of the general trend in this market is the student desks on sale in department stores. The deluxe models, which cost over $500, have built-in alarm clocks especially equipped with timers for speed tests, high and low intensity lights, swivel executive chairs, globes that light up, and in one case even a built-in calculator. That may seem a bit much even to most Japanese, but the sale of special educational equipment—from children's microscopes to butterflies ready for scientific mounting—is a regular feature of Japanese department stores.

It is estimated that the sale of study aids and equipment has recently grown into a billion-dollar annual business, thanks to the growth of university aspirations and the prosperity of Japan's middle class.[18] With over three-quarters of a million students applying each year and several million just a few years from taking entrance exams, the market is large. Almost all candidates are likely to buy at least a few study guides.

There has also been a national boom in practice tests (*mogi shiken*) and the related service of computerized counseling. Until the late sixties, before public high schools were committed to downplay exam preparation, boards of education and high schools administered general practice tests modeled on university entrance examinations. This was done to measure student ability and provide guid-

18. See *Nihon Keizai Shinbun* (April 16, 1974), *Osaka Shinbun* (December 17, 1974), *Chubu Keizai Shinbun* (October 30, 1974), *Nishi Nihon Shinbun* (July 26, 1974), *Nikkei Sangyo Shinbun* (April 16, 1974), and the *Oriental Economist* (July 29, 1978) for articles on this industry.

*Students taking a practice examination*

High school students taking a practice exam offered by a private company. Typically, students take these exams at least three times during the year prior to making application to universities. The companies that give the tests provide detailed feedback on what to study and where to apply.

ance in the application process, as well as to give students practice in taking examinations. All this came under a cloud of disrepute during the late sixties, in the era of social criticism and student radicalism. Suddenly private testing companies, which had been offering practice tests, experienced rapid increases in the number of subscribers to their services. Nearly all high school seniors aiming at college now subscribe to this service.

Taking tests is obviously something of a learned skill: presumably, the more one practices, the better one becomes. High school seniors typically take two or three of these tests prior to making their applications, and *rōnin* students, who do not have teachers monitoring their progress, typically find it valuable to take a practice test every month. Test companies have sophisticated computer programs that analyze individual test results, indicate the types of mistakes made,

and point out areas requiring the most study. The diagnostic possibilities are probably only just beginning to be developed. Because so
many candidates now take these practice tests, they are the most reliable data bank against which to evaluate a student's chances of entering any particular university. The subscriber routinely receives,
along with his test results, a statement of the probabilities of acceptance to any of the schools under consideration.

Even greater growth has come in the business of cram schools
(juku) which offer supplementary education after school.[19] A 1976
poll of thousands of Japanese children revealed that 60 percent of the
urban student population in grades seven, eight, and nine were enrolled in a cram school or were being coached by a private tutor.[20]
Further, the poll showed that 40 percent of all fourth, fifth, and sixth
graders in Tokyo were going to a juku. And one in ten of the country's high school students was shown to be attending yobiko,[21] the
advanced analogue of juku.

These tutoring establishments are diverse and interesting. Some
belong to franchise chains, owned by large companies, that enroll
thousands of students. So lucrative and flourishing was the business
in the mid-1970s that a movie company, several publishing firms,
and a department store all entered the market to set up their own
franchise systems.[22] Most cram schools are quite small, however,
typically run at home by housewives and former teachers. Many
university students who contract their services to juku also make
money on the side tutoring children privately, often in conjunction
with some agency. Nine percent of the middle school students in
Tokyo have private tutors.[23] In juku the focus is high school entrance or, in the case of juku for upper elementary school students,
entrance exams to the elite private schools that admit students in
seventh grade, as Nada does.

The chains and some of the smaller juku try to develop distinctive
teaching qualities. Each seeks to make its atmosphere and program

19. English-language articles on cram schools include Kondō (1974), Riggs (1977),
and Rohlen (1980). In Japanese, see Endo (1975) and Mainichi Shinbun Shakaibu
(1977).

20. Mombushō (1977). A more recent survey by a private research organization
found three-quarters of Tokyo's fourth, fifth, and sixth graders going to juku. Mainichi Daily News (February 12, 1981), p. 3.

21. Mombushō (1976), p. 59.

22. Nihon Keizai Shinbun (April 16, 1974).

23. Mombushō, Daijin Kanbu Chōsa Tōkeika (1977).

*Cram school*

A cram school (*yobikō*) in Tokyo that specializes in English instruction.
Note that the great majority of students here are boys, as is typical of supplementary education above the ninth grade. (Courtesy of *Asahi Shinbun*.)

more effective, and it seeks public notoriety to ensure a flow of applications. Some have elaborate teaching devices, others continually
give tests, and some go in for a psychological approach close to that
of the United States Marine Corps. As might be expected, the larger
cram schools advertise the number of their clients who successfully
enter Tokyo and other top universities. Some cram schools target
particular schools and even departments in their search for a special
segment of the market.

Private tutors and neighborhood *juku* have been around for a long
time. Special schools for *rōnin*, where they prepare while waiting for
another chance at the examinations, have also been part of the general education scene for quite a while. But private academies that
focus on fulfilling the tutoring function on a sizable scale, with the
sophisticated special methods and equipment made possible by large
organization, are a development of the late sixties and seventies. In
effect, the growing demand for supplementary education to help children get past the examinations has fostered new mass-production
techniques and new, more competitive approaches to the matter of
preparation. One franchise system centered on math claims to be

reaching over three hundred fifty thousand children.[24] Some of the smaller schools are so intense as to require attendance of more than twenty hours a week, plus most vacation time.[25] The top *juku* have entrance exams themselves and are rumored to be more crucial to success than regular school. With popular interest high, parents cannot ignore the cram school phenomenon, for it could mean the difference between success or failure. No proof exists that cramming helps, but exam competition and anxiety about what the competition is doing drive the market. Most parents deeply regret sending their children to *juku*, appreciating full well the loss of fun and innocence involved, but they fear their children will lose out in the race without such extra stimulus.

This phenomenon illustrates better than any other the potential for escalation in what could be termed the university entrance arms race.[26] The extent to which some will go in order to prepare is awesome. And the extent to which some parents will encourage or permit the sacrifice of time and money to this undertaking is truly frightening. What Americans might regard as the lunatic fringe— students memorizing whole English dictionaries or doing seven hours of preparation a night for a year—actually sets the pace in this sort of competition. Moderation is a losing strategy as long as entrance examinations measure the gross absorption of knowledge and the perfection of problem-solving and test-taking skills.

Schools and education officials have attempted to restrain the inclination to excess. They regularly condemn cram schools and, as we have noted, they ended public practice tests. Excessive concern with exams has been highlighted as a major national problem. But public school restraint has only created a vacuum in which the cramming business has expanded. Keen entrepreneurial instincts are now shaping and further intensifying the competition, and the majority of parents are going along with this trend.[27] Despite the

24. *Oriental Economist* (July 29, 1978).
25. Mainichi Shinbun Shakaibu (1977).
26. I might add that one does not regularly hear occupations discussed between adults and youngsters, as is the custom in the United States. Students learn to aim at universities more than at archaeology, marine biology, the legal profession, and the like.
27. It is interesting to note in this regard the debate in the United States surrounding claims that special cramming can improve SAT scores. In Japan, such a debate would be very widely followed, and the burden of proof would lie with those who would deny the claim. In the United States, little popular interest has been aroused by the issue.

high quality of public schools, education expenses are a large part of most family budgets, and the investment of time and money in preparation at one stage compounds the incentive to protect the investment at the next stage. Captives of their own ambitions and anxieties, parents and precocious scholar-gladiators cause the new "exam industry" to thrive.

## Summary

Institutions develop, are molded, and survive largely in response to forces in their social environment. The social environment of postwar Japanese secondary education has been dominated by university entrance examinations. What was an elite phenomenon three decades ago has now become a national preoccupation. We have gained some sense of the breadth and intensity of this phenomenon by noting such manifestations as the extraordinary attention it receives in the media, the undeniable employment rewards that success brings, the readiness of so many young men to become *rōnin*, and the spectacular development of the cramming business.

High schools can only be understood in the context of the fundamental realities that direct the lives of their students. In Japan, for more than half the students, examinations are a central focus of their existence. For Nada, Okada, and Otani students, the priority of exam preparation is quite clear, and their teachers cannot but respond to this imperative. Whatever original ambitions for university may have been held by the vocational students of Yama and Sakura have been considerably blunted. They have stumbled on exams already and have been judged academically below average, so the university exams are not a motivating goal, but a rather cruel mirror reminding them of their inferior studies. The vocational schools themselves also suffer from a form of second-class citizenship, stemming from the nonacademic nature of their courses.

The bifurcation into different paths to adulthood for boys and girls is also dramatically advanced by choices made about educational goals and the appropriate amount of exam preparation. Despite coeducation and equal opportunity, a major separation of the sexes takes place during high school. This separation is not intended by educational policy but occurs as a response to the intense competition to enter universities.

The existence of most American high school students is shaped by a significantly different reality. University entrance exams are of crucial concern to some American youths, to be sure, particularly those from the upper-middle class, those attending academically strong high schools (mostly private and East Coast), and those with parents who are keen on reaching or maintaining educational status. But this group is far from the majority. Most students who go on to higher education in the United States are not preoccupied with entrance exams. They can find a place in a junior college or college simply by completing high school. Only for our best colleges and universities is there significant competition, and the manner of the competition greatly reduces the likelihood of success through cramming Japanese-style. A personal love of reading or a natural ability in science and math or an artistic talent or leadership are all important individual factors in our admissions approach. For the Japanese, the matter of gaining acceptance to a good university is like running a marathon or conducting a prolonged military campaign. Planning and stamina over a twelve- to fourteen-year period are required. And most parents realize this.

The popular preoccupation with entrance exams also shapes Japanese definitions of education. Despite the continuing public policy goals of developing democratic education, this intention at the high school level is largely overwhelmed by the more powerful pull of exam-oriented concerns. The criterion of efficiency in preparation, of meeting competition by gearing education to the examinations, reaches deep into nearly every corner of high school education. Nada, a powerhouse in this regard, is clearly a popular model; without a doubt, half of Kobe's parents would gladly pay the school's tuition fee if their children could get in. Citizenship, individualism, equal opportunity, creativity, social morality, strength of character, and other goals bequeathed by the Confucian heritage and Western example are not denied, but their significance fades considerably in the face of the more urgent demands for efficient preparation.

A division arises here between public values and private interests, between idealism and reality. The public, idealistic goals remain central to the rhetoric of politicians, officials, teachers, parents, and students. And they are all sincere in their desire that education further the development of democracy and promote individual growth. Yet, when the chips are down, most parents want success for their own children more than anything else. A gap thus develops between parents and educators, one that has great significance to the question of reform. The growth of supplementary education and the rise to prominence of private schools like Nada has been noted. When the public side reforms, the private side grows and prospers. Because so many anxious parents are willing to pay additional costs of keeping their children in the race through private education, public sector efforts to reduce the grip of examinations are regularly stymied and even become counterproductive because they encourage parents to shift more and more reliance to private means. Prosperity increases this tendency, which can be clearly observed in the recent history of Japanese secondary education.

Are we not witnessing in all of this something highly indicative of Japanese national character? Many important virtues—diligence, sacrifice, mastery of detailed information, endurance over the many preparatory years, willingness to postpone gratification, and competitive spirit—are tied together at a formative period and are motivated largely by a rather selfish individual desire to get ahead (or as many put it, "to not fall behind"). Whether the desire is the parents' or the child's is never that clear, and this too seems characteristically Japanese. This desire is hardly individualistic in the sense of stemming from individual choice or the uniqueness of personality. Rather, it comes as part of a great mad rush, the product of group psychology, and it focuses on the goal of social status rather than on some more personal ambition. The entire process tests the ambitious student sorely, but the lesson learned in the cathartic experience is to knuckle down, to restrain one's instincts for pleasure and personal preference. Walking the prescribed straight and narrow path, wherever it leads, is the way of the successful student.

Conduct is one thing, but private thoughts are quite another. Exams measure conduct, but intelligent students are not robots. The private world of Japanese students is one full of imaginings and often bizarre images. One needs only to glance through the comic books that are so popular among teenagers to realize that they have a fondness for the extraordinary, the weird, and the obscene that stands in stark contrast to their outward conduct. Boys avidly consume illustrated stories about lethargic and often grotesque misfits prone to crude speech, slovenly living, flatulence, sexual misdeeds, and nihilistic senses of humor. They also take to comics that depict heroic boys, full of energy, fighting evil characters who threaten beautiful girls or old people or the nation. In none of these cases do the stories approach realism. A final characteristic, then, of Japanese psychology that I see tied to the exam syndrome is a rich and distorted inner life seemingly encouraged by the strict and demanding exterior world. The American response would be to encourage the expression of this inner life and thus to close the gap, but that would spell disaster for the Japanese student. Students learn to keep conduct and private thought a safe distance apart. Individual uniqueness and feeling are not for immediate public consumption.

# 4

# The Social Ecology
# of High Schools

Now that people are classified by ability, the gap between
the classes has become wider. The upper classes are, on
the one hand, no longer weakened by self-doubt and self-
criticism. Today the eminent know that success is just reward for their own capacity, for their own efforts, and for
their own undeniable achievement . . . As for the lower
classes, their situation is different, too. Today all persons,
however humble, know they have had every chance.

MICHAEL YOUNG
*The Rise of the Meritocracy*

VIEWED FROM the perspective of social structure, education is like
a giant railroad roundhouse located between families and entry
into adult society. Children from diverse social backgrounds are
shifted around and differentiated among the "tracks" within the
school system, and finally, having been sorted into categories of presumed skill and ability, they leave for different adult careers. The
modern mass processing of children in universal education not only
generates great uniformity of training, experience, and aspiration; it
also differentiates entire age cohorts and prepares for their allocation
into the larger social structures of employment, class, and status.
We have already considered the last stages of this process, marked by
university exams and their fit with employment. To gain a full overview, we also need to consider the stages of education prior to high
school, those that link family background and elementary education
to high school entrance.

Knowing what differentiation occurs in the first nine years of public education puts into perspective the five high schools we are considering. And taking one step further back to consider the question
of differences among Japanese families will put the entire Japanese

educational roundhouse in better perspective. At issue, of course, are the eternally important questions of social mobility, social class, equality of opportunity, and the role of education as a key institution linking the social structure of one generation with the next. If we assume, as Japanese do, that change in social position and rank is limited after school graduation, then education is indeed crucial to our understanding of Japanese social structure. The high school level marks the point of most fundamental differentiation within Japanese education. It epitomizes many of the polarities and illustrates many of the factors characteristic of the overall social spectrum.

Difference and equality are, of course, matters of degree. No school system and even no single school could possibly sort and differentiate students on a strictly individual basis. The very numbers involved preclude this. Nor is there any real possibility of totally ignoring individual differences throughout the entire course of education. Strict equality remains an ideal, yet when and how differentiation occurs does vary greatly from society to society. A comparative framework is required, one that clarifies the distinctive qualities of the Japanese approach in terms of the criteria used and the discontinuities created. We also want to know at what age children are differentiated, and what this does to their self-esteem and their relationships with one another; further, on what basis they are sorted, and what notion of justice is applied. Is there much advanced warning of impending differentiation? How closely does tracking parallel differences of family background? Does it affect school and peer solidarity? These are questions of great importance to an understanding of our five high schools and of Japanese society in general.

## Family Background: Japan and the United States

Japan has a population that is racially, ethnically, and linguistically homogeneous. The one significant ethnic minority, resident Koreans, makes up less than .5 percent of the total population.[1] These immigrants arrived during Japan's colonial rule of their homeland, which ended in 1945. Although few are citizens, they are now almost entirely second- and third-generation residents and are quite assimilated in terms of language and public conduct.[2] Japan has

1. See Mitchell (1967).
2. Rohlen (1981).

taken in virtually no foreign workers or immigrants since 1950. The other large minority, the Burakumin, is racially and ethnically Japanese.[3] Similar to the situation of lower castes in India, this group was socially isolated and given the lowest forms of work for centuries prior to their legal emancipation in the Meiji period. Today they number between two and three million, or less than 3 percent of the population. Some Burakumin continue to reside in particular neighborhoods and to identify publicly with their own minority, but many have "passed" by changing residence and identity. Both minorities have lately achieved reluctant recognition in Japanese public education, and in places like Kobe, which has large numbers of both groups, minority relations are the source of much tension below the surface.[4]

All the same, Japanese high schools do not have minority problems on a scale anywhere near those in the United States. The minority situation in the United States, for example, involves at least the 22 percent of the children in public schools who are black or Spanish-speaking. Also, although nearly 10 percent of all adults in the United States are foreign-born,[5] the Japanese have essentially refused entry to refugees since 1945 in order to preserve their social homogeneity.

Japan is also a capitalist society, one that has not developed elaborate systems of social welfare or income redistribution; yet research indicates that it contains relatively small differences in household income.[6] This is a complex matter, especially when international comparisons are made, but studies indicate that before- and after-tax income distribution in Japan is more egalitarian than in the United States, Germany, France, Canada, or the United Kingdom regardless of the specific measure applied. Particularly notable in this respect is that the bottom two deciles, the poorest 20 percent, have a greater share of the national income in Japan than in any of the Western nations above.

A large part of the explanation for this is Japan's low unemployment rate, which was below 1 percent for the late 1960s and early 1970s and has not risen above 2 percent since the oil crisis of 1973.

3. See De Vos and Wagatsuma (1966).
4. See Rohlen (1976) for an account of one explosion of minority and political discontent. Brameld (1968) and Shimahara (1971) also offer accounts of Burakumin and schooling.
5. *United States Statistical Abstract, 1977.* Washington D.C.: United States Printing Office.
6. Sawyer (1976).

Japan does not have great pockets of severe poverty, and social disorganization is minimal compared with the United States and much of Europe. Most of the country's unemployment, moreover, is centered on workers over fifty-five years of age, meaning that unemployment is not a factor seriously affecting the development of human capital. Few families of high school students[7] and few young workers suffer the effects of unemployment. In the large industrial societies of the West, unemployment rates are higher, and the age structure of unemployment seriously affects the young.[8]

Families can also be differentiated by the character and quality of parenting. On average, people marry two years later in Japan than in the United States, and the mean deviation in age at marriage is much less.[9] Japanese parenting follows a more common pattern than in the United States. Proportionally few Japanese children are born to very young parents.[10]

Perhaps the greatest difference between the two countries lies in the divorce patterns. In the United States the rate is over 90 divorces annually per 1,000 existing marriages, whereas in Japan the rate is a low 2.7.[11] Whereas 5 percent of Japanese children grow up in single-parent families (more than half because of the death of a parent), 19 percent of all American children now grow up in single-parent families. Slightly more than half of all Japanese mothers work, but only one-quarter work away from home, whereas over half of all American mothers work away from home. Whereas less than 1 percent of Japanese are born out of wedlock, 17 percent of American births were illegitimate in 1979.[12]

These striking contrasts provide a portrait of parenting and child-rearing in Japan that is much less differentiated than in the United

7. Rōdoshō (1978).
8. For example, 25 million Americans were living below the poverty level in the United States in 1975, and nearly half of them were below the age of eighteen. (*CBS News Almanac*, Maplewood, N.J.: Hammond Almanac Inc., 1976, p. 235.) In 1977, 7,900,000 children were recipients of aid to dependent children, according to the U.S. Department of Health, Education and Welfare.
9. In Japan the average age at marriage for males is 27 and for females 24.7 (1975), whereas in the United States it is 23.8 and 21.3, respectively.
10. Nearly 20 percent of all infants born in 1976 in the United States were to mothers under the age of twenty. U.S. Department of Health and Human Services (1980).
11. Kōseishō (1978) and United States Department of Health and Human Services (1980). To put the matter differently, there are almost five times as many divorces per capita in the United States as in Japan. The divorce rate is rising faster in the United States than in Japan.
12. Ibid.

States. The impact of family differences on Japanese children should also be relatively small: such clearly adverse influences as poverty, minority status, and divorce affect a much lower percentage of the nation's school children. Another indication of the general homogeneity is that an appreciably larger percentage of four- and five-year-olds in Japan is sent to kindergarten than in the United States. The figures for the two countries are:

Kindergarten Attendance

|       | United States (1976) | Japan (1979) |
| ----- | -------------------- | ------------ |
| Age 4 | 41%                  | 79%          |
| Age 5 | 81%                  | 85%          |

SOURCE: Mombushō, *Waga kuni no Kyōiku Suijun: 1980 (1981)*, p. 10.

Overall equal opportunity is greatly affected by factors of this sort, as they set the stage for difference in school performance.

The Japanese portrait of demographic homogeneity, relative income equality, and absence of great differentiation in family background seems nearly ideal as a foundation for mass secondary and higher education. It means that (by American standards at least) a remarkably large majority of children start school on much the same footing.[13]

Over 90 percent of Kobe's children enter first grade reading the Japanese syllabary.[14] Since textbooks for their level are written without Chinese characters, they are functionally literate from the beginning. To keep pace in reading they need only learn a reasonable number of new Chinese characters each year. Surprising as it may seem, given the complexity of the language, keeping children learning at the same rate throughout elementary education is much less difficult in Japan than it is in the United States. One does not find separate reading groups in classrooms, or many children frustrated by their inability to read textbooks. In fact, Japanese teachers visiting American grade schools are regularly surprised by the great amount of time devoted to reading.[15] In Japan other subjects, like math and sciences,

13. The Japanese Ministry of Education has shown no interest in broad studies of the relation of family background to school performance.

14. This is according to a survey conducted by elementary teachers that was reported to me at the Kobe City Education Research Office.

15. See Bereday and Masui (1973).

are given the time that Americans devote to reading, and because the pace is fast in these subjects, keeping up is more difficult. Class size in Japanese grade schools is large (generally over thirty), yet children still are able to stay together, not only within a given class, but across the entire nation. Certainly the nature of the written language plays a role here,[16] as does the near absence of dyslexia in Japan.[17] But all the same, we are considering a school system that succeeds in moving children ahead very quickly in terms of basic skills and that in the process does not produce unmanageable differences in individual levels of achievement. That this is accomplished with relative ease is evidenced by the level of development also attained in art and music. Children can *all* play two simple instruments, one wind and one keyboard, by the end of sixth grade. Who could doubt the crucial importance of a homogeneous population, stable families, and relatively equal distribution of household income in making these impressive results possible?

The tracks leading into the Japanese educational roundhouse are few and orderly. Education does not have to serve as an instrument of socialization for diverse ethnic and racial groups. Nor does it face as great a challenge in compensating for disparities in family income. The roundhouse therefore operates very efficiently. Japanese teachers in most schools cope with manageable amounts of individual variation. Planners can create curricula for entire student populations without doing great disservice to large numbers at one or another end of the ability spectrum. Fewer resources need to be allocated to remedial and compensatory programs. Schools need not focus on offering equal opportunity because most children begin together and are supported by essentially the same kind of family situations. Such homogeneity may make Japanese schools less fascinating and colorful. It also makes them very effective.

The enrollment of the typical Japanese elementary and middle schools is, thus, comparable to schools in prosperous American suburbs. As in our upper-middle-class suburban school systems, there is variation among children and families, to be sure, but its impact is manageable.

16. This point is argued in an unpublished paper by Hiroki Kato and debated by Norman B. Overly and Benjamin Duke in *The Educational Forum* (January 1977).

17. Makita (1968). His conclusions probably understate the incidence of dyslexia, yet the entire school system operates as if dyslexia does not exist.

Comparing this relatively homogeneous base among families with the differentiated hierarchical and rather inflexible employment arrangement on the other side of education, an important characteristic of Japanese education is revealed. The educational system does not serve as a "melting pot." Education provides a standardized experience that shapes all children in a common direction, but its content does not present a radical change from what children are learning at home. Family and school reinforce one another easily.

## Compulsory Education

Until the completion of ninth grade and the end of compulsory education, Japanese children receive a public education that is delivered with remarkable uniformity.[18] Fully 99 percent are enrolled in public elementary schools (compared with 87 percent in the United States), a strong indication of the centrality and influence of the public system. Three reasons explain the high degree of uniformity.

First, Japanese metropolitan areas are not severely segregated by income and residence.[19] Most urban areas contain a notable degree of residential heterogeneity by American standards, and emerging suburban areas in Japan are regularly (and voluntarily) incorporated into cities for the greater administrative services that long-established cities offer. Public schools are not exactly the same, and parents and teachers note differences, but rarely are the variations great enough to cause parents to shift residence for the sake of education.[20] The pattern of variation among public elementary schools in a Japanese metropolitan area shows a smaller overall range and a much higher clustering near the mean than the typical American metropolitan pattern. Prior to high school, little can be found comparable to the American phenomena of prosperous suburban and impoverished urban school systems, of de facto segregation of minorities, or of great differences in the content and quality of schooling.

Second, Japanese compulsory education is guided by detailed na-

18. Cummings (1980) is a valuable and far more complete account of this aspect of Japanese compulsory education.

19. Though there is ample statistical material on Kobe neighborhoods to document this, I know of no comprehensive study; but no one familiar with American and Japanese cities would deny the difference as presented here.

20. This conclusion is based on my three-year acquaintance with the city of Kobe and its educational system.

tional standards and a fixed curriculum.[21] Across the entire nation, students of the same grade are expected to learn the same materials in the same time frames with the help of the same textbooks, television programs, and other teaching aids. The pace is undoubtedly geared too high or too low for some individuals and for some school populations, but the iron rule of national standardization works to systematically preserve a general level of equal opportunity. Even the design of schools and the arrangements of classrooms and facilities are greatly standardized by national leadership.

Third, wide and inclusive administrative districts, both prefectural and big-city in scope, cause resources to be allocated evenly over large numbers of schools.[22] Local and national funding is distributed quite evenly within each prefecture and large city. Teachers regularly rotate among schools throughout wide areas, and equipment and other necessities are equalized on the same broad basis.

Public schooling in the United States arose first on a local scale, and local autonomy has remained a highly regarded principle. Throughout the last century of expansion, the institutional potential for significant differences in the funding, staffing, and guidance of our local school districts has been maintained while actual inequality has grown as the American population continued to pursue patterns of residential segregation. Our localism in education has most certainly encouraged our general pattern of inequality. In contrast, the modern Japanese educational system originated with national impulses. The Meiji leaders set up the entire arrangement, which was administered by a single central authority until 1945. From the beginning, every effort was made to standardize compulsory education because it was seen as a crucial tool in shaping an entire new citizenry. Japanese parents have never made residential choices on the basis of education, nor could they create superior schools by creating their own separate communities. Some have sent their children to live with relatives near outstanding schools or in other ways "jumped" residential districts, but even this practice has almost completely ended.

Japanese compulsory education may have certain inherent advantages in attaining equality of delivery compared with the American system; nevertheless, a close look at the urban landscape in Kobe

21. See Cummings (1980).
22. Ibid.

reveals some significant differences in the sociological composition of neighborhoods. Kobe is a long, narrow city located between Osaka Bay and a mountain range that closely parallels the water's edge for about twenty miles. It is a city on a slant, so to speak, because immediately behind the port and industrial areas along the water's edge, the land begins to rise, continuing upward for hundreds of feet until the mountainside is too steep for building. The oldest residential areas just above the port give way to those built during the immediate prewar decades. New high-rise apartments stand still higher up on land only recently cut out of what had been forested hillsides. The city has also grown recently by adding new territory on the far side of the mountain and to the southwest, as these areas have shifted from largely agricultural use to become the sites of large new apartment complexes.

Within this general framework there are neighborhoods that stand out clearly. Distinguishing the industrialized strip along the water's edge are low-income neighborhoods. At least three areas near the water have concentrations of Burakumin and Koreans, and smaller pockets of the two minorities are scattered elsewhere. Yet a twenty-minute walk up the mountainside takes one into older, well-to-do residential districts marked by sedate stone walls and elegant shrubs. These neighborhoods, too, are small and strung out roughly in a line that parallels the water. Because the city's school districts are drawn by lines that run from the bay up through the foothills, cutting across sociological divisions, various types of neighborhoods often share the same elementary and junior high schools. The newer areas on the city's outskirts, which contain high-rise apartments and tract developments, have little of the older city's heterogeneity. Their school populations are almost entirely middle-class, with a sprinkling of local farm children, and the schools fall near the mean in terms of academic performance. In sum, Kobe does have distinct kinds of neighborhoods, but those that are notably poor or rich and those with minorities are small, scattered, and integrated educationally by judicious drawing of district lines.

I know wealthy parents who would prefer not to send their children to the local public elementary school, but private school options are few. The lab school, operated under the auspices of the education department of Kobe University, takes only the brightest of the city's seven-year-olds; the other, an attached grammar school of the private Konan University, leads primarily into that university. Thus, most well-off parents learn to live with equality in public elementary education, choosing instead to invest in *juku*, private tutors, and other aids to success on entrance exams.

Only a few exceptions to these generalizations need be noted for the junior high school level in Kobe. A few middle schools are widely mentioned for having discipline problems, which are attributed mostly to their large numbers of Burakumin and Korean students. The elementary schools located around Kobe's two largest minority neighborhoods send their students to three particular schools out of the city's eighty-three junior high schools. In Kobe, I regularly heard comments from teachers and parents about these three schools, which had reputations for delinquency and violence. Concrete confirmation of such problems came from teachers in these schools, who received extra pay and were viewed by the local Office of Education as serving in hardship posts. All three cases of assault on teachers in Kobe in 1974–75 occurred in these junior high schools. Not surprisingly, officials steered me away from visiting them despite regular requests.

Just as the city possesses a few seriously troubled schools, so it has a few outstanding schools. I was treated to a week-long visit to its showcase junior high school, one of great vitality and order that regularly stands at or near the top in academic, cultural, and athletic performance. In the days when children could get away with "jumping" districts, this was Kobe's elite public middle school, and it retains its image and style. Yet these schools are but a half-dozen out of eighty-three.

The structuring of differences begins in earnest with high school and rests not on residential criteria or aptitude tests, but on measured mastery of school work. Our point that Japanese elementary and junior high schools offer essentially an equal education may have a few exceptions and may rest largely on fortuitous historical factors (authoritarian instincts have created "democratic" results); nevertheless, the fact is that up until tenth grade, the Japanese populace is neither tracked nor sorted in any manner. Children of differing family backgrounds and abilities sit together, play together, and work together in urban schools that are very much the same the nation over. Nor is there tracking of any kind within these schools: quite the reverse, in fact. In the schools I visited, teachers sought to mix and balance abilities in each classroom. They wanted to create a spirit of comradeship and egalitarian sharing.

All of this is reversed at the high school level, where entire schools are differentiated by the presumed ability of their students, where tracking is the essential ingredient in the overall structure of schools, and where instead of offering equal education, high school offerings are responsive to and limited by the specific abilities of their students. From lumping, the system shifts to splitting.

## Entering High School

For historical reasons already noted, the residence principle for school attendance was not applied at the high school level during the post-war period of reform. A one-district, one-school arrangement was established for some (comprehensive) rural high schools and in one large city (Kyoto), but everywhere else an awkward compromise known as the "large district system" prevailed. In Kobe, three large areas containing numerous public high schools were delineated as districts, and all public schools in each were open on a competitive basis to any resident of the district. As public high schools were built, they were added to one of the existing districts. The city's twenty-two private high schools all continued to offer entrance exams to any applicant regardless of residence. The high school world thus remained one shaped by entrance competition. It assumed much the same differentiated structural and attitudinal character we have noted of Japanese universities.

Although the attention of Western scholars has focused primarily on the problem of college entrance in Japan, and particularly on the formation of future elites, the time of high school entrance represents an even more crucial juncture in the total process of educational stratification. Virtually the entire youth population is involved, and the educational tracks into which students are shunted at this stage are both more diverse and more fundamental than at the college stage to the overall structure of society. The ranking of high schools in a given locality is as clear—if not clearer—to all citizens as is the ranking of universities on a national scale. At the local level, which high school a person attends carries lifetime significance, and the finely etched stereotypes of student character associated with each high school become an indelible part of individual identity. At the high school level in Kobe, the various spectra of differences in such things as academic ability, career prospects, family background, and school reputation are all interwoven into a single, hierarchically ordered fabric. And these differences have marked significance for the actual conduct and ethos of each school. Urban high school subcultures are as close to social class stereotypes as can be found anywhere in Japanese society.

Kobe's three large public high school districts contain six schools each. The ranking among the six is clear and unquestioned. Each district has a "best" public high school at the top and a night high school at the bottom. The order of rank has seen almost no change from decade to decade. Reputation is a self-fulfilling prophecy. The school drawing the best applicants has no trouble retaining its high reputation, and the schools at or near the bottom can do very little to change their destiny. It is no accident that the top public high school in each of Kobe's three districts is the oldest, dating back to the first public boys' middle schools established in the city. New public high schools, for lack of a reputation, take their place at the bottom of the ladder in their category (academic or vocational). Structure thus reflects history. The rule among public high schools is that status and quality are functions of relative age.

Even the lowest ranked of the public academic high schools, however, occupies a better than average position in the ranking that also includes Kobe's private high schools. Many of the city's private high schools, despite their academic classification, are held in low esteem. The students who attend most of them are those who failed to enter a public, academic high school.

There are many kinds of private high schools, especially in Kobe, where private schools are numerous. Forty-four percent of the city's students are enrolled in private high schools, compared with 30 percent nationally.

Many of the city's private schools are old, some dating back to the time in Meiji when the port of Kobe was a foreign missionary and commercial center. The city's oldest girls' schools were originated by foreigners for religious (Christian) purposes. Several of them became rather exclusive and remain so today. A second tier of private girls' schools was established on much the same model, but without a Christian or foreign base. A separate group of schools was established in the 1920s for boys of well-off families who failed to enter the public middle schools of the time. Nada is one. Thus, private schools arose to fill prewar gaps in public secondary education, gaps below the elite boys' middle schools. The occupation's reforms did not affect them greatly except to grant them more freedom than before the war. Not one in Kobe became coeducational.

Nor were private schools aimed at academic superiority, and only some of the girls' schools achieved a finishing school flavor. Until the meteoric rise of Nada and several other boys' schools in the sixties, no private high school in the region attracted top students. And matters have not changed much since. Only four private schools in Kobe (including Nada) presently rank with or above the better public academic schools.

Most of the students who attend private schools are not proud of the fact. Even those private schools with the worst reputations offer college preparatory courses, however, and to many parents they are preferable to public vocational schools. Even among the less desirable private schools there are significant differences. A few have such bad reputations for delinquency that they rank below even the vocational schools.

In spring 1975, there were 15,112 students graduating from junior high schools in Kobe, and all but 5 percent initially indicated a preference to go on to high school. A poll of these students the previous autumn revealed that fully 80 percent wanted to matriculate to public academic high schools. The rub came in the fact that only slightly more than six thousand places in such schools were available. Two of every three wishing to obtain an inexpensive education leading to university entrance were destined to disappointment. They faced a choice between two evils: public vocational school or a private high school offering a second-rate college preparatory curriculum.[23] Those who could not afford private school, of course, chose a vocational school. And students failing examinations to the lower ranked private schools (the precise numbers are unavailable) also ended up in

23. The cost of private school is not generally matched by better quality. Most private schools are in chronic financial trouble, and only the best schools are exceptions. Private schools must ask more of teachers, and class size is greater: as already noted the average is fifty-four students per class, compared with forty-two in public day high schools. The Hyōgo prefectural average student/teacher ratio for private high schools is twenty-five to one, whereas for public schools it is seventeen to one (Hyōgo-ken Kikakubu, 1976).

vocational schools. The tendency of applicants to flow down to lower levels created a surplus of applicants for the city's vocational schools. Those refused admission even to one of the public vocational schools clearly belonged to the bottom decile of the ninth-grade population. Their fate was to enter a night school like Sakura or to take employment. Night schools kept their admissions period open into the new school year and waived district residence requirements to be sure to catch as many of those falling through the grate as possible.

If we add to this general portrait of preferences the 1–2 percent of students who have entered the elite private schools like Nada before ninth grade, we have a complete overview of the social geography of high schools (see Fig. 1).

Are there sex differences in the pattern? A greater proportion of boys (12 percent) than girls (6 percent) take jobs or are idle following graduation from ninth grade. Similarly, more boys (5 percent) than girls (1 percent) enter night schools. The very bottom decile appears to be largely male. There is a larger proportion of females (28 percent) than males (24 percent) in daytime vocational schools. One of the most conspicuous differences is in the proportions attending private high schools. Roughly twice as many girls as boys in the prefecture attend private high schools, most of which are in and around Kobe. It is impossible to be absolutely precise here, as many Kobe students go outside the city to private high schools, some even commuting to schools in neighboring Osaka Prefecture, and many nonresidents in turn attend Kobe's private high schools. Nevertheless, the general pattern is for about 22 percent of the boys and 34 percent of the girls to matriculate to private high schools. This indicates the willingness of Kobe's parents to pay to keep their children, especially their daughters, from taking early low-status work. They may not seek university educations for them, but they want the respectability of a high school degree.

The proportions are slightly reversed when it comes to public academic high schools. Among all those leaving junior high school, 42 percent of the boys and 41 percent of the girls succeed in entering public schools like Okada and Otani. In fact, the best public academic high schools regularly enroll a ratio of fifty-five to forty-five males to females. The pinnacle of the arrangement, the very elite private schools, are all male. The general pattern to be noted here is that disproportionate numbers of males do either very well or very

**Figure 1**
Futures of Ninth-Grade Graduates in Kobe, 1974

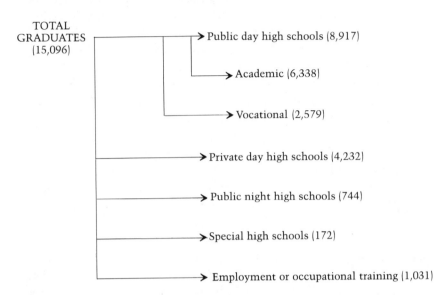

SOURCE: Data from *Sotsugyosha no Yukue, Gakkō Kihon Chosa-Chugakkō/ Kōtō Gakkō* (Kobe: Hyōgoken Kikakubu, 1976.)

poorly, and females tend to be overrepresented in the middle and lower middle areas of the structure.

This raises the question of the criteria used to select students for high school entrance, and whether there is room for manipulation. I found that private schools conduct examinations that closely follow the university pattern, but the lesser schools among them do not limit themselves strictly to the exam results. An offer by a parent to make a donation, or good contacts in the community, has been known to help. Such cases are unheard of for the better private schools, however, and are not a major point of concern.

Public high school entrance is more complicated. In much of Japan, public high schools give examinations just as Kobe's private schools do.[24] The decisions are therefore quite straightforward and crisp, but problems arise in managing the application process. A rational approach would be for schools to offer their tests in descend-

24. For a discussion of Tokyo's entrance exam system and its reforms, see Rohlen (1977).

ing rank order, allowing students to continue taking tests until they finally enter a school. In actual practice, however, students can apply to only one public high school. As a result, miscalculations are possible. Ambitious parents and students, often against teacher advice, can overreach and apply to a public high school for which the chances of entrance are too slim. Failing this one-shot chance, they must locate a suitable private school or even, in extreme cases, choose to have the child (typically a boy, of course) do a year of "high school *rōnin*" before applying as a freshman the next year.[25]

Hyōgo and some other prefectures operate under a more elaborate system that puts greater weight on the judgment of junior high school teachers.[26] In theory, many distinct factors are made relevant; but although grades, an aptitude test, teacher recommendations, and a conventional entrance exam are all taken into consideration, the crucial determining factor tends to be the supervising junior high school teachers. They arbitrate the application process, sending forward to the better public high schools only the names of those students virtually certain to gain admittance. With the top private schools already closed, they are obliged to carefully shepherd their good students into some academic public high school. Controlling the risks of one-shot application means coordinating rather closely with the admissions officers of the top public high schools. Only a city-wide informal system of such cooperation explains why almost exactly the right number of names are sent for the entrance examinations of top public schools as will finally be accepted. This coordination links some twenty junior high schools in each large district with the district's four public academic high schools. When it works, the fallout of good students is small, and the public is none the wiser.

The teachers' role is very different in the case of students destined for private, vocational, and night schools. There is little they do other than provide information on the schools and estimates about how competitive the entrance situation will be. Ironically, the numerically most competitive entrance exams occur in the lower half of the overall school rankings. I do not have the figures, but some

25. High school *rōnin* have been a regular, if minor, aspect of the Osaka school landscape for many years.

26. This account is based on interviews with middle school teachers. All, incidentally, preferred this system to an unmanaged, open application process and felt that it is a fair and less anxiety-producing arrangement.

public vocational and private schools turn away sizable numbers on occasion. Managing the upper half with such finesse only serves to put the problems of insecurity more squarely on those students in the lower half of the academic spectrum.

Teachers make their judgments according to a student's grade rank and score on the prefecture's aptitude test. Parents have access to this information, and improper bias on a teacher's part could be exposed. Each year a few parents do disagree with a guidance counselor's assessment, insisting that their child's name go forward to a school ranked higher than the teacher suggests. In such cases, parental prerogatives take precedence, and teachers use the typically unfortunate results to try to control similar parents the next year.

A small amount of unofficial "affirmative action" is also accomplished in this informal process. Specifically, the recipient high schools can and do set quotas on particular well-off junior high schools with the intent of tipping the scales a bit in favor of students from schools located in poorer sections of the city. But this is not publicly acknowledged and would be difficult to document.

Whether entrance exams or a teacher's judgment about grade rank are the central criteria, the basic lesson in the high school entrance game is the same: work very hard in school or you will end up having to pay for private schooling just to get a diploma, or even worse, miss the chance for college altogether. That 95 percent of Kobe's students are advancing to high school is no evidence of utopia having arrived, for a large number aspire to a kind of high schooling and level of achievement that remains out of reach. The education level of the entire generation has advanced, but elitism and social hierarchies have not been fundamentally altered by the rapid growth of secondary education.

Competition and the anxiety over entrance to high school is no longer an elite or even a middle-class phenomenon. In Kobe, virtually all children are involved. As our attention passes from areas of high academic performance to the bottom one-third of the junior high school population, we find parental concern shifting from the goal of university attendance to that of saving the family money in the process of gaining a high school diploma. In 1975, private high schools charged approximately $700–$1,000 per year plus a sizable entrance fee. In Kobe the majority of parents shouldering this burden do so because their children performed below average academically.[27] Poor performance is clearly punished by the system. Because there is a solid correlation between poverty and poor school performance, it follows that the costs of private schooling are likely to fall heavily on families least able to afford them. These families are not only reluctant to carry an extra economic burden, but they are often anxious that their children should avoid the problems of delinquency and peer group troubles associated with the worst private schools. The fact that they send their children to high school at all is vivid testimony to the powerful drive at all levels of society for attaining at least a high school education.

### Family Background and the Five High Schools

The composition of local high schools in Japan is thus one of academically induced differentiation that generates schools with remarkable concentrations of talent and schools that are carrying an assortment of a city's most troubled and least accomplished students. The five high schools we are considering are a sample of the top, the middle, and the bottom of this hierarchy.

At issue is the question of how Japanese society is reflected in the spectrum of high school differentiation—or, more precisely, how differences of income, occupation, parental education, and other household influences show up across the five schools. This in turn tells us a great deal about the role of lower schools in producing equal opportunity and social mobility in contemporary Japan.

I asked second-year students in each of the five high schools to fill out questionnaires on family background. I was warned by the faculties of several schools against inquiring directly about income, and the faculty of one school asked me not to inquire about one's father's education. Clearly, the Japanese are more sensitive to the implications of these matters than are Americans. The questionnaire also inquired about what I felt were useful diagnostic items, such as *juku* attendance and whether students had their own rooms for study at home. The scheme was to use the hierarchy of the five high schools

27. The reforms undertaken in Tokyo (Rohlen, 1977) have partially ameliorated the problem of cost burdens on the poor, but the trade-off was the loss of more top students to the best private schools.

as a benchmark to discover the general degree of correlation between family background and academic achievement.

Teachers often refer to the importance of family differences; and yet as we have seen, there is much about Japanese society and education that contributes to equal opportunity. By implication, at least, the relative social and cultural homogeneity of Japan, the high degree of institutional equality present in compulsory education, and the low correlation between income, residence, and schooling up to tenth grade should produce a result that confirms an "ability over background" thesis.

My survey, however (Table 6), revealed that regular and quite impressive differences of family background distinguish the five schools. These differences point unmistakably to the fact that socioeconomic variations play a significant role in shaping educational outcomes in Japan. The process of educational sorting that begins with high school expresses these differences more clearly than residential or employment patterns. I can think of no other inclusive social institution in Japan that comes closer to a simple class structure than the structure of urban high schools in cities like Kobe.

Consider the evidence. Nada students clearly come from stable, well-off families. Virtually all have their own rooms in which to study. Three-quarters were sent to tutoring schools when in elementary school, indicating careful parental planning and high aspiration. With few exceptions, the Nada boys have but one sibling. Okada and Otani students also come from stable, small families. As a group, their parents are not as well educated as Nada parents, but they look firmly middle-class when compared with the parents of Yama and Sakura students. Only one boy in a hundred at Nada comes from a family with four children, but nearly one-quarter of the Yama students have three or more siblings. One in every seven vocational students is missing a parent. The use of tutoring to supplement elementary education also shows a consistent decline from Nada to Sakura. One out of four vocational school students does not even have his or her own study space. The percentage of working mothers is higher for the vocational students, and the kinds of work the mothers do are generally of lower status. The working Nada mothers may be doctors or teachers; mothers of Yama and Sakura students tend to be factory workers, saleswomen, and home pieceworkers, and a few

**Table 6**

Family Background of Students in Five Kobe High Schools, 1975

|  | Nada | Okada | Otani | Yama | Sakura |
|---|---|---|---|---|---|
| Average number of siblings in family | 2.1 | 2.3 | 2.4 | 2.8 | 2.9 |
| Percentage of working mothers in sample | 15% | 22% | 21% | 30% | 34% |
| Percentage of students missing one or both parents | 1% | .07% | 2% | 13% | 15% |
| Percentage of students' fathers with university education (including *senmon gakkō*) | 60% | not available | 33% | 6% | 2% |
| Percentage of students with their own room for study | 99% | 86% | 77% | 71% | 58% |
| Percentage attending tutoring or cram school at some time; during elementary school | 91% 74% | 78% 43% | 68% 37% | 37% 40% | 39% 24% |
| Percentage of Burakumin in student body * |  | 1.4% [†] | 2.2% [†] | 4.9% [†] | 5.8% [†] |
| Percentage of Koreans in student body * |  | 2.1% [†] | 1.3% [†] | 3.8% [†] | .5% [†] |

* Based on statistics kept by each school's officials for 1975.

[†] For each school, left to right, the numbers are as follows. Burakumin: 18 out of 1,215; 27 out of 1,220; 60 out of 1,229; and 12 out of 206. Koreans: 26 out of 1,215; 17 out of 1,220; 46 out of 1,209; and 1 out of 206.

work as bar hostesses, according to teachers. Small family shops are also common among the families of the vocational students. All these considerations point to the same general conclusion: that the high school academic ladder reflects household socioeconomic stratification.

Our five schools are sharply differentiated by parental levels of education. The parents of children who were high school students in 1975 belong largely to a generation that attended secondary and higher schools during and just after World War II, when many educational careers were disrupted. In the immediate postwar period, only those whose families could afford it or those who were very talented were able to attend university. Between 1940 and 1950 roughly 10 percent of each age cohort of males was able to advance to higher education, and more than half were going to the more expensive private universities. The fact that fully 60 percent of the fathers of Nada students gained a higher education at that time indicates that they either were academically talented or came from families with incomes in the upper quarter of the population. It is not known what proportion of the Okada fathers attended university, but the rate is bound to be similar to that at Otani (33 percent), considering the general similarity of family background profiles for the two schools.

Moving from Otani to Yama, we find a precipitous decline in the percentage of university-educated fathers. Yama looks very much like Sakura Night School by this measure. Both sets of vocational school parents possess educational records that put them well below the national average for their generation. The great majority of these fathers essentially stopped their schooling with the eighth grade. Teachers in the two vocational schools recognize this fact, noting that most parents cannot help their children with their homework. The large gap between the academic and vocational schools in parental education raises questions about the balance in our sampling of high schools. It appears that we would have a fuller picture if we had one low-status private academic high school in our sample. It might provide a more evenly graduated pattern or correlation between background factors and school rank.

The matter of parental occupation is more difficult to organize statistically due to the infinitely complex issue of categorization and the variety of vague euphemisms utilized by students, especially when the work carries some stigma. Each school's student information cards, while also vague, provided the best picture. In a class of forty-five from Yama and a group of one hundred from Nada, the following descriptions were supplied to the schools by families.

### YAMA

| | |
|---|---|
| "company employee" | 18 |
| home business (shops, factories) | 6 |
| "office worker" | 5 |
| metal worker | 5 |
| out of work | 5 |
| deceased | 5 |

| | |
|---|---|
| taxi driver | 4 |
| construction | 2 |
| factory laborer | 2 |
| postal worker | 1 |
| sailor | 1 |
| longshoreman | 1 |
| restaurant worker | 1 |
| golf club employee | 1 |
| welder | 1 |
| music teacher | 1 |
| ship repair | 1 |

## NADA

| | |
|---|---|
| "company employee" | 41 |
| "company executive" | 16 |
| self-employed | 11 |
| doctor | 10 |
| public employee | 8 |
| teacher | 3 |
| unclear | 3 |
| professor | 2 |
| Christian minister | 1 |
| industrial worker | 1 |
| policeman | 1 |
| small manufacturer | 1 |
| barber | 1 |
| deceased | 1 |

A similar inventory for Sakura, the night school, indicates a higher proportion of fathers in agriculture, transport, and construction. The category of "company employee" is very small. All of this, of course, is consistent with the overall portrait of fathers' educational background.

The distribution of minority students across our five high schools largely fits the overall pattern. Fully 60 percent of all the Burakumin students in this sample are attending either Yama or Sakura, two schools that represent but 30 percent of the total enrollment sample. In other words, the chances that a Burakumin student will go to a vocational high school are twice the average. Other research in Hyōgo prefecture confirms that the Burakumin as a group do rather poorly in school. Koreans, however, are distributed more evenly in our sample. The story of Koreans in Japanese education is a complex one, but the crucial point is simply that they face serious discriminatory barriers *after* high school. However, Korean families do manage to support their children in education to the degree that they fare about as well as the average Japanese up to the point of high school entrance, and this is strong testimony to their dedication to educational paths toward social advancement.[28]

In Kobe, the concentration of Burakumin and Korean students in vocational schools like Yama is a notable fact. One in ten students at Yama is either Burakumin or Korean. Several vocational schools in the city had serious minority problems in the early seventies that closed down classes for weeks. In one case, classes were suspended for several months while an outside Burakumin activist group and some faculty members led an intense schoolwide effort to root out and confront discriminatory attitudes among teachers and faculty. And Yama itself experienced a protracted conflict between the principal and the faculty over the admissions of Koreans. In rural Hyōgo prefecture (with the nation's second highest concentration of Burakumin) there are high schools with large Burakumin enrollment, and they too have lately experienced problems, not disciplinary but political ones, as adult Burakumin activists struggle to gain supremacy over Burakumin student groups in the schools.[29]

Although minority problems have troubled some schools, most Kobe high schools have not been disturbed. Disruptions are least likely to occur where the dominant goal is preparation for university entrance exams. The power of the exam system even shapes the distribution of minority problems in public education.

## Summary

The Japanese system of education is a single track through ninth grade.[30] Compared with the United States, differences among households and between individual schools and districts are not great. Entrance to high school marks a point of considerable discontinuity.

28. Rohlen (1981).
29. Rohlen (1976).
30. Japanese students, you will recall, produced lower mean coefficients of variation than students of any other country on the international tests of math and science achievement.

Urban neighborhoods are relatively heterogeneous, but after ninth grade students are segregated, like with like, into high schools regardless of residence. The egalitarian and inclusive qualities of compulsory schooling are followed by a now nearly universal secondary system marked by strenuous sortings and rankings. Students are shunted out into a hierarchy of schools, each with its own subculture. Education has nearly as many tracks at this point as there are high schools in a particular locality.

The Japanese child learns early of this impending point of judgment. The sober realities of competition and differential rewards are an informal part of the upper grade school and junior high school years. Parental warnings and whispered gossip, the advice of tutors and *juku* teachers, and the media fanfare given to exam competition are all at work shaping attitudes throughout this period. Childhood in contemporary Japan is an experience of progressively deepening seriousness. By fifth grade, teachers have become rather stern, and the ratio of male teachers progressively increases. More and more students are going to *juku*. Upon entering middle school boys are required to shave their heads as a badge of their serious commitment. Grades and tests become central. A few have already made it to elite private middle schools, and their neighbors watch them going off proudly each day. By the time of high school application, every boy and girl is acutely aware of school rankings, and all find themselves being placed in the system. High school entrance is a momentous turning point, calling forth competitive instincts and hard work. Social innocence, or what remains of it, ends. The school each student enters implies a judgment, and its subculture is a portent of the social world to which he is destined. The label received is nearly indelible. No wonder the carefree joys of early primary school are fondly remembered by Japanese, who particularly love to attend grade school alumni gatherings.

Contrast this with the American conception of progress from grades one through twelve. We see increasing work and increasing academic difficulty, to be sure, but we couple this with an expectation of increasing independence and freedom. Everyone must go to high school, so no privilege is involved. But doing well in high school makes a big difference for the individual's future. Good grades and SAT test scores are important. But to only a small minority of American students are they a dominant concern. Teachers hope to "motivate" the rest of the students. High school is ideally a time for the flourishing of friendships, romance, creativity, and independent choice. Finally, our high schools are rarely viewed as symbols of academic stature. Rather, they are taken as poignant symbols of the concern and largesse of communities.

In Japan, the recent near universal enrollment in high schools has not been accompanied by a greater mixing of students. Just the opposite has occurred: as more schools have been constructed, each has come to enroll a narrower segment of the total population.

We face a basic paradox. At least, it is a paradox if we seek easy characterizations of what is being produced by Japanese education. In essence, we find the egalitarian and unifying experience of compulsory education juxtaposed to the equally profound experience of being sorted into clear, nearly immutable strata of hierarchically arranged and quite different high schools.

In theory, a meritocracy is a social system that offers equal educational opportunity, makes it frankly competitive, and then uses the order of ability or merit produced to stratify individuals according to the many grades of work in society. Japan probably approaches this ideal more than any other society today. One result is the Japanese habit of seeing society as composed of wafer-thin status distinctions. Education is the most crucial determinant of this stratification.

The statistics herein on family backgrounds from our five high schools illustrate just how far the present system is from perfect mobility. The stratification of the parental generation appears to be largely replicated in the stratification of the next generation. Family background does carry great weight in shaping educational outcomes in Japan, and although the national government has studiously avoided a serious investigation of this question, some recent Japanese studies corroborate quite closely the results of this one.[31]

Because education has often been pointed to as contributing greatly to equal opportunity in Japan, it is important to point out evidence to the contrary.[32] The heart of the problem seems to be that although

31. E.g., the work of Fukaya Masashi as reported in Rohlen (1977), p. 55.
32. This section is a comment on the numerous studies of social mobility in Japan that emphasize the positive role of education. In my opinion, by using father and son comparisons but not asking the basic question of the relative stratigraphic position of the son's occupational and educational "achievements," the real mobility involved remains obscure. See Tominaga (1970). Cummings (1980) summarizes this more recent thinking and research on the issue.

enormous change has occurred in overall educational attainment and in occupational status from one generation to the next (that is, sons can rise above their fathers' levels of accomplishment), most of this is the product of general industrial advancement that has opened up more opportunities in general: rapid economic progress has readily allowed sons to supersede their fathers' social status. Most Yama students, simply by finishing high school, are doing this, and so are the 40 percent of Nada students who will go to university although their fathers did not. But intergenerational comparisons involve a definitional sleight of hand when used in a context of rapid economic development. There are many more managers and skilled workers now and fewer farmers than in the previous generation. There are many more high school and university graduates too. The more basic question is one of mobility in relative social position. We have found that Yama students remain largely in the bottom quarter of their generation, precisely where most of their parents were. Even those Nada students whose fathers did not go to college appear largely to come from the highest levels of society by other criteria. My impression is that intergenerational changes in concrete social rank as measured against the total structure have not been as great as changes between fathers' and sons' educational and occupational status. One can be the high-school-educated, salaried employee son of a farmer with a sixth-grade education and not have moved up in an absolute sense at all.

This is a very significant point, for it reflects on the effectiveness of Japanese education in creating greater social equality. Despite its many egalitarian qualities, a meritocratic system is still affected by the power of household factors beyond its control. Institutional equality and exam objectivity participate in the creation of educational outcomes in what must be termed a passive manner. They create no additional biases or differentials over and above those that already exist between households. Public education, however perfect, cannot "generate" social mobility in an active manner, short of affirmative action programs. These do not exist to any degree in Japan. In sum, despite the homogeneity of the population and the relatively small degree of family differences, parenting makes a profound difference on educational outcomes, and real intergenerational mobility is not as great in Japan as many have been led to believe.

Further, the rate of change in education and occupational structure slows with slower economic growth; a near plateau state has arrived where about the same percentage of each generation will be going on to higher education. The shape of the occupational world will also change very slowly. Combine these trends with the rising influence of private education, both elite private schools and *juku*, and it is quite possible that a trend toward greater influence for household factors is at work. Already in the last decade, an increasing proportion of national university students is coming from the top 10 percent of the households in terms of income (Table 7). Money appears to be making more of a difference. The ideal of open social mobility in Japan is faced with a serious challenge as private avenues to exam success open wider. This may be the real significance of Nada.

So far, popular thinking has not judged public education as biased in favor of wealth or status. Japanese generally believe in the fairness of objective entrance exams. And while the teachers' union points out the problems, most teachers I spoke with individually prefer the present system to any form of affirmative action or reform of the meritocratically generated hierarchy of high schools. Parental interest in every conceivable kind of aid to exam preparation, the *juku* being the most prominent, also demonstrates their recognition and firm conviction that families make a difference. Most middle-class Japanese seem privately convinced that school performance is a reflection of the character of the student and the household. Divorce or many children or lack of parental discipline, they intuitively feel, are not the fault of the school system or society, but of the parents themselves. Quite naturally, they think, these factors affect a student's ability to do well in school. Schools to them are not instruments of social leveling, but arenas of fair competition. Good students, people say, come from stable, hard-working, and, most of all, concerned families. To the popular Japanese mind, if families are well-off, their success is merely further illustration of the same point: good family character.

There is no denying that for just about every rich doctor's son in elite Nada High School, there is an average-income school teacher's son. Yet the enormous difference between the number of doctors and teachers in the total Kobe population and the likelihood that teachers' children are an anomaly in terms of educational achievement are not widely considered. Japanese teachers are particularly keen educators at home.

Ironically, the belief that there is adequate equal opportunity in

**Table 7**

Percentage of Students from Five Strata of Households in Japan, Based on Income Differences.

| | 1961 | | 1965 | | 1970 | | 1974 | |
|---|---|---|---|---|---|---|---|---|
| **National Universities** | | | | | | | | |
| I (lowest income) | 19.7 | } 39.9 | 16.3 | } 31.4 | 17.3 | } 31.2 | 14.4 | } 25.6 |
| II | 20.2 | | 15.1 | | 13.9 | | 11.2 | |
| III | 15.4 | | 18.6 | | 17.7 | | 16.0 | |
| IV | 18.5 | } 44.7 | 22.5 | } 50.1 | 21.2 | } 50.4 | 24.3 | } 58.4 |
| V (highest income) | 26.2 | | 27.6 | | 29.2 | | 34.1 | |
| **Private Universities** | | | | | | | | |
| I | 6.4 | } 15.6 | 4.8 | } 11.6 | 5.8 | } 11.9 | 6.1 | } 12.6 |
| II | 9.2 | | 6.8 | | 6.1 | | 6.5 | |
| III | 12.3 | | 11.1 | | 13.3 | | 11.6 | |
| IV | 19.2 | } 72.1 | 20.9 | } 77.3 | 22.3 | } 74.8 | 21.2 | } 75.8 |
| V | 59.2 | | 56.4 | | 52.5 | | 54.6 | |
| **Total Four-Year Universities** | | | | | | | | |
| I | 11.0 | } 24.1 | 8.3 | } 18.7 | 8.5 | } 16.5 | 8.0 | } 15.5 |
| II | 13.1 | | 10.4 | | 8.0 | | 7.5 | |
| III | 13.5 | | 13.4 | | 14.4 | | 12.6 | |
| IV | 19.1 | } 62.3 | 21.7 | } 67.9 | 22.0 | } 69.0 | 21.8 | } 71.9 |
| V | 43.2 | | 46.2 | | 47.0 | | 50.1 | |

SOURCE: Data from Mombushō Gakusei Seikatsu Chosa (Ministry of Education student life survey), reported in a number of issues of *Kosei Hōdō* (published monthly by the Gakusei Hodoka of the Mombushō).

NOTE: Each stratum represents 20 percent of all households in Japan.

the school system is most strongly held by those who make every effort to get their children into a "better" school. There will always be the exceptional case of "rags to Tokyo University" that illustrates this notion.

Perhaps because public schools have dominated quality education for so long, the Japanese do not think of money as buying privileges. For the same reason, no scholarship system to private schools exists. We are discussing an educational system in which the crucial difference affecting achievement has been seen traditionally as ability and effort, parents and the family environment properly affecting effort. Ability is innate and cannot be changed; only effort makes a difference. Exam preparation has been, and still is, viewed as essentially hard work. Those willing, able, and encouraged in the effort are, according to the popular view, the ones who succeed. Money alone cannot purchase ability or inspire hard work, but it can provide a more efficient context for effort in the forms of *juku*, tutors, and private schools. Its actual impact on educational outcomes, however, remains debatable because ability and effort remain largely unassessed. What we do know is that the children of the wealthy are doing well, by and large, in education. Whether this has more to do with money or with parental attention also remains unanswered.

A second caveat is the simple one that although the development of social classes has not been notable in Japan, consciousness of class can be detected in such subtleties as the interaction between people of different backgrounds and privately stated comments about social realities.[33] Compared with Westerners, the Japanese pay less attention to the economic basis of class differences and focus more heavily on educational considerations. The social gap between Kobe's high- and low-status high schools is indeed great—a separation as large as between nineteenth-century classes, European or Japanese. The gap is certainly not just academic. Past and future status, income, and power are involved, and between the elite schools and the vocational schools there is a significant difference in self-esteem and personal conduct. Certainly the sense of identity, the confidence, and the general life patterns of Nada students are a world apart from

33. See Nakane Chie (1970) for the argument that Japan is not a class society. The opinion that it is dominates most Japanese sociological thinking. Cummings (1980) argues that "cultural" class differences are pronounced, but that education is a major factor teaching egalitarian values and offering equality of educational opportunity.

the disorder, frustration, and low self-esteem that characterize Yama and Sakura. If Japanese society were characterized primarily according to the structure of its secondary and higher education, a class analysis would be most appropriate.

The magnitude of the subcultural differences between types of high schools makes them the modern equivalent of nineteenth-century industrial classes. Yet this stratified order emerges only at the time of high school. Compulsory education strictly denies it. In fact, the educational experience of the elementary years teaches equality and the norms of group solidarity in a thorough manner. A profound discontinuity is created at grade ten, one that marks the intersection of two distinct and equally important principles of Japanese society: group solidarity and hierarchy. With high school, the two become more complexly related.

In work institutions—companies, the government, and so forth— the horizontal strata of individual rank and status are meshed with and moderated by powerful ties of small group solidarity, institutional affiliation, and vertically arranged interpersonal relationships. Companies have powerful ideologies of family, and internal class divisions are not as apparent as in Western work organizations. Unions include both blue- and white-collar workers, for example, and most are company-based rather than occupation-based. Managers often have a personal history of union membership, and a remarkable percentage of top managers were once officers of their company's union. In this manner, Japanese work institutions largely suppress overt class consciousness and structure.

Secondary education thus appears unique in its broad expression of class divisions. It includes nearly the entire adolescent population in one hierarchical reality, a reality that is not forgotten following high school, when individuals take their places in work institutions. The classes formed here are educational, as compared with industrial.

Thus education up to twelfth grade leaves a complex legacy of social experiences, one that combines inclinations to group solidarity and great initial equality with a sharply etched sense of ability ranking and a three-year term in a class system of high schools. The solidarity and group intimacy of elementary school is primal and emotionally powerful. Egalitarianism is the institutional mode of the early years. It is prior to and of longer duration than the subsequent sorting into the hierarchy of high schools. The interplay of these elements and their relative prominence in actual behavior are subsequently orchestrated by adult institutional arrangements. All are part of Japanese modern consciousness, and the potential for recombinations and changing emphasis is great.

# II

## THE INSTITUTION
## AND THE EXPERIENCE

# 5

## Space and Time

From the first, education was an American religion. It was
and is. In education we put our faith . . . even in architecture
we proclaim our devotion, building schools like cathedrals.
HENRY STEELE COMMAGER

U RBAN public high schools in Japan have been built according to
some formula that has no legal or other explicit authority, but
that nevertheless has made them all very much alike physically,
much more so than American high schools. The shortage of land, a
sense of appropriate form, and a broad agreement on efficient size
have no doubt combined in the history of school design to the effect
that most urban high schools have about twelve hundred students
and a faculty of forty or fifty sharing one or more plain three-story
classroom buildings surrounded by a small athletic field, a gymna-
sium, sometimes a swimming pool, and often a small greenhouse.

Simplicity has always been valued in Japanese architecture, but
otherwise the aesthetic sensitivities for which the Japanese are famous have not contributed to the country's modern school architecture. Insufficiency of funds coupled with a Spartan attitude toward
schooling has resulted in buildings that are as uninspired, drab, and
gloomy as were nineteenth-century factories. If Americans proclaim
their faith in democratic education by building high schools "like
cathedrals," the Japanese express their intent (a no less religious one)
that high schools be a sober introduction to adulthood by creating
school buildings like military barracks.

Three-quarters of a century ago, in the ramshackle dormitories of

Japan's most elite higher schools, asceticism was exuberantly celebrated, as Donald T. Roden observes.

> The late Meiji higher school students championed their artificial state
> of "relative deprivation" as a test of manly determination to live un-
> selfishly in fraternal harmony. Nothing was more effective in enhanc-
> ing the sense of belonging to the community than the awareness among
> students that they must join together in withstanding the adversities of
> uncivilized life.[1]

Something of the same ethic lay behind the response by a graduate
student friend of mine to my dismay at the total defacement by student radicals of a new university building. He disagreed, saying that
for Japanese students the seriousness of education is undermined if
the surroundings are attractive. "Learning loses interest when physical conditions are excellent." He implied that a sense of commitment is lacking.

School architecture anywhere cannot avoid being institutional to
a degree. It is governed by the large numbers and the inalterable fact
of classroom instruction. Americans, however, often try to marry
the pragmatic with the inspirational by rearranging the boxes, inter-
spersing them with open space, introducing flexible partitions, opening them up to the outside, and in other ways disguising their institutional essence. The Japanese have not felt this need. They seem
to want the unadorned pragmatism to be the inspiration.

All five of our Kobe high schools are at least twenty years old.
There are new high schools being built today with some improvements (the concrete is not weather-stained and the floors are lino-
leum instead of wood), but even the best new high schools evidence
none of the dramatic design, the individuality of conception, or the
colorful architectural vitality of postwar American school architecture. Everything remains guided strictly by the idea that a school is
a three- or four-story collection of standard-size rectangular classrooms linked by hallways. Students go there to sit and listen and become sober adults. High schools do not offer an expansive atmosphere
of creativity. Their architecture fits the teacher-centered approach
quite neatly.

Japanese high schools seem to lie under a permanent prohibition
against any kind of decoration. Elementary and even junior high

1. Roden (1980), pp. 111–112.

schools in Japan enjoy collections, exhibits, and the like in their hallways. One especially bright middle school even had an impressive collection of tropical fish displayed in tanks outside the principal's office. But at the high school level, everything of this sort vanishes. Hallways are absolutely devoid of anything except signs and room numbers. Classrooms are equally barren. Gray is by far the most popular wall color, yet, as if to prove that there is a variety and independence of choice in these things, some schools have chosen light brown or serviceable cream. Whatever the color selected, it is applied liberally over the entire school, leaving a wandering visitor with the impression of being below decks in a ship of the line.

It is rarely, however, a shabby kind of monotony. The sparseness of furnishings and impeccable orderliness remove any chance of that. All is well swept, and that is about what is required to keep things neat. There are no lockers in the halls and no student lounges that require steady maintenance. The bathrooms and minuscule cafeterias are as sturdy and simple as possible.

One thing that postwar high schools do not lack is sufficient light. Each classroom has an expanse of windows running along one side. There is little reliance on artificial lighting, a contribution to the very low overhead costs of Japanese schools. Nor do schools rely on central heating. Classrooms are equipped with gas heaters that, when used, take the chill off; but not everyone uses them, and they work only if the doors are closed. A trade-off is involved in which classrooms are warm but stuffy and smelly. Japanophiles have praised the way traditional domestic architecture invites nature in and provides intimacy with the change of seasons, but sitting in many a cold, damp schoolroom through one winter caused me to favor the unaesthetic kerosene stove. Schools actually resemble Japanese farmhouses in their practical simplicity, but unfortunately most are made of concrete. In today's Japan, the blessed are workers in large offices who spend their days in fully heated and air-conditioned comfort. Students endure an environment of inelegant harshness, summer and winter. With the arrival of spring and fall, however, the windows are opened, and Japanese classrooms assume a joyful airiness that no modern office building could possibly match.

In the West, there is a tradition of remembering one's alma mater for the beauty of lawns and ancient buildings. Nostalgic memories for Japanese come from different sources. The discomforts are glori-

*Otani High School*

One of two classroom buildings (on the right) and the gym at Otani High School. The playing fields are in the foreground. The simple modular design of the classroom structure is very typical. I have never heard of anyone using the observatory on the roof.

fied. Difficult times together evidence the appropriateness and worth of the educational experience. School gates are also powerful symbols. They signify success in passing entrance examinations and represent the school's status and prestige. Those that pass through together join a fellowship that many will cherish for life. Passing through the school's gate for the last time is memorable and is referred to time after time. The moment marks an end of innocence.

A peek into the principal's office reveals that it is surprisingly large and ornate. Its walls are filled with pictures, plaques, trophies, and inspirational messages. A set of stuffed chairs and a sofa are gathered intimately around a low coffee table, with the principal's desk in the background. The furniture is typically covered with white linen lace that gives the whole setting a tidy Victorian air contradicted only by such objects as a large, gaudy cigarette lighter on the coffee table of one office that dispensed an imposing three-inch colored flame. Even though the principal works at the desk in the rear of the room, the impression is of a place for entertaining visitors. Indeed, this is one of the key functions of the principal, who must greet and consult with parents, the parent-teachers association, school board officials, delegations of other principals, journalists, and even an occasional foreigner like me. The principal's office is an oasis of antiquated plushness in a desert of educational puritanism where important people, puffing innumerable cigarettes, talk about adjusting the school to the outside world.

Next door is the much larger teachers' room, where forty or so desks are cramped together. These desks are home base for all but the physical education teachers. File cabinets are woefully inadequate, and desks are loaded high with papers, dictionaries, and textbooks. Many other Japanese government offices also use desk tops as filing cabinets. Everywhere one turns there are piles of documents, some no doubt indispensable, which miraculously do not get lost or ruined and do not blow all over the room when doors are opened.

Because teachers do not have their own classrooms, they have no opportunities to decorate them with educationally inspiring material. Rather, each has a desk cheek by jowl with the desks of other instructors serving the same grade. Privacy and independence at work are evidently of little concern. Teachers who wish to confer confidentially do so in the science labs or in neighborhood coffee shops.

Nor is the teachers' room a haven from students. Between classes and after school, students venture in, most rather cautiously, to ask questions, threading their way among the teachers' desks and around those standing about drinking tea or enjoying a cigarette. It appears to be a cozy atmosphere, and often it is, but enmities can lie barely below the surface of such close living, and junior teachers live constantly under the critical scrutiny of their seniors.

Next to the principal's office on the other side is a smaller room containing the school's administrative staff, five or six people who keep the students' records, order equipment and supplies, maintain the school physically, administer many routine personnel matters, serve as receptionists, and do all the accounting. They assist the principal and have very little to do with the teachers or students. There is no traffic in and out. Students, parents, and other visitors, including teachers, deal with them through a reception window that opens onto the hall outside the principal's office. Their relationship with the school in general is aptly represented by this limited and narrow concourse. They make no policy and are not linked to the teaching profession by lateral transfers either way. Proximity to the principal is not a source of power. They have their own union separate from the teachers, and quite clearly teachers view them in the way professionals view lowly clerks in their offices. The fact that the administrative staff will not be encountered again in this book is indicative of its place in the school system.

When the bell rings at the start of a new period, a few teachers can be seen pulling attendance lists from the rack by the door of the teachers' room and scurrying off to class. The classrooms where they lecture surprised me by their drab simplicity. No maps, travel pictures, collections, famous quotations, or items of curiosity grace the walls. Above the front blackboard there is the inevitable cardboard chart of the weekly schedule of classes. In a few classrooms a vase with flowers stands on a corner table, the voluntary contribution of some, inevitably female, student. In Yama, the commercial high school, a few rooms have posters of movie stars and rock singers pinned up high on a wall. But these are exceptions, and teachers show some irritation about their presence. Otani's principal once remarked that he would like to let the students paint their own classrooms as a means of tying them more closely to their school. But he never acted on the idea. I suspect he feared they would not exercise enough restraint to keep the experiment within the narrow bounds of propriety and good taste.

In each class hour, a complement of forty to forty-five students is taught by a single teacher. Japanese high schools do not have team teaching or independent projects or any of the innovations that might transform the convention that a classroom is where one teacher instructs a set of students. Each hour is devoted to a single, standard subject. Each classroom is a homeroom, and students of the same homeroom stay together in the same classroom for most of the day. For an entire year they take all their courses together, including physical education and electives.

Homerooms of the same grade level are grouped together on the same floor. Thus, not only is the location of any student at any time easily determined, but if there is a disturbance, the homeroom and grade of the perpetrators is quickly discernible. Schools everywhere are like egg cartons, with each compartment a classroom. Japanese high school students have a clearly designated compartment for the whole day, one that corresponds with his or her social location in two basic reference groups: homeroom and grade. American high school homerooms, by contrast, are of little consequence. An American student's locker is typically his or her most permanent physical location, and student groups are continually forming and disbanding from one class period to the next, both within and outside classrooms. Whole grades are rarely together physically even at assemblies in American schools.

The art and music rooms and the science labs seemed more congenial to my American expectations. These are the two types of classrooms to which students migrate, leaving their homerooms for these special environments a few times each week. Educational materials are sitting about, and a tangible approach to learning of the sort I recall from my own high school experience is visible. Some biology teachers are amateur botanists, and their labs and greenhouses are places of verdant interest. Art teachers use their rooms to display what they think beautiful or instructive. I remember being especially amused by a collection of plaster of paris copies of the busts of great Europeans glaring down from the shelf in one art room, giving it the appearance of a nineteenth-century French classicist's studio.

These rooms are the exception in an otherwise remarkably sparse approach to instruction. Objects of curiosity would probably prove distracting from the major goals of the educational enterprise: university entrance exams. Japanese high school teachers certainly enjoy the company of interesting objects connected with their subjects. Many are scholars and collectors in their own right, but personal fascination is restrained. Japanese high school teachers do not evidence much feeling of need to stimulate their students.

Not all Japanese students are interested or motivated, to be sure. The motivated and able are preparing for exams, the less able and less motivated already have some idea of their limitations. American high school education is regarded as a time for discovering and nurturing potential, for sparking intellectual growth in young people just beginning to find themselves, whereas in Japan it is a time of tightening study routines and skills and preparing for examinations. The recent extension of high school education to slower students who are not ready for this kind of finishing has not been accompanied by a pedagogy oriented to awakening their curiosity. It is noteworthy that Yama's students, not their teachers, were putting posters on the walls.

Standing back to visualize the overall pattern of offices and classrooms, it becomes clear that the teachers' room is the school's hub. Teachers come and go to their classes, and students with questions and problems head for this central point. This is the pivot of school organization and communication, and its atmosphere sets the tone for the school. When the teachers are businesslike, cooperative, and friendly among themselves, the school as a whole follows.

An administrative link connects the teachers with the principal, but the relationship is irregular and varies greatly from school to school. Many principals are frequently away, and some are on poor terms with their faculties. Others are tired or timid. In such cases, the door between the teachers' room and the principal's office sees little traffic. It is the faculty, as a group, that is the heart of most Japanese high schools.

A striking quality of the overall physical pattern is its inherently simple efficiency. The ratio of total floor space to numbers of students is low by American standards: 1) few rooms are ever empty; 2) the density of desks to space is perhaps twice what it is in the United States; and 3) teachers and administration require little additional space. Many teachers and students complain about being cramped, and principals incessantly lobby with offices of education for more space. But to an American observer what the Japanese are able to accomplish without impressive plant and equipment raises profound questions about the effects of our inclination to solve problems with more brick, glass, and concrete.[2]

The placement of all classrooms of a single grade on one floor is noteworthy. It establishes the physical basis for an organizational approach in which the academic disciplines are subordinate to supervisory responsibilities. The faculty, instead of belonging to academic departments, is organized according to duties as homeroom teachers of particular grades. Teachers who share responsibilities to the same grade sit together in the teachers' room. This replicates the general physical arrangement of classrooms.

---

2. Our school architects would in fact like to create buildings with dimensions that encourage a sense of freedom and pastoral beauty. Robert Sommer (1974), one of the most articulate and persuasive, condemns our typical schools as "hard" and "tight," qualities that dehumanize. What he might say of Japanese schools, which are tighter and harder, remains to be seen, but clearly the Japanese see Spartan training as "humanizing"; and Japanese classrooms are places where much group socializing does occur. Sommer's assumption that human qualities grow best in soft, open spaces is, if not uniquely American, nevertheless only one of many views on the subject.

A high wall surrounds every one of our five high schools, closing it off from the surrounding neighborhood and the city. Security at night and on Sundays is a simple matter of locking several gates. Students come and go through these gateways. There are no grassy lawns or parking lots marking the schools' borders, as in suburban America.

Premodern Japanese cities were never walled, but homes, work-shops, temples, and government buildings were typically set in their own walled space. The traditional Japanese city was less marked, in other words, than the institutions that comprised it. Today the walls surrounding high schools, like those around homes and modern fac-tories, accomplish the same thing. They establish and underline dis-tinct institutional entities and encourage a self-contained, centripe-tal orientation. In the United States we talk of breaking down the invisible barriers between school and community. We encourage work-study projects, outreach programs, field trips, talks to students by community representatives, and outside volunteer work. Our schools properly belong to a community.

The walls around Japanese high schools tell a different story. With only one minor exception, I encountered no efforts to bridge the school-community gap except at the principal's level. Outstanding sports teams and records of success in university entrance exams do stir civic pride, but that is all. Open houses are limited to parents and friends, and sports events draw few spectators. The relation be-tween school and town is distinguished by a deep concern among teachers with their school's reputation, which primarily means that they worry about the conduct of their wards off campus. Like other Japanese institutions, this one tries to tie personal identity closely to the group and is sensitive to how its members are viewed by outsiders.

The wall is but a symbol of a deeper quality. Student turnover is low, for public academic high schools will not accept transfers. It is not uncommon for families to leave students behind to complete high school when fathers are transferred. A stable pattern of institu-tional membership is created. In Japan, constancy and intensity of fixed relationships are valued. The special framing of the school ex-presses a deeper set of assumptions and prefences that are signifi-cant, not only to schools, but to social institutions in general.

Inside the wall, playing fields occupy most of whatever open space there is. The fields are small and worn by extensive use. Grass is out of the question. Different teams must often share the same general space, and they do this with surprising courtesy and ease. I have seen ten players practicing on one tennis court, and soccer and baseball teams practicing together on the same field.

One also finds a tiny garden tucked away in some corner of the school buildings. A few rocks, some shrubs, a cherry tree or two, and perhaps a shaped pathway stand as mute reminders to the students of the Japanese love of nature. At Yama there is a bench under a wisteria arbor that is popular with girls after school, and at Otani the garden area is kept and enjoyed primarily by girls. The little garden in an otherwise modern utilitarian space is also typically Japanese. Even grimy factories often have a little area of rocks and azaleas squeezed in somewhere. Amid all the ugly secular hustle and bustle, Japanese institutions are not complete without an endearing touch of green quietude.

## Time

Schools in a very real sense teach us modern time. Only when we start school do we begin to experience an extraordinary need for regularity that centers on the clock. Schools begin and end at set hours, meals can be taken only when the clock allows, and activities are all fixed by the daily schedule. A decade or more of going to school and we are all perfectly prepared to abide by the sense of time that runs through the organizational life of industrial society.[3]

In school, furthermore, we learn that time is serious. It is productive and it is social. That is, being late or being confused about time is a social disturbance that affects others and causes the group to be inconvenienced and less productive. We learn in school the rhythms of the days, weeks, and years. Balances are fixed between work and rest, between different forms of work, between sitting and exercise. Difficult subjects are mixed with "fun" ones. Balances are sought between passive and active learning. In American education we make sure to build in "free" time.

Schools thus set a pace that prepares the young for adult society. They establish the crucial categories of time, and they shape the meaning these categories have as they contrast and interrelate, as

3. Thompson (1967) offers a lucid portrait of the place of regular clock time in the development of working habits fostered by industrialism and the place of schooling in the implantation of such clock-governed regularity.

they affect different social groups, and as they become fundamental assumptions of a modern cultural system. High schools come late in the educational process, so their special interest lies in their proximity to adulthood. How they structure conventional time tells us a great deal about the final preparations for adulthood.

Classes in Japanese high schools begin at 8:30 six mornings a week and last until 3:00 in the afternoon Monday through Friday and until 12:30 on Saturdays. A brief ten-minute homeroom meeting precedes classes. Six periods of fifty minutes each follow, with a half-hour lunch break at 12:30. Since most students remain at their desks to eat lunches they have brought from home, the tiny school cafeteria suffices, and there is no need to stagger lunch periods or to view the lunch hall as a major trouble spot in maintaining order in the school.

High schools, Japanese or otherwise, because their assumed purpose is to teach specialized knowledge in a coordinated manner to sizable numbers of students, are inevitably organized by two fundamental considerations: grade level and subject. The intersection of teachers, students, textbooks, and so forth all follow. The crucial ordering device is the hour-long class period, axiomatic in all kinds of high schools. If, as in Japan, the crucial motivating force is the next entrance examination, then the primary purpose of teachers, by implication, is to disseminate information to students. It is the duty of the students to absorb the information in preparation for examinations. For this arrangement to work most efficiently, students should be passive and teachers active.

Also following the universal pattern for high schools, knowledge and skills are segmented into subjects in which teachers specialize. Subjects are broken down into courses to create what Dan Lortie describes as the "single cells" of instruction. The division of knowledge into separate units is notably conventional, arbitrary, and unchanging in Japan. The curriculum is compartmentalized and the Japanese keep the number of compartments to a minimum. Time is thoroughly segmented and defined, with the curriculum serving as the central gear in a complex machine of time-compartmentalized activities. Because time is precious, order is reinforced, and social organization achieves a high level of immutability. Teachers in Japanese high schools do not have the same student all day. Rather, the teachers go before different classes and thus large numbers of students. The experience of a "single cell" is rather impersonal. Nor do teachers question the boundary lines between subjects or seek to create interdisciplinary offerings or try to concoct new subjects. What personal experiences, wisdom, humanity, or ethical insight they have to offer students must come during the interstices in the subject grid.

The high uniformity greatly simplifies the task of coordination. Teachers easily keep together because they follow a fixed national curriculum. They pass students along to the next grade level who are prepared as expected. Coordination between levels is easy. The lack of variation and surprises makes for a monotony that Americans would find oppressive, yet the orderliness of Japanese schooling is a crucial source of their efficiency in preparing for exams.

A school week consists of thirty-four class hours. Because the high school curriculum is based on national standards, with a given type of high school and grade one can readily determine what subjects any student is studying. The famous boast of a French minister of education that he knew what page of what text every French child was reading at any hour of any day could almost be made of Japanese high schools.

Furthermore, since there are no study halls or free periods and no use of class time for independent projects or library work, all students are attending scheduled classes with a teacher for every one of the thirty-four hours. In some academic schools students actually do use the library, but on their own, at lunchtimes and after 3:00 P.M.

Only nine class hours a week are set aside for what are not mainstream academic subjects: boys have four periods of gym and girls have two periods of gym and two of home economics.[4] They both have two hours of an elective (music or art), one hour of health, an hour-long homeroom meeting, and an hour of faculty-led "club" activity. The remaining twenty-six hours of instruction are devoted to hard-core subjects. In academic high schools this means English, Japanese, math, science, and social studies. The precise proportions of each differ with grade level. A graduate of a Japanese academic high school has had essentially three full years of each of the five

---

4. Home economics is today more the social science of family life than the traditional course in cooking and sewing. Female students are taught the rudiments of nutrition, budgeting, child care, etc. Many social problems in these areas are raised. One might best characterize the course as an introduction to the family and to household management.

basic subjects. Vocational high school students have the same core subjects (with less difficult textbooks) but take them for fewer hours each week; vocational subjects are substituted for nine to eleven hours of academic subjects. Vocational schools still require three years of English, Japanese, math, and social studies, but only two of science. At every level the Japanese high school week is indeed an intensive one.

Comparing it with the weekly schedule of American high schools is no easy task because there is such great variation from school to school in the United States. Our private schools aiming at better universities insist on almost as many required academic subjects as do Japanese academic high schools. But I have not discovered any that have as many as twenty-six hours of class per week in basic subjects. In suburban American public high schools, oriented largely to higher education, the list of required courses today rarely includes more than one year of science, two of math, and two of a foreign language. In such schools neither English nor social studies is required in all years, yet both subjects regularly attract more students than science and math do. Less than half of the average American high school student's courses are now required. As a result, only a quarter of the students are taking science and math during any semester. Our typical student is graduated with one year of biology or general science and one or two of math. Fewer than one in ten has had a physics course.

The electives offered in American schools are, however, correspondingly much richer: driver education, foreign languages, typing, music, drama, social problems, journalism, drafting, cooking, independent study, psychology, ceramics, auto repair, anthropology, photography, work experience, and so forth. A typical suburban American high school offers about two hundred courses over two semesters, whereas a Japanese high school offers twenty-five to thirty for one year. The difference in approaches to schooling represented in the two curricula is profound. The typical American approach has been sponsored by at least three characteristically American concerns: the comprehensive high school ideal, an acute sensitivity to individual differences in talent and interest, and an inherent preference for systems that provide individual choice. The Japanese curriculum rests on very different concerns: a separation of academic and vocational schooling, a preoccupation with keeping up with the highest international standards as they reflect on Japan's future economic security and national pride, and a belief that setting high national standards is the only way to fully use and develop the nation's only significant asset: people.

Japanese high schools are not flexible in regard to time. During class periods students do not go to the bathroom or sign out of school or engage in individual tasks or do administrative errands. They store personal belongings under their desks. The school day is not complicated by short periods or classes getting out early or field trips or classes outside on the lawn. Everyone is geared to one basic routine. And this routine is the same nearly every week of the school year. As socialization in orderliness, nothing could be more effective.

The major potential source of disorder during class periods in Japanese schools is the absence of a teacher. In any public school, on any day, there are classes doing "self-directed study" (*jishū*). As we have seen, Yama and Sakura students often have difficulty staying quiet or even staying in the classroom given this opportunity, and supervision by teachers from neighboring classrooms is often necessary. Why no substitute teachers? Clearly, the commotion and disturbance are not great enough in most schools to force the Ministry of Education to hire substitutes, but the heart of the issue is a complex political tug-of-war between the teachers' union and the administration, to be discussed later.

The nine hours of nonacademic subjects, especially the gym periods, are times when students do things differently. They can sing or paint or work clay, and they run around yelling in team sports. In gym, art, or music, teachers are not incessantly delivering lectures, and in these activities students have some opportunity to express themselves. It is interesting to note, however, that even these times have an academic component. Physical education teachers give a series of lectures on health, and home economics teachers have largely moved their subject from an earlier emphasis on the domestic arts to one that stresses the economics, sociology, and psychology of the family. Music and art have a historical element. The Dewey-inspired American experts who wrote the occupation's program for educational reform would be quite disappointed, for the creative and practical activity they so strongly favored has been given a very limited part of the curriculum.

The teachers of nonacademic subjects are in a clear minority within the faculty, and they remain on the edge of faculty affairs. Half of the women teachers in our five schools teach nonacademic

*Cooking class in an academic high school*

A home economics class in an academic high school. This required course is only for girls and is conducted while boys take two extra hours of physical education.

subjects, therefore their influence as a group is even less than their small numbers would indicate. Curricular time and its implicit values thus help shape faculty relations and politics. Order is coupled to convention and to "serious" subjects.

The annual school calendar tells the same story. The Japanese school year begins in April, "at the time the cherry trees come into bloom," and ends in mid-March.[5] Vacations occur in summer (six weeks), at New Year (two weeks), and in late March at the end of the school year (two weeks). Students also miss about two weeks of school each year for public and informal school holidays. In all, they are in attendance forty weeks a year, at least four more weeks annually than their American public school counterparts. The six-day school week and the shorter vacations make Japanese schools a more regular and pervasive aspect in the lives of Japanese youth. In comparison with the hiatus of summer vacation in American education, the year seems virtually continual.

5. The blooming of the cherry trees has been the traditional first theme of elementary school textbooks—another example of the ties of education to classic Japanese sensibilities.

*Physical education class for girls*
Boys and girls are separated. Note the uniforms and the general orderliness.

Young Japanese go to school for approximately sixty days more each year than their American counterparts. Using the American five-day week as a standard, this means that Japanese students get three months' more schooling each year. During the three-year period of grades ten, eleven, and twelve, they attend class the equivalent of one year more. By this kind of calculation we arrive at a remarkable and sobering fact: over the twelve years of elementary and secondary education, the Japanese student actually receives four more years of schooling!

If we couple this with the rigors of the curriculum just examined, we see there is good reason to argue that a Japanese high school diploma is the equivalent of an average American bachelor's degree. I found this conclusion hard to believe at first. But the more I looked at the fundamental facts, the more convinced I became that the majority of high school graduates in Japan would compare well with the majority of our university graduates in terms of basic knowledge in all fields and in math and science skills. There are areas of weakness in the Japanese curriculum, and undoubtedly our best university students are quite advanced; but in dealing with averages and educational basics, the Japanese secondary accomplishment is simply of a different magnitude than the American accomplishment.

Attitudes toward vacation are also different from those in America. Teachers are not officially on leave during vacation periods. They are considered on duty and are paid even during summer vacation. A few faithfully attend school during this time so that students can use the sports and other facilities, but due largely to union protection most do, in fact, take vacations. That makes teachers one of the few Japanese occupational groups that is well paid and that enjoys long vacations. It is no surprise that teaching is a relatively popular profession.

Parents, on the other hand, would like teachers to show more devotion during vacations. Japan does not have a tradition of family summer trips, summer cottages, and summer camps. Parents find even a six-week vacation a long time. Many parents feel that only high school seniors, preparing for university exams, know how to use their summer vacations. They attend some tutoring academy or concentrate on reviewing subjects that need work. Homework is typically assigned for summer vacations. The rise of summertime *juku* programs to fill this void is a further indication of the Japanese inclination to keep leisure time narrow.

The great separation between "free time" and "going to school"—between work and play, between being subject to an organization and being "on one's own"—so central to American thinking about the basic categories of activities that divide our lives—finds much less nurturance in the Japanese school calendar. School is the unequivocal central pivot of a student's existence, not just one pole of it, making vacations properly brief periods for rest and renewal. It is firmly a part of American popular culture that school is stuffy and boring, that vacation is fun and healthy, that weekend leisure is a sacred right. These opinions are occasionally voiced in Japan, too, but they are still largely opinions. Surveys reveal that few Japanese workers take all their paid vacations, and managers generally work very long hours. Free time has not been cultivated extensively. As youth, Americans have some opportunity to live out a bit of the Tom Sawyer dream, even as they work at a summer job; but urban Japanese grow up harnessed both to study and to a single organization. No dream of ultimate innocence and freedom is given credence by the school calendar.

That Japanese are so serious and diligent, that they do well on international tests of math and science while learning a great deal about art, music, geography, and history, seems less remarkable when one considers the time allocated to the educational enterprise. European school systems are also more intense in curricular terms, yet the percentage of students pursuing an academic curriculum at age seventeen is proportionally smaller than in Japan and the school year is not generally as long. What would be considered a superior level of learning and thus be representative of, say, the top 10 percent of students in the United States or Europe is what is experienced by the majority of academic high school students in Japan.

There are but a few special activities that break this routine. The annual school calendar includes a set of events and ceremonies that are standard for high schools across the land. Each year begins with an all-school assembly in which entering freshmen are welcomed, new teachers are introduced, and the principal delivers an inspirational talk. After each vacation, a brief version of this ceremony is held to mark the return to studies. Similarly, just before vacations begin, assemblies are held to warn students to be careful while not in school. In all of these, however routine and conventional the format, several central themes are stressed: 1) the school is a community in which all share a social duty (to nation, city, and family) to serious and hard work; 2) bad behavior causes inconvenience to others and reflects on the school's name; 3) improper actions after school hours and away from school reflect badly on everyone; and 4) life is full of opportunities, but only by beginning early to anticipate the realities of entrance exams (or job requirements) will students be able to share in them.

The great events of the year are the Culture Festival (*bunkasai*) and Sports Day (*taiku taikai*). Each involves the entire school, with parents and friends invited as spectators. The Culture Festival includes a variety show in which each homeroom performs a musical serenade or skit. In the evening there is an open house, with exhibits of student and teacher art work displayed in homerooms decorated by the students. The preparation put into the Culture Festival and its attending excitement make it a high point of the year. Rehearsals (during homeroom periods and after school) begin at least two weeks before and take up considerable time, and the decorating of homerooms lasts late into the night prior to the open house.

Sports Day is also great fun. Classes are pitted against one another

*Tug-of-war between classes*

A giant tug-of-war between classes during Sports Day at a Kobe high school. Flag waving is a common form of cheerleading in Japan. The flags are all hand-painted for the occasion.

in a day-long series of relays and team events that occasionally includes a team of teachers. At intermission, humorous floats and demonstrations by student clubs are offered as entertainment. The day is organized into the form of an olympiad, with opening and closing ceremonies that have all participants marching in and out, a set of welcoming addresses, and a solemn oath of sportsmanship given by the student council president.

These two events are so far from the routines and atmosphere of the normal school day that they can cause teachers considerable anxiety. A major worry is that in their excitement, students will become rowdy or improper. The presence of outsiders as an audience further loads these occasions because teachers are under close scrutiny for the behavior of their wards. The result is intense teacher supervision and a high degree of practice and preparation. The schools under consideration here differed, however, and anxiety and supervision were in inverse relation to the academic rank of the school. At Nada, teachers were hardly in evidence at the Cultural Festival. At

*Homeroom skit rehearsal*

Scene from a homeroom skit rehearsal before the Culture Festival. Presentations by each homeroom are given before the whole school in the auditorium.

Otani there was some anxiety; but at Yama the whole event depended on the teachers. Remarkable to me was the degree of detailed preparations that teachers insisted on for events that Americans would see as largely casual and spontaneous.

I was pleasantly surprised by the rich humor and playfulness of the students. I had assumed them to be more docile and serious from observing them in class. Teachers prefer them restrained, but I was greatly relieved to discover a side of Japanese adolescence that fit my own best memories.

The junior class trip, an event with some of the same "turn the world upside down" qualities, is the third highlight of the year. The classic form of the trip is a visit to a big city like Kyoto or Tokyo, where all four hundred or so students stay together in some hotel specializing in school excursions. The official purpose is to introduce points of historical interest and cultural pride to the students— in short, to help sophisticate them. But in fact, these trips are more like an extended slumber party. The students stay up most of the night, to the chagrin of their chaperones, and they drowse off the next day as their tour buses go from one famous place to another. For the participants, getting pictures of friends and souvenirs for the family are goals far more important than drinking in ancient culture. Harried teachers suffer a constant fear of losing someone. They worry that boys will sneak off at night for a drink or a peek at some pornography shop, or that a fight with some local students might start, or even that a boy and girl will discover some possibility of cuddling together. The potential for trouble on this kind of trip has increased throughout the post-World War II period as high school enrollments have grown and as Japanese youth has become more brazen. The raison d'être, on the other hand, has weakened as television and family travel have made visits to the big cities commonplace.

Rural high schools still follow the civilizing routine, but city high schools are turning to a new approach to the class trip: a ski vacation! The idea of a whole class going to the mountains for five days of group lessons seems a bit implausible at first, but teachers and students both like the change. For teachers a ski trip is more easily supervised than a city trip. The students get so worn out skiing that they sleep more at night. And staying in an isolated, snow-covered dormitory offers no opportunity for a surreptitious night on the town. Broken legs and the extra expense are problems, but even the most unathletic teachers prefer standing around on skis in the sunshine to marching through famous temples and shrines for the sixth or seventh time. As for the question of relevance to education, I was simply informed that learning to ski is in line with the Ministry of Education's new emphasis on creating a citizenry that can enjoy leisure as well as work hard. Japan has become a country that needs to encourage its citizens to enjoy themselves.

The school calendar ends with a quiet graduation ceremony. This is not a big celebration, for it comes at a rather somber time for seniors, when university acceptances are being announced. Destinies diverge. There are the disappointed and the elated. Many students face a year of *rōnin* study on their own. Under these conditions it is hard to generate a mood of celebration, and leaving friends is a sad occasion. The school marks the occasion with a formal ceremony; the students do not elaborate with their own parties or other events. Americans like to celebrate the end of the ordeal of school; Japanese like to celebrate getting into the next one.

*Ski lessons during the junior class trip*
Students have rented identical equipment, and each has an identifying number and his or her school's name on the racing bib.

The yearly calendar also includes an occasional schoolwide cleanup, a time-out for class pictures, class health checks, and such. Sports events are of little significance unless the team is outstanding. Interscholastic competition does not draw many spectators. There are no "big games;" nor are there scheduled school dances or other social events. Only when the best baseball teams in the country meet in a national tournament is there a great furor.

Contrast this with the classic American high school calendar, where the majority of events are essentially generated by students—dances, rallies, sports contests, election campaigns, club-sponsored assemblies. The faculty arranges graduation ceremonies and special assemblies and teachers supervise student activities, but ideally the students run things. With few exceptions, participation in anything but classes is voluntary, and "school spirit" is needed if these events are to succeed. In American high schools, the calendar of extracurricular activities is far richer, and our high schools are regularly judged as much by their sports teams and the character of their social events as by their academic quality. Excitement is a goal, not a worrisome by-product. We have pep rallies to breathe life into school spirit. Teenage, not adult, tastes set the tone. The assumption of voluntary action lies at the heart of the American approach.

Although schools in both cultures have formulas for events, less depends on convention in the United States. School events and ceremonies are readily changed, and most are abandoned if student support lags. Japanese school events, on the other hand, appear uniform and constant. They depend on tradition and teachers. The Confucian appreciation of formality in ritual as expressive of the moral order lingers in Japan, just as our democratic and Protestant heritage inclines us to events with a grass roots spontaneity that is informal and emotionally expressive. The basic cultural symbolism of school events is quite different in the two societies.

## *Summary*

As with most modern institutions, the basic arrangements of space and time are foundations upon which the school enterprise rests. The most ingrained of learned patterns are those that become totally routine and soon slip below conscious awareness. In this sense, what students learn from the school's structuring of space and time contains lessons more basic and certainly more thoroughly taught than the content of any textbook or lecture.

From spatial arrangements Japanese students learn the notion of distinct, inward-looking groupings. The school, the faculty, and the homeroom each has its own exclusive space marked off and reserved for continuous group interaction. Students also learn a Spartan ethic. The atmosphere carries an implied message that serious intentions are expected. Teachers are not entertainers any more than the school's physical form is inspirational. Nor do the spatial arrangements speak of freedom of choice, flexibility, or openness to the flow of social change. School architecture embraces gray institutional reality.

School schedules teach that the regularity of things has no individual exceptions. Order is based on the group. Everyone in a homeroom, a grade, and a school marches to the appropriate tune. Students are reminded that the central feature of their lives is school. Vacations and weekends are short and invaded by schoolwork. From class to class and year to year, all the time available is filled. As with Japanese farming, which uses every bit of land, educational scheduling is intense. And nearly all class time is strictly academic.

In a very real sense, schools pace society. They set the rhythms that people grow up with, and they teach the segmentation of time into various components. After spending delicious three-month summer vacations growing up, who can help but dream for them again as an adult? The rhythms and segmentation of the Japanese high school complement very neatly indeed the working order of industry and modern organization. If that order in Japan is particularly intense and disciplined we should not be surprised. Even company sports days and exhibits of employees' art work echo the school calendar's two major extracurricular events.

We are talking here about a regimen that nearly all Japanese now experience. Social boot camp lasts until age eighteen. Only with college is the age cohort divided into two groups: those who are rewarded for hard work (or family income) by four years of university-sanctioned leisure to think and explore, and those who go from the regimentation of high school directly into the regimentation of employment. At eighteen or nineteen the officer corps emerges, and university experience comes to symbolize the relative luxury due the successful elite. More flexible time, greater choice, and even less simple surroundings come with higher education. An analogy comes to mind between the corporate executive's spatial and temporal prerogatives and those of university students. Only by passing the university entrance exam does part of the population begin to experience what will become the prerogatives and perquisites of higher adult status, such things as greater discretionary time, more choice, and a sense of responsibility for society, not just to it. In the United States, these prerogatives are more a matter of immutable class distinctions than markers along the overall path of socialization.

The contrast with our own schools is revealing. We Americans have all heard the refrains: "High school is the best time of your life," "Enjoy your freedom while you can," and "Sweet sixteen." Romance, friends, going out every Friday and Saturday night—these are the memorable ingredients of adolescence. Many American students do part-time work, get their homework in on time, and study hard for grades, but the level of schoolwork and the proportion of all students who are truly serious about school is small—and such students often keep their diligence a secret from their peers. Our students' sense of time is generally leisurely and diffuse. For most of us, it is only after high school, when taking a job or entering college, that we begin to feel we have to "buckle down" and "face reality."

# 6

## Organization

> Once organized, if a society is to maintain itself, the young must be shaped as to fit into the roles on which the society's survival depends.
>
> JAMES C. COLEMAN

B ECAUSE schools stand along the formative path to adulthood, everything about them is scrutinized as influential in the socialization process. A case in point is school organization. Reformers from Plato on have proposed that schools should model the ideal social order so that impressionable students will learn the desired values and behavior patterns and will, as adults, advance the cause. The assumption here is that school organization is in effect a miniature of society, one with great (if often unconscious) didactic power over the way each generation ultimately conducts itself. This was certainly the logic behind the strenuous American efforts after World War II to change the authority structure of Japanese education, to introduce coeducation, to create a single track through twelfth grade, and to establish comprehensive high schools. The occupation's emphasis on student clubs, student government, and teachers' unions was part of a general effort to reshape school social organization and to exemplify democratic ideals.

Although in the field of education there has been a recent focus on memorable examples of social ideals institutionalized in school organization (for example, Summerhill, the Chinese and Soviet examples of socialist schooling, the schools heavily influenced by Dewey), it must be remembered that schools are not like societies in many fundamental respects. Schools have but two very distinct status groups (teachers and students) with very different interests, rights, and duties; they contain relatively small populations; they have but a few very standardized activities; their reward and control systems are rather limited; they affect teachers and students very differently; and they are only indirectly subject to external forces. It is more appropriate to see them as functionally specialized units of a larger social whole. It is interesting to think of them as "miniature societies," but above all, they are judged by their effectiveness as schools.[1]

At the heart of every Japanese high school is a simple set of activities: classes, events, and after-school programs. These are organized by an equally simple set of social groupings. The faculty is arranged to supervise the students in virtually all their activities, and students find their social place as members of homerooms and, if they choose, clubs. Almost nothing of significance occurs outside the jurisdiction of these organizational entities.

The student populations of the five high schools considered here are not all the same, but observed closely, a basic and widely common pattern is perceptible. The three daytime public schools all have between 1,100 and 1,200 students, and faculties of 60 to 65. More than half of all Kobe's high schools fall within this narrow range.[2] The exceptions are mostly private schools, evening schools, or newly built schools. Sakura, for example, has only 270 students and 16 teachers, and its population has been shrinking with the growth of daytime high schools. Student-teacher ratios remain consistent across most schools. In our sample of five, the ratio is 18 to 1, exactly the average for all Japanese high schools.[3] Classroom size does vary,

---

1. Ethnographic accounts of American schools, especially of social organization, are so numerous now that only the most outstanding can be mentioned. Classics in the field include Waller (1932), Coleman (1961), Cusick (1973), and Bronfenbrenner (1970). Bidwell (1965) contains a useful overview of collected readings expressing the anthropological approach to school organization that includes Spindler (1974), Roberts and Akinsanya (1976), Wax et al. (1971), and Ianni and Storey (1973). No ethnographic accounts of Japanese high school organization exist, but for middle schools see Singleton (1967). Also of considerable interest for its portrait of the American teacher is Lortie (1975).

2. The variety in size among American secondary schools is much greater. We have, first of all, differing grade spans. In 1977, less than half of our high schools followed the classic nine-to-twelve pattern. The national average for enrollment in our ten-to-twelve grade span schools (those most similar to Japanese high schools) was 1,193, almost the same as in Japan. Dearman and Plisko (1980). This average, however, is produced by numerous quite large and quite small three-year high schools.

3. Student-teacher ratios in American secondary schools are nearly identical once the daily absentee rate of about 8 percent is figured in. Ibid.

however, between private and public schools. Nada and most private schools have about 55 students in each class, whereas daytime public schools have 44. Night schools like Sakura often have just 10 to 15.[4] The class sizes observed in Kobe are neatly in line with the national statistics.

## *The Faculty*

Just as the teachers' room is the hub of the school, so the faculty is the center of the school's social organization. Instruction and homeroom duties require only about fifteen hours a week (quite low by United States standards),[5] but teachers are expected to perform many other duties. Fifteen hours spread over six days a week means that a teacher is in class less than one-third of the time he is paid to be in school, a situation that compares well with the typical teaching load of an American junior college teacher. This also explains why, despite reasonable teacher-student ratios, class size remains high. Large classes make for fewer teaching hours.

Teachers shoulder many administrative burdens without receiving extra remuneration, however. The formal organization of the faculty is built on these administrative tasks. The supervision and coordination of homerooms is central. In a typical high school, each grade contains about four hundred students divided into nine homerooms. The faculty is divided accordingly into three subdivisions, each responsible for a different grade. At the core of each subdivision is a set of nine homeroom teachers, with three or four senior teachers serving as leaders and staff. In the teachers' room these twelve or thirteen teachers sit at desks arranged together, and the desk of the head teacher of that grade faces the rest. Teachers can easily confer on matters relating to their common responsibilities for a particular grade. They organize the special activities of the grade as a whole, such as the junior class trip. Most of the course instruction for each grade is done by this set of teachers; they are expected to stay with the same grade over the three years it is in the school. Although the composition of homerooms is reshuffled annually, and teachers therefore supervise different students each year, the overall continuity be-

4. This is the opposite of the case in the United States, where public school student-teacher ratios are slightly higher but class size is much smaller. Dearman and Plisko (1980), p. 71.

5. The general rule in the United States is five hours of instruction per day, totaling twenty-five hours a week.

tween a set of teachers and a grade is great. The system links one set of teachers to one group of students for the duration and gives the teachers responsibility at the end to help their wards locate good jobs or the right universities.

Obviously, teachers of the same grade must work together closely to share information and coordinate their handling of common issues. It was often pointed out to me that homerooms of a single grade are all located together on one floor of the school. Two points were stressed about this. First, poor control by one teacher inconveniences others of the same grade. Second, teachers along the same hall actually share supervisory duties for a set of classrooms. A grade is arranged physically to resemble a neighborhood, and teachers who are absent or are poor disciplinarians or are sloppy in recordkeeping or are uncooperative in arranging special grade events cause inconvenience and stand out. By packaging duties in this manner, the organization ingeniously puts peer pressure behind tight management.

Nevertheless, levels of solidarity in individual grades of different schools vary widely because of the many potential divisions among teachers. I found it informative to ask if the grade supervisors went out for dinner together after work, as is the general custom in Japanese companies and government bureaus. The range of replies was startling. Some supervisory groups took overnight trips together and regularly maintained close relations through special activities; yet the same question drew incredulous looks in other schools, where teachers flatly stated that relations were barely cordial. The techniques of generating small group solidarity are not unknown to teachers, but unlike most company situations in Japan, high school faculties are often fragmented.

In high schools, to begin with, instructional responsibilities are fulfilled on a strictly individual basis. Perhaps one-fourth of all high school teachers in Kobe moonlight at other jobs (particularly tutoring), and because there are no formal rewards or punishments for failing to help out in extracurricular work, some teachers do no more than teach their classes and wait for 3:00 P.M. to arrive. Moonlighting is widely condemned by outsiders, but its debilitating effect on faculty morale is rarely mentioned by teachers, who are loath to criticize the private behavior of others. On this point school faculties significantly differ from Japanese business organizations, where considerable discipline is applied to support group morale.

Other sources of dissension include politics and periodic transfer.

As in Japanese corporations, long careers in the same school system are punctuated by regular transfers. Lifelong employment is the expectation, and most males follow this pattern. Transfers within the public system are a necessary corollary of lifelong employment because they renew organizational discipline, but new arrivals, especially senior teachers, are not easy to integrate. Authority among teachers rests largely on informal criteria that develop slowly with time.

Female teachers account for about 15 percent of high school faculties. Of the six or so women in a typical high school, one teaches girls' physical education and another home economics.[6] Although women are treated with greater respect and given heavier responsibilities in schools than in private Japanese businesses, they remain on the edge of the informal faculty system. Their numbers have grown somewhat lately, however, and Kobe appointed its first female high school principal just after I had left.

Such internal differences make the job of head teacher for each grade particularly important, as head teachers are leaders of the basic cooperative units. If they can generate integration in their small groups, faculty relations are on a good footing. It is notable that this position is elective. The candidates must, of course, be experienced and respected. It is their task to ride herd on the teachers, who in turn ride herd on the students. Factions sometimes compete to put their candidates in office. Elections then foster political schisms, and, at times, philosophies of teaching and administration are put to the test. Whether a head teacher favors stronger discipline or a more relaxed approach, whether ideological issues will be taken up in homerooms, or whether teachers stay late or are allowed to go home early often depend on who is elected. Most elections are approached cautiously because the job is so sensitive.

As elsewhere, faculty committees proliferate. I found eight the average number, covering responsibilities for everything from supervising the library to beautifying the school grounds. These are permanent units with full administrative responsibility over such issues as career guidance, discipline, and minority problems. Teachers assigned to the important committees are not relieved of responsibilities within the grade subdivisions and are expected to work hard

6. American high schools have a much greater proportion of female teachers, and only a few vocational subjects are still male preserves. Approximately half of the secondary teachers in the United States are female.

at their tasks. Committees are also the places to shelve teachers who are unsuited to leading homerooms or who need a rest.

The usual core of the American high school faculty—the academic department—does not exist in Japan. Teachers of the same subject are coordinated by a senior teacher assigned to lead them. Responsibilities include supervising the training of new teachers, upgrading teaching of the subject, and, often, leading informal discussions on topics of common interest. Together these teachers decide on the textbooks they will use and the pace they will keep.

As in most countries, high school teachers have a strong personal interest in the subjects they teach. The subject was the teacher's major in university; he, or she, was hired for his mastery of it; and as a rule he actively keeps up with it. Many older Japanese high school teachers publish articles or books in their subjects. Although assignments take teachers from school to school, one's tie to one's subject remains unbroken. It is the basis for a distinct citywide network of teacher relationships centering on regular seminars and study meetings, which are often made into recreational events. Friendships among teachers of the same subject are legion, and their socializing typically exceeds that among teachers of the same school. Physical education instructors and teachers of English especially flock together, as their specialities and experiences are the most distinctive, but friendship groupings exist within all subjects. When I moved from one school to another, I was always sent with introductions to other teachers in such subject-based networks.

Despite the pull of academic interests, supervising students is the central focus of faculty organization, and the potential for fragmentation into small cliques of teachers is held in check by the emphasis on homeroom and grade affairs. The formal structure of the faculty, in other words, puts school as a whole ahead of more private academic interests.

Compared with American high school teaching, the degree of standardization of subject matter is high, and preparation is accordingly less. Teachers spend little time developing new courses, and their preparation of teaching aids, supplementary materials, and field trips is minimal. Administration is time-consuming, but only some teachers carry this burden. Although administrative service is expected of all, the fact is that no formal rewards or punishments exist to ensure performance. The situation resembles university committee work in the United States, where some shirk responsibility and are unpunished and others labor mightily with little or no reward. Japanese teachers are given tenure when they are hired, as are other government officers and regular employees of large companies in Japan. They receive pay increases solely by seniority unless they take principal and vice-principal jobs. Such posts mean de facto salary reductions because people who hold them must retire at sixty, whereas others need never retire. Almost no stipends are offered for less important administrative tasks.

Japanese companies use promotion as a motivating factor.[7] But in high schools only peer pressure, personal pride, and informal leadership have influence. A visible minority of teachers in public high schools do not respond to any of them. Young teachers, the most idealistic and responsive to peer influence, are generally assigned to homeroom duty and are put under the tutelage of the dedicated and capable older teachers. The key committee positions are staffed with motivated senior teachers, and the lazy, the jaded, and the incompetent are assigned to the scattered smaller tasks having little or nothing to do with the basic order and morale of the school. As a consequence, some teachers are very busy, while others do precious little. Their paychecks do not reflect this difference, and this provokes considerable cynicism, resentment, and disapproval. The heart of faculty organization—shared administrative duties—is a serious problem.

Friendships can also be important. In Japan, the way to understand informal relations is to inquire about after-hours socializing. Called *tsukiai*, relaxed talking and sharing of drinks and food in a separate location marks a degree of personal familiarity that is not readily achieved at the workplace. Some teachers of the same subject and those active in the union spend some of their free time together. Hobbies, bachelorhood, or having attended a common school are other foundations for friendship. Sometimes a senior teacher will befriend a younger instructor of the same subject and become a kind of patron (*oyabun*) for him or her. Such leadership might then extend to political matters and even beyond their tenure together in the same school. I found the majority of teachers, however, to be rather private and disinclined to socializing with their colleagues. Such independence would very likely cripple a managerial career in

7. For descriptions of work relationships in Japanese companies, see Rohlen (1974), Dore (1973), Atsumi (1975), and Clark (1979). For descriptions of work relationships in Japanese government bureaucracies, see Noguchi (1974) and Skinner (1978).

a Japanese business organization, a point several teachers made in explaining their career choice.

There is an independence about teachers that especially stands out in a nation where employment usually means deep group and organizational involvement. In the classroom, teachers have great autonomy. Unlike businesspeople, they are not obligated to socialize and cultivate relationships for promotion or to get cooperation from others. If they choose to look through bookstores or to sit at home watching television at night, their careers are not jeopardized. The union further buttresses the independence of teachers, for it has on occasion demanded stipends for extracurricular work and, failing this, it has defended the right of teachers to avoid such duties.

Yet compared with American high schools, what stands out are the sociocentric qualities. The faculty assumes full responsibility for student behavior and discipline, and it is organized around this common task. In the United States, it is typical to find disciplinary and morale issues delegated to a separate administrative set of offices, freeing teachers to concentrate on their classroom duties. The single large teachers' room in Japanese schools is in fact the social nerve center of the school.

What part does the principal play? The fact that there is no simple answer is itself quite revealing. By law, principals have ultimate responsibility and thus presumably ultimate authority. They may attempt to influence virtually all aspects of school life. But in practice few tend to be active in the school's daily affairs, either because they have delegated authority to the faculty or because the faculty is not responsive to their rulings. Strong principals are few. They are opposed by the union and are unwelcome to those teachers who enjoy autonomy. Principals can be absent from their schools most of the time, as some in fact are, without incapacitating the administration.

Only the principal, however, can deal with the Ministry of Education, the parent-teachers organization, the news media, and local citizens groups. A principal's major occupation is to act as the school's external representative, striving to obtain resources for the school (new facilities, larger budgets, the best teachers, more equipment) and to fend off disruptive pressures (disgruntled neighbors, unwanted school board policies). It is as a public figure and educational leader that a principal has status.

Much less regularly, principals enjoy status and respect among the teachers. The hostility of the teachers' union can be one relevant factor. Another is that principals are typically in their later fifties, nearing retirement. They rarely enter the job with the goal of building a personal reputation, as is the case among many American school principals. If they are not particularly energetic, respected, and dedicated, they are likely to want to complete their careers with as little trouble as possible. Few make much of an impression on their schools, but some do make a difference.

As in most small institutions, the principal's authority is great on paper, but in practice it rests on the ability to influence and lead the teachers, particularly the senior ones. Principals cannot order them, but they do try to get reliable senior teachers elected to key positions. Running a high school is inherently a political job, especially given the strength of the union and the formal independence of teachers. Principals do not enter office with great power, however; and unlike Kobe's primary and middle schools, where male principals can domineer younger female teachers, at the high school level high-handed principals will be challenged. Many older Japanese, bothered by the postwar erosion of authority in the schools, blame this on a failure of will among school administrators, but the story is more complex as we will discover in Chapter Seven.

### The Homurūmu

Because classes are all taken with the same homeroom group, and mostly in the same room, during every school day a student is a member of but one group. This adds considerable tedium to the day, but the system is admirably tidy. Each student has a constant physical location and reference group. Supervision is easy, and the social environment experienced by students is stable and intimate. The Japanese have borrowed the word "homeroom" from the American high school organization, but they have given it their own character.

Students are allocated to homerooms with an eye to balance. Academic talent is evenly distributed. The entrance system makes each school population internally quite homogeneous, and tracking is unnecessary. Because of the segmented approach to high school entrance, egalitarian principles can prevail in each school's organization of classes. Indeed, an egalitarian spirit is encouraged, and teachers are very proud of it. Some of the social distinctions like those between "brains" and "dumb jocks" that divide American high schools are largely avoided. Equality of this kind may be specious, as it depends on a more basic system of discrimination, but it is important to note that at the school level it does help substantiate the idea of group unity among the students of each grade and homeroom.

Students remain at the same desks in the same classroom virtually all day. When a period ends, the great hourly reshuffling so central to the American experience of high school is simply unknown. Between classes some students do go out to the bathroom or to talk in the halls, but the level of confusion (and tardiness) is minimal. The Japanese apparently prefer such order at the price of some monotony of environment, whereas Americans would no doubt trade a dose of disorder to avoid what we would assume to be the stagnation of immobility.

American students often report feeling alienated or painfully anonymous amid the mass of students flowing to and from classes in our larger high schools. Japanese certainly find peer society less imposing. The homeroom environment gives each student a fixed set of classmates who are soon accustomed to one another. They do not choose to be together, but familiarity is a natural outcome. In American schools there is always an effort by friends to register for the same classes, but this only illustrates how different the two organizations are. Peer relations are less of a preoccupation in Japanese high schools for many reasons, but in part this is because there is no opportunity to choose classes or connive to take them with friends. The fear of social rejection that is so high among American students actually depends on the opportunities during the school day to choose or be chosen. The greater social security in Japan is gained at the price of variety. In a most concrete manner, a group focus is achieved at the expense of student mobility, independence, and individual initiative.

Students are responsible for their homerooms. Care of the room, including sweeping the floor and setting things straight after school, is everybody's job, at least in principle. Little tasks are parceled out so that everyone has some formal role to play. One student wipes the blackboards after each class, another carries messages to the teachers' room, and others represent the homeroom on committees. In one high school, an American visitor counted fifty-four such jobs among a group of but forty-one students.[8] The largest joint undertak-

---

8. Reported by Sarah Sandford in an undergraduate research paper recounting her experiences as an exchange student in a private girls' high school in Japan.

ing is the homeroom's participation in the annual Culture Festival. This is very time-consuming, and much emphasis is placed on everyone's pitching in. Homeroom teachers often see that positions of some leadership are rotated so that the less involved are pushed into greater participation. Having to cooperate is a source of irritation at times, but it is also an important foundation for socialization to group membership.

The homeroom is not a social club. Students mostly just sit together listening to teachers drone on and on. They do share a half-hour lunch period and a daily ten-minute homeroom. They have the same teachers to gossip and complain about and the same tests for which to prepare. Although homerooms participate in the school's Culture Festival as an entity, the homeroom has no parties, outings, campaigns, or other gatherings.

Students typically eat their box lunches sitting together in the homeroom; and this is when things get lively. Popular music blares over the school's public address system, and all sorts of raucous activities occur. In one Otani homeroom on one day, a Ping-Pong game is being played on top of some desks shoved together, a student in the hall is practicing his trumpet, a group of girls are talking in one corner, and several boys are playing chess in another part of the room; in the midst of all this, some students are actually catching up on review work before a test scheduled for the afternoon. It is warm, and students hang out the windows calling to friends below. Teachers do not seem to mind the noise. They eat their own lunches at their desks in the teachers' room or go out for lunch near the school. Students generally accept the teachers' sense of order when they are present, but when they retreat, students create their own lively world, and adolescence as it is known in America is easily recognized in Japan, too.

Only once a week, during a fifty-minute "long homeroom," is time set aside to discuss school or personal problems under the guiding hand of the homeroom teacher. Most teachers are rather inept at leading group discussions of "real life" issues, however, and few long homerooms are notable. Yet, under active tutelage these sessions can become powerful forums for self-discovery. I witnessed one such session in Yama that deserves attention here although it was quite unusual in intensity.

The teacher involved was a young Marxist who believes the homeroom is a critical agent for social education. Following announce-

*Otani first-year homeroom posing for a formal portrait
with several of its teachers*

All students wear their uniforms for the occasion, and a serious look is appropriate. The cherry trees in back are in full bloom, indicating that the school year has just begun.

ments focused on the upcoming Culture Festival, he stepped forward and gravely addressed the students. My notes covering the session have been considerably abbreviated.

> We have a really serious problem in our homeroom. A sixteen-year-old boy with a bright future, Tamura, has just been given a week-long expulsion from school for smoking. We didn't want to do it, but there is no question that it was needed. He may even flunk and be held back a year if things don't improve. I want you to break up into your small groups (*han*) and discuss this problem. Tamura is going to be gone for a week. What does this mean to him? After ten minutes I will ask each leader to give me the group's opinion.

In the group nearest me, two girls remarked earnestly that they didn't know Tamura was smoking in school. One said, "Teacher knew. It is his fault for not stopping Tamura." Another added, "We all knew he was smoking, but he can't stop. The teacher should have warned him."

Scattered comments were reported by the group leaders. "We couldn't reach any conclusion." "We want to know why Tamura wasn't warned by you." "He'll have trouble getting caught up in his work. It's a vicious circle." "We don't think the punishment is going to serve any purpose." "He'll fall behind in his work."

The teacher answered that he did not think Tamura's smoking would lead to such serious consequences and that it was partly his fault, but that partly it was an unavoidable development. "But if all of you don't work to help him fit in, nothing will be resolved. You know he quit the track team recently because he felt no one liked him. Human relations are important to people, you know. How many of you knew he was smoking in school?" (About half the hands went up.) "Once you've gotten in trouble and have been punished, it's easier to get in trouble the next time. Another vicious circle. I want the groups to discuss what you might have done to prevent this."

The group nearest me: "He always talks like this to us. Tamura wouldn't have stopped, whatever we might have done. What does the teacher want us to say, anyway?" Silence and then some jokes I couldn't understand. "All the boys smoke. Everybody knows that." (Out in the hall other homerooms began getting out early, and there was noise and running about. Some students peeked in.) "If we tell him to stop, he'll be cold to us. It won't help." "Tamura is weak-willed. He wants to be part of the gang, and he does what others are doing." "He may have wanted to quit, but he can't." "Girls are different." "I warned him many times. He wrote down a promise to quit by a certain date, but he smoked too much to quit. He's my friend, sort of; he used smoking to look tough." "All men smoke, so why not boys before they're out of high school?" (The noise in the halls continued.)

"I think you are taking this matter too lightly," said the teacher. "We'll stay after school an extra hour to discuss this." "Close your eyes. Sit up straight. Now quietly think about this." After a few minutes the teacher asked for comments.

"Can I say anything I want? Frankly, I feel sorry for Tamura. All the boys smoke but he got caught."

"He won't be able to come to the Culture Festival, will he? That makes me sad. I hope we can keep this from happening again. It's all our responsibility."

"We should be thinking about the others too; those who haven't been caught yet."

"All the boys smoke. I wish they would stop before they get caught." (Students stand to make their comments in Japan, and many of the girls seemed on the verge of tears as they spoke. Obviously, they did not address the class often, and certainly not on this subject.)

The teacher asked who smokes in the homeroom. Four boys sheepishly raised their hands. A comment was thrown out: "Some girls are lying. They smoke too." The teacher asked for the four boys to stand up. The first bowed his head and would say nothing. For several minutes there was silence as the teacher looked at him. The next said, "I smoke. That's that. I'd like to stop, but everyone does it, so I can't drop it." The next confessed bravely, "I'll probably get caught too. I don't want to, but I don't know the answer." The fourth said, "Tamura's problem is lack of friends. As for me, I'm finding smoking less and less interesting." Finally, the boy who was silent spoke. "I guess I'll go along smoking. I'll get the same as Tamura. I started in middle school. One time I quit for a while, but . . ."

A girl stood and blurted out, "If our homeroom has a poor atmosphere, it's the fault of those who don't cooperate and join in. I get angry when the rest of us are blamed for Tamura's smoking. He's not a good member of the homeroom. It's his fault."

The teacher told the class that he had visited Tamura's house the previous night and talked with him and his parents until 10:00 P.M. He said Tamura had promised to stop smoking. He then turned the subject to the Culture Festival, asking the small groups to consider its purpose.

In the group nearest me, a girl began, "At first I didn't want to join in. Ueda's parents are getting divorced, you know, and I couldn't feel right about making a celebration. But now it's interesting." No one else had much to say, so they chose this girl to represent their group's opinion. (The students were getting tired of the whole discussion, which had been going for about an hour and a half.)

When this girl stood to report to the whole class, she said, "The goal of the Culture Festival is homeroom unity. Some work hard and others don't pitch in. I feel sad and lonely because of this. We have to have unity."

Several said they thought the Culture Festival a waste of time and doubt that it has any meaning. One spoke of it as just another thing students are supposed to do. (Clearly, impatience with the situation was making students more and more frank and aggressive in their comments.)

"You are all just saying the same thing, aren't you?" said the teacher, prodding them to greater frustration. "Wasn't Tamura on our festival committee? Is there any relation between that and his punishment? Between the goal of unity and why he got into trouble? Don't you think all of you are responsible, because there's been so little cooperation getting ready for the festival?"

A student angrily demanded of the teacher, "Tell us what *you* think!"

He replied, "I want you to decide this yourselves." He sent them back to their small groups once more.

The group nearest me: "We should drop out of the festival. We have no homeroom unity and therefore there is no meaning to it all." "Maybe Tamura was worried about this, that we were not cooperating with him."

The small groups reported: "We want to go ahead. If we quit, Tamura will be hurt. He'll feel it was his fault we quit." "We feel it is better to quit because we're not getting along." "We'd like to continue." And so on; all mentioned unity as the goal, and the majority said they would like to try to establish it but were dubious.

The teacher recounted how recently an excellent high school baseball team had withdrawn from the national championships when someone in the school was arrested for stealing.

> Isn't that true group responsibility? Aren't you avoiding such responsibility when you choose to go on with the festival? Will things between you and Tamura get any better this way? Frankly, with your present attitude I would prefer that you go on, yet deep down I am disappointed. At least do the festival with unity. That's the least you can do. And don't forget the other four smokers.

(Many breathed a sigh of relief.) More small group discussion followed: "This is giving me a real headache." "I definitely don't want to do it. All we do is follow what the teacher says." "I don't know what to think."

When the groups reported a mixed reaction, the teacher asked if they weren't getting tired of senseless discussion and if they were ready to make up their minds.

One boy stood and said that the girls do just what the teachers say and don't think for themselves. The room was filled with heated mutterings, which the teacher finally silenced. One of the more outspoken girls raised her hand, "How can you criticize us when you are one of the selfish ones that never cooperates?" She finished in tears. (Over the loudspeaker came a request that all teachers gather in the teachers' room.) There was silence for four or five minutes. Those who had just spoken had their faces down on their desks, and one girl was weeping. Several girls tried to heal the wounds with comments like, "He at least speaks out frankly." Others, who didn't want to be involved, kept quiet. The boy criticized stood up again. "I overstated what I meant just now. You know I wanted to join the drama group. But it was all girls and that made it hard for me to join. I've felt very lonely about not participating." (Everyone looked sad.) A girl asked, "Why didn't you join the girls?" Like all the other boys, this one was a tough-looking boy with greased hair and a zoot-suit look. "I'm not the kind who can just join, not unless it is made easy for me." The girl who criticized him pressed for an explanation. Neither could look at the other. Many girls were crying. One boy tried to resolve the conflict between the two. Silence followed. The girl, trying to hold back her sobbing, said she didn't think the explanation was sufficient: the boy would have to try to do better and couldn't rely on some excuse.

Suddenly, the teacher sharply criticized the whole group for a bad attitude and left for the teachers' meeting. This long homeroom had been going on for over two hours. After the teacher left, the students decided to remain in the Culture Festival.

Rarely is a foreign adult visitor like me introduced to the world of adolescent feelings that lie below the orderly events of a school's routine. In a few homerooms, the teacher will cause the feelings to surface, as occurred in this case, but in most instances teachers stop far short of creating such an atmosphere. Most teachers and students prefer the comfort of polite reserve. Teachers lead some sort of discussion each week and serve as counselors for their students if approached, but much of this is perfunctory. The dramatic side of student relations often escapes the teachers' attention altogether. At Yama, student problems like smoking are great enough so that teachers cannot easily ignore them; but in academic schools I encountered little emotional expression.

Homerooms are also the basic units of student government, as they are in the United States. Student representatives are elected, and committee members are appointed from homerooms. Student government at this grass roots level is hardly a hotbed of democratic practices, however. Elections rarely involve more than one candidate for a job. A rule of rotation and the notion of duty combine to make the actual elections anything but the legitimating last step in appointments reached by discussion. It is quietly arranged that someone will run and be elected homeroom representative because he or she has the time and the willingness and lacks past service in the job.

Nor is student government very important. Schoolwide officers, as with homeroom representatives, are typically elected from a fixed slate selected by the outgoing officers and their faculty advisors. The problem is finding individuals willing to serve. Conspicuous leadership is not sought by young Japanese, and no glory accrues to officeholders. Officers serve in a spirit of duty, rather than the spirit of politics or student rights. Unlike the situation in American high schools, being student council president is neither a sign of popularity nor a help in getting into college. Student government does not supervise behavior, judge students, or lobby for greater rights. Mainly it just helps organize the annual events and coordinate homerooms.

The homeroom has not become a model of democracy, as some occupation authorities had anticipated, but all the same it is of considerable importance in Japanese discussions of high school education. The homeroom is important to those Japanese who would have high schools become places of broad human learning. Besides providing a home in the school for each student, homerooms are the place where teachers meet with students, not as specialists in some subject or as drill masters in the training for university entrance examinations, but as advisers presumably well acquainted with their students. The long homeroom represents the only formal opportunity in the high school schedule to discuss such problems of fundamental importance to students as their own development as people, the ethics of living together, and the problems of society. Only during this hour can the teacher offer his or her own experience and cause the students to reflect on theirs. Only in the homeroom hour can discussions be free of the authority of textbooks. The homeroom is where the education of "the whole person" is supposed to occur. Yet one hour a week set aside for this is hardly more than a token amount, and there is much criticism and complaint in some quarters about this. Those teachers opposed to the entrance exam system especially rally to the homeroom's neglected potential.

It is useful to recognize a significant difference among schools on this subject. Nada makes almost nothing of homerooms and has no long homeroom in its schedule. In the academic high schools, filled with students from stable backgrounds who are well socialized to cooperation and good conduct, homeroom issues are often rather trivial. The importance of the homeroom teacher increases significantly at the vocational school level, where more students are seriously in need of guidance and opportunities to discuss their problems.

## *Clubs*

At 3:00 P.M., the shadow of classes lifts from the school. The transformation is amazing. Homerooms are quickly cleaned up, and students head for club (*kurābu*) activities or begin to wander homeward in small groups. The halls near the school's exits, the playing fields, and the rooms in which clubs meet become animated. The sound of music comes from open windows, and athletes yell to each other as they charge about. No one assessing Japanese high schools can fairly represent them without looking beyond the arduous business of curricular instruction to the life of the school from 3:00 to 6:00 P.M..

Extracurricular organizations and after-school activities were certainly not unknown to prewar Japanese education, but the occupation authorities gave them a new and much more central role. Following the American example, student clubs were interpreted by the occupation as valuable training grounds for independence and democracy. In them, the theory went, students learn to govern themselves and to take initiative. In the same manner as a democratic society is composed of various independent entities, so student clubs are building blocks of a student community. And in the name of democracy, the Japanese proceeded dutifully to encourage *kurābu* of all sorts in every junior and senior high school across the land.

Had the Americans known more about prewar student clubs, especially those among high school students, they may have been less enthusiastic in pushing them. Prewar clubs (and many postwar university clubs, too) were characterized by the strict authority of the senior boys over their juniors. This hierarchical order was accompanied by hazing and severe discipline. Even today, students occasionally die under the harsh training conditions some clubs create.

Largest and most active are the sports clubs. Among them the most popular are volleyball, baseball, Ping-Pong, judo, soccer, and tennis. Girls belong to many of these, but they generally practice and compete separately. Cultural clubs, as they are called, are typically numerous but are small and less active. Music groups (folk, guitar, rock, and chorus), some led by the music teacher, are prominent after-school fixtures. Typically, the academic high schools have some sort of science club. Among the most popular clubs in the better high schools is the English Speaking Society. Art, drama, and literature are usually represented, and in rare instances one can find service clubs. Few cultural clubs meet more than once a week, and those without faculty supervision are usually plagued with attendance problems. By contrast, sport clubs meet every day. They face regular interscholastic competition and enter local tournaments. Sports generate most of the vitality in the after-school scene, and for this reason the American expectation that clubs would be sources of democratic education seems to have been misplaced. Sports teams are hardly democratic in Japan.

Political education is an explicit intention behind one variety of club. In schools where the Burakumin and Korean minorities are well represented, special minority study clubs led by politically active teachers can be found, each minority with its own club. The Burakumin study their place in Japan's history and discuss how to deal with discrimination. The Koreans study Korean culture and a bit of their now largely forgotten language. The teachers who set up these clubs are invariably part of one or another left-wing national organization seeking to use the clubs as a basis for recruitment and training among high school students. Although the numbers involved are small and the clubs limited to only a few schools, the potential for conflict between different political sponsors is not to be taken lightly. Communist teachers, for example, have been locked in confrontation with the powerful and radical Burakumin organization, Kaihodōmei, allied to the Socialist Party. This is an ironic drift away from the American intentions for these clubs.

As part of my questionnaire survey of second-year students in the five schools, I asked about club participation. Unlike students in the United States, Japanese students can be members of only one club at a time, and nearly all memberships are expected to last for the duration of high school. Membership rates ranged from 44 to 77 percent over the five schools. To my surprise, participation at exam-oriented Nada was no lower than at other schools. About one-half of the students of any particular Japanese high school belong to a club, and at least one-quarter stay around each afternoon to engage in an organized activity. Most of the faces belong to those playing sports and are the same day after day.

It is customary in academic high schools for the leadership of club activities to transfer from the seniors to the juniors at the end of the first trimester since: starting with summer vacation, seniors should begin their concentrated study schedule aimed at the impending university exams. Furthermore, in top academic high schools, as many as 10 percent of the students (mostly boys) are attending *yobikō* in the afternoons. The ideal of the well-rounded scholar-athlete has become unthinkable given the present examination pressures. Reluctant bookworm though he may be, it is the pale and underexercised exam "pro" who is going to succeed and make his family proud.

Only some teachers are active with clubs. By law, teachers are expected to work a full day, all presumably helping with such activities, yet the majority disappear shortly after 3:00 P.M. There are no special stipends for extracurricular duties, and administrators insist that regular salaries cover a full eight-hour work day. Having stayed around various schools until they were locked up in the evening, I discovered that it was much the same small group of teachers who were the last to leave most nights. Many are physical education teachers, and the rest are mostly young. The major sports clubs are coached by this group. Occasionally, the music teacher and some older teachers burdened with heavy administrative tasks will stay quite late too, but on the whole the faculty divides into a majority that departs soon after classes and a minority that remains late.

The ideal high school teacher is, of course, close to students. The Tokugawa ideal was one of sharing a total existence with students, and the prewar ideal was one of unselfish service and dedication to the nation's young. As the school day is now arranged, however, about the only opportunity for serious personal contact with students is after class, when students can approach teachers for help or share some club activity that provides familiarity. The teachers who stay late gain rapport with at least some students. The first to leave, by contrast, are almost always lacking in significant relationships with students. They are labeled "*salariman* teachers"—teachers who work for salaries, as in business, rather than out of devotion—a poignant phrase that juxtaposes the ancient ideal and the modern bureaucratic reality.

The Otani volleyball team is practicing in the twilight of a cold November afternoon. The coach, standing on a ladder, throws down the ball with all his might toward a waiting boy, making sure it is just out of reach. The boy dives to retrieve, sliding across the hard ground to get a hand under the ball. The coach quickly throws another ball as he climbs back to his feet. The ball hits the ground, and the boy hestitates to make a fruitless second dive. "What! Give up already? Get back in line! We can't have that sort of attitude on this team. Okay, Kono, let's see what you can do. You guys sure are slopping around today!" The coach always yells like this during practice. It is getting dark, and lights are coming on in houses around the school. It is cold, and the boys are tired. Practice goes on as long as possible. Just before the gates are to be locked, the coach calls the team together. They sit on the ground and he talks softly. He congratulates them on trying hard and tells them to get a lot of rest before the game on Saturday. He smiles and tells them they are coming together as a team, but they still have a long way to go. On the way, he overtakes one boy on whom he was especially rough. Putting his hand on his shoulder, he tells him to keep trying. The experience of sports clubs is totally different from that of lectures in class, and the teachers are different too. The dominant influences after school are the physical education and fine arts instructors; both take a hands-on approach to learning.

Clubs largely do not maintain the authoritarian flavor of their prewar antecedents, but the matter is worth pondering at some length. Most sports clubs do have a developed sense of seniority. Older students are addressed respectfully as *sempai*. In some clubs, juniors must doff their caps and greet their *sempai* crisply if they meet on the street. Senior students carry great responsibility for the club and for instructing the younger members. Seniors can speak roughly to their juniors, who must be deferential in return. Trivial but sometimes onerous tasks are given to the junior members.

In boys' sports clubs, the potential for extremism lurks. Volleyball, rugby, mountaineering, and male cheerleading in particular have traditions of being rugged, and their leaders can fail to draw the line short of excess.

Group factors legitimate much of the discipline that is imposed. Club activities extend thoughout the year, so a team, even if it has a set season for competition, practices together for twelve months, unlike in the United States. Continuity of membership is related to commitment, group identity, and the development of strong internal bonds. In the larger and more active clubs, poor attendance is subject to punishment by exclusion or second-class treatment. If a member leaves, he is not likely to be allowed back. Many clubs also have strong OB ("old boy"), or alumni, loyalties. OBs keep in touch often and come back for practices and games.

Although seniors are firmly in control, decisions generally involve an open discussion among all members. Membership means a wide sharing of understanding and responsibility. More than the home-room, the club epitomizes the classic pattern of the Japanese small group in its jealous preservation of unity. The intensity of relations among members of a single club is the Japanese equivalent of friend-ship cliques in American high schools. But major differences exist. American student cliques rarely cross grade lines, but the backbone of Japanese club ties is the relationship between seniors and juniors. Also unlike friendship cliques, clubs are open to all who wish to join. They are also anchored physically in the school and are generally su-pervised. Neither status nor dating are significantly related to club membership.

These ingredients do make for a replication of the basic prewar club pattern, yet there are moderating factors: the close guidance of teach-ers, the presence of girls on many teams, and the general inclination (since the war) to pull back from excessively hard training. I am told that in several private schools of low standing in Kobe, violence-prone bullies are said to control certain clubs and run them like gangs. In my own experience, I witnessed nothing that approximated such extremes. Much of the problem with the prewar clubs was that they lacked adult supervision. Student leaders were under great pressure to prove themselves, and hazing became a yardstick of their dedication.

Team sports seem destined to an ambiguous place in "liberal" edu-cation. They contrast with the learning style appropriate to the individualist and democratic ideals. Some Americans see the two as antithetical. Sports training teaches discipline, not reflection, and it involves sacrifice for a group. Team spirit supersedes individual inclination. In academic learning the ultimate measure of performance is verbal, but in sports it is physical. Academic learning is accomplished largely by isolated study, whereas teams are inherently cooperative. In any school system dedicated to liberal democratic ideals, sports teams may appear as islands of a foreign culture.

In Japan, the issue of sports is complicated by the examination syndrome. To become an exam pro means devoting time to a painful regimen, not too different from hard sports training. The Japanese view the two as analogous in terms of sacrifice and discipline. Each is a modern version of an ascetic route to personal stature. Each is popularly said to enhance spiritual (*seishin*) strength. Thus, sports and exam-oriented study are really parallel practices in a cultural sense, and the two stand together in contrast to the laissez-faire ideals of schooling based on freedom and personal choice.

One striking piece of evidence of cultural affinities between sports and exam preparations is the similarity between the special techniques of cram schools and the volleyball team practice just mentioned. The shaved heads, the harsh lectures, the raised voices of the leaders, the strict discipline, the constant challenges, the focus on competitive spirit, and the friendly pat on the back from the coach belong to both. Compared with dull lectures, both are animated by a sense of drama and excitement. That many budding exam pros like the charged atmosphere of their cram school and find public school boring should not come as a surprise. The same preference for the atmosphere of sports clubs over class lectures is common among many high school boys, and in idealizing school sports clubs Japan's popular culture confirms this general preference.

I also must admit to finding club activities, sports or otherwise, the most pleasant and encouraging part of the Japanese school day. They give expression to youthful and buoyant qualities—enthusiasm, humor, and motion—and contrast sharply with the static and monotonous six-hour regimen of classes. Clubs offer opportunities to make friends and to be recognized for something besides test results. I recall two girls who were the entire membership of a folk song club. They practiced after school sitting in a stairwell. My first impression was of a forlorn effort on the verge of extinction. But,

*Rock band club practicing*

A rock band club practices in a classroom without teacher supervision; students drop in to listen.

stopping to listen, I was touched by the fact that they were singing songs that expressed how they felt, and they were having fun together. Down the hall was a rock band with all the electronic paraphernalia and eccentric posturing of that species of entertainment. They, too, were absorbed and happy in their common interest. Japanese teenagers need clubs for such things. Their homes are too cramped, and there are precious few other places where they can meet without spending too much money or getting into trouble.

A very real question, then, is why more students do not join clubs. The exam pressure is one explanation, and another is lack of sufficient faculty help and encouragement. Clubs often flounder without reliable faculty leadership. In all but Nada, student leadership is notably weak, a product, I believe, of the general educational emphasis on passive, teacher-centered learning. Viewing clubs as opportunities for students to learn to organize themselves sounds fine in the abstract, but leaving clubs up to students too often results in disorganization and lethargy. I came to resent the *salariman* teachers.

Clubs and homerooms are quite different, yet both are small groups that last throughout the school year. Both provide the student with social anchoring. And their quality depends heavily on some teacher's interest, in the absence of student capacity for self-government. Both teach the lessons of group participation. Both reflect the importance of leadership more than egalitarian process.

## *Peer Group Influence*

The reader familiar with research on American high schools will naturally wonder where adolescent culture enters the picture. We know that some of the powerful influences on the American high school student are clique membership, social status, sexual relations, and so forth.[9] In fact, the culture of American high schools is best described as the interaction of two very different and influential subcultures: the teachers' and the students'. On the subject of adolescent culture in Japanese high schools, we can be short and sweet.

Three facts stand out: 1) adolescent social life in Japan is not very developed; 2) high schools are not greatly affected by what social life exists; and 3) the influence of social life in schools is inversely related to the importance of exams. The first and third points will be discussed later. It suffices here to say that individual friendships are important; adolescents follow distinct fads and fashions; and Japanese teenagers yearn for peer contact. But independent group activities (parties, going out together, hanging around) and status rankings (created by cliques, dating, invitations, fraternities, sports, elections), which are at the heart of the American teen subculture, are of little consequence. One more reason high schools are not much affected by peer group life is that schools offer few opportunities for autonomous student social relations. Homerooms and clubs, the major points of social contact, are subject to teacher scrutiny, and neither is founded on a principle of free association. Both have fixed purposes that define relationships. High schools do not create opportunities for dances and other purely social activities as they do in the United States.

It is worth recalling here that Japanese high schools were not co-

9. See, e.g., Coleman (1961), Smith (1962), and Cusick (1973).

educational before the war, and they have never been viewed as community recreation centers. Parents do not want their teenagers encouraged in coeducational socializing. Each school day is busy and thoroughly organized.

As many have pointed out, the border between the high school and outside peer group influences has nearly collapsed in many parts of America. That teenage values, pressures, and behavior form in the streets and on weekends and then enter schools as a distinctive force is well known.[10] But the problems that come with this situation have grown. Over 80 percent of American metropolitan high schools, for example, reported crimes committed on school grounds to the police in 1974–75. The longstanding contradictions between popularity contests and academic purposes now pale, however, in the face of the invasion of drugs and violence into high schools. Cities now employ security forces to patrol the schools in the same way police patrol the streets. The problem of border maintenance is a general one, but it is greatest in urban situations where the drugs are harder, the violence is more common, and adolescent subcultures are more hostile.

In milder form, the same problem can be seen in Japan's lower status schools. Vocational and low-ranked private high schools have border maintenance problems because some of their students are involved in delinquent activities. In the worst high schools (usually private), teachers fear violence, student gangs prowl, and extortion occurs based on physical threats. Perhaps one in fifteen urban high schools has problems of this sort, and about one in four suffers such milder border maintenance difficulties as smoking, discourtesy, inattention, tardiness, and truancy.

### Student-Teacher Relations

One of the most profound discoveries for me when I began visiting Japanese high schools was that teachers regularly refer to students as *kodomo*, "children." I was surprised not only by the idea, but also because in spite of four previous years spent in Japan, I had not real-

10. United States Department of Health, Education and Welfare, National Center of Education Statistics, *The American High School: A Statistical Portrait* (Washington, D.C.: U.S. Government Printing Office), p. 38.

ized that to Japanese the category *kodomo* extended to sixteen-, seventeen-, and eighteen-year-olds.[11] That high school students might no longer be children or that they should be treated as adults are not ideas consciously considered. The official age for adulthood in Japan is twenty, and cities across the land have public ceremonies (*seijin-shiki*) celebrating the transformation to adult status. Perhaps this is an explanation, but the crucial point is the basic cultural difference between Japan and the United States.

The implications are truly profound when we compare this sense of age in Japan to the American understanding that high school students are, if not adults, largely adult and properly viewed and treated as adults. Teachers as a rule lean quite readily to the point of view that extending the rights and duties of adulthood to teenagers is sound educational practice. American parents may have trouble releasing their hold on their children, but in most respects teenagers are "no longer children" in their eyes. We see the high school years as a time when sons and daughters gain independence rapidly, experimenting with alcohol, drugs, sexuality, cars, and earning their own money. Mixed signals on all these issues are sent by adults, who struggle to find a fitting definition to a fast-changing situation. We cannot think of adolescents as children, yet they still have a way to go to qualify fully as adults. Such words as teenagers and adolescents help bridge the gap.

Japanese high school teachers in no way encourage their students to regard themselves as adults. In fact, it is their duty to prevent them from experimenting with adult pleasures and vices. Students are reminded of their obligation to family, school, and society. No one suggests they have rights.

It is a teacher's job to assume a parental attitude. The ideal teacher is one who is devoted and involved but not an equal or a pal. Of the two sides to parenting, affection and discipline, it is the latter that most parents want teachers to provide. In fact, Japanese parents typically look to the teacher for the discipline that they feel their affec-

---

11. In this regard, consider the results of a 1976 poll of eighteen- to twenty-two-year-olds conducted by Nihon Hōsō Kyōkai. Asked when they first felt like "adults" (*otona*), over 40 percent said they were not yet adults, 20 percent replied when they took their first full-time employment, another 20 percent answered when they graduated from high school or entered university, and 10 percent said when they turned twenty. Almost no respondents chose a time prior to leaving high school. Reported in Sōrifu, Seishonen Taisaku Honbu (1977), p. 281.

tion for their children prevents them from exercising fully. I have in my notes many instances of either parents asking a high school teacher to shape up their wayward or unmotivated child, or of teachers going to parents and telling them what must be done to bring a student back into line. Teacher coordination with parents is not always close, but it is always assumed that the two share a common perspective and position vis-à-vis the child. Teachers are encouraged to be close to students, but not as friends; and teachers are rarely interested in being popular with students.

Students address teachers as *sensei* (teacher), a term of considerable respect. Although they can give the word a twisted pronunciation that makes it insulting and funny, I only heard this in schools with delinquency problems and used only to the faces of a few very weak teachers. Although the Japanese language can be elaborately respectful, students generally speak to teachers in a simple, respectful manner. By being hesitant and shy they show their deference. Teachers use intimate terms of address (*kimi* and -*kun*) to reciprocate. This also follows a basic Japanese pattern in which superiors mark status differences while stating affection for a subordinate. The English equivalent might be: "Professor Elliot," followed by "Yes, Johnny."

Japanese teachers offer guidance and supervision covering student conduct away from school. Rules that prohibit smoking, motorcycle riding, and drinking are not restricted to school, for example, and teachers are expected to chastise rule-breaking students whenever they are encountered. I have been with a teacher who warned students against loitering when he met them on a downtown street. The long arm of the school can be a blessing to delinquents caught doing something like shoplifting, because some stores call the school rather than the police. Teacher supervision also extends to part-time work and vacation jobs. Most Japanese high schools have policies governing what kinds of jobs are appropriate for their students. Teachers may veto jobs and employers. The fear is that some work situations will corrupt a student's morals. Indeed, a theme that does run through many cases of teenage pregnancies, prostitution, and crime is recruitment of young part-time employees of snack shops and bars by older men, including gangsters. Teachers are expected to prevent such contact. Preventing accidents is another responsibility that weighs heavily on teachers. Prefectural and city offices of education will often punish the teachers supervising extracurricular activities if accidents occur. The fact that accidents happen accidentally is not the point, but rather that a teacher has near absolute responsibility for the safety of his students. Principals have even resigned to take responsibility for serious injuries connected with their schools.

Teachers complain about this policy of *in loco parentis*. They cannot actually supervise much of what their students do in a big city any more than they can prevent accidents on a junior class trip or during sports practice. But many are thus overly cautious about anything unusual or innovative that students want to try. Such expectations for teachers are unrealistic—and they fall much more heavily on teachers in schools with high levels of delinquency.

Homeroom teachers in particular are expected to watch over their students. By spending three consecutive years teaching and supervising the same group of four hundred students, considerable mutual acquaintance is achieved. Problem students and those who seek close contact with teachers receive attention in this arrangement, and they are known to the entire group of teachers supervising the grade. But many students are reserved and give no cause for intervention. To reach these students, homeroom teachers assign diary-like essays, which they carefully read for evidence of underlying problems and worries.

Even the most diligent and attractive homeroom teachers, however, become very close to only a few students each year. Neither the teachers' room nor a classroom of forty-three students is an especially fruitful context for personal intimacy. A few students will call on their homeroom teacher at home, and many teachers visit their students' homes when problems arise; but, more typically, supervision is at arm's length and waits on events.

The excellence and dedication of some teachers is usually known within the Office of Education, and if they make no mistakes their diligence will put them in line for administration work and eventually a principalship. But they will not be paid more or promoted quickly or recruited away by other school systems, as in the United States.

A nostalgia for an idealized past, when relations between students and teachers were close, is still present, but the contemporary bureaucratic context provides little that inspires dedication in teachers or respectfulness in students.

## *The School As Moral Community*

The ideal Confucian school paralleled traditional Japanese ideals for families, villages, and other basic social groupings in crucial respects. Its key ingredients were: 1) orderly, intimate relations centering on common identity, purpose, and interests; 2) dedicated leaders and loyal followers sharing hardships and joys; and 3) a group-centered existence that generates high morale and motivation. It was considered good for schools to be marked by a respect for internal hierarchy, a minimum of bureaucracy, a distaste for politics, a sense of autonomy, and high teacher involvement with students. Duties, not rights, were important: they expressed a cooperative spirit. Severity was appreciated because it strengthened character. The school articulated with the social environment by creating highly socialized, productive individuals, strong of character and socially concerned.

Even now this image is neither farfetched nor antiquated to many Japanese. In fact, the country is experiencing a revival of many traditional attitudes and values expressive of a nostalgia for the simpler, "more Japanese" ways.

Otani's principal is addressing the students during the ceremonies opening the new school year. "You may have seen me going around the school with a knife last month. I spent a lot of time scraping gum off chairs and desks." He lifts up a paper bag and tells everyone that it is filled with gum.

> I did this because a parent mentioned to me that Otani students do not care for their school as much as those at X High School [a grade above on the academic ladder]. I decided to see for myself, and he was right. I felt rather ashamed going around collecting this stuff, but I can tell you the gum is pretty much gone now.
> I know many of you love this school and I want you new students to learn to love it. We are starting a new year and I want the older students to offer good guidance to the new students. Can we all agree to take better care of our school, just as we would our own homes? That is how we will show our love for our school.

Expressed in this brief section of the principal's talk are many elements of the traditional legacy. The principal's devotion in going about humbly scraping gum off the bottom of chairs reflects his role as super-parent, generating guilt and reform through extraordinary care. Beginning with his own example and continuing with the request that the older students lead the younger ones is the notion of a familial hierarchy. No rules banning gum from the school are announced, nor are punishments set out for sticking it under the seats; only moral example and group sentiment are relied upon to solve the problem. Confucius would have approved. Otani is obviously quite a distance from attaining this ideal, but the path forward is neither bureaucratic nor democratic nor socialistic so much as it is Japanese and Confucian.

Other echoes of this perspective had been heard at a graduation ceremony the month before. The principal was dressed in tails. Bowing deeply, he intoned,

> Congratulations. You have completed all of the required courses.
> The word commencement in English means a beginning. You are entering new paths in life as university students or as working members of society. You must continue to work hard. From the bottom of my heart I pray for your future welfare.
> Recently I received a letter from a student graduating this year. I want to read it to you:
>
>> I have never had a chance to talk to you, the principal of my school, during the three years I have been here. I wanted to talk to you to find out what kind of person you are. You are probably not a fearsome man. But you are not easygoing, either. I want you to know this is how I see you. From now on during the rest of my life, I will do my best. I want you to know this too.
>
> I go around the school supervising every day, but instead I should have opened my heart and talked to each of you. Please excuse me. This is my last chance to talk to you. Please write me; you can always count on an answer. If you have troubles or you have failed, please write. Make your troubles the beginning of your success.

He then told the story of two friends, one who was accepted at a good university, one who was not. The second was unhappy and jealous, as their teacher had told the two they had an equal chance. But the successful friend apologized deeply, saying he was sorry the result could not have been the reverse. His friend reflected on his jealousy, "No wonder I failed. I had the wrong attitude. It was good I failed." The principal continued, "When things don't go the way you expect, you come to life's true turning points. They say Japanese wood is especially strong. Do you know why? Because of our hot summers and cold winters. Be full of energy and remember it is life's hardships that give strength."

Again the principal had stooped low (at least symbolically) and evoked a traditional ideal: intimacy coupled with severity. Reciprocity came at the end of the same ceremony, when students sang a prewar student song, "Aobatoshi," expressing the ideal of respect and affection for self-sacrificing teachers.

The school itself is the focus of most values, for in a moral sense it symbolizes the common good. Schools have public identities, of course, and a school's reputation is part of the teachers' and the students' identities, but these external considerations are of much less concern than is the quality of internal relations and activities. Cooperation is valued above all. It is obviously crucial to the running of the organization and a mirror of attitudes and morale. The complex daily management of a thousand adolescents can be achieved only when students behave in reliable ways. No amount of authority alone can force order on a school. Nor can disorder long be tolerated, especially among the Japanese, who have a relatively low tolerance for confusion.

There is an aesthetic to the culture of the school that is magnified in large public events such as Sports Day and epitomized in little interactions: a friendly greeting, a teacher staying late to help, flowers in the classroom. Cooperation and good will are concrete, aesthetically pleasing sentiments, and their opposites—sloppiness, inflexibility, thoughtlessness, poor planning, disdain or lack of care—are disturbing and ugly. It is important to appreciate that orderliness in a Japanese school does not evoke some authoritarian image in the eyes of most, but rather is pleasant evidence of benevolence, high morale, and successful instruction.

Clearly, most teachers and students appreciate smooth, coherent behavior. It evidences goodwill and social warmth. But casual sources of unreliability—impoliteness, forgetfulness, laziness, and so forth—are obtrusive and irritating. They become disquieting signs of disrespect for the common good. It is the job of teachers to build a community by squeezing them out. This is what the chewing gum talk was about.

Precision in schoolwide events is another sign of a school's moral state. The degree of preparation and control of details that go into Sports Day amazed me. It is a lighthearted event, yet the day before it at Otani, in physical education class, the whole school practiced marching in and out of the playing grounds. A minute-by-minute schedule of events was printed and distributed to all participants to assure coordination. Teachers lined up participants at the side of the field, waiting to go into action long before their turn came. Though a few boys sitting around roughhoused, over a thousand students spent an active day patiently sitting and watching races until their turns came to compete. Strenuous supervision was not needed, but all but one teacher were in attendance and alert. The principal, in his opening address, had asked the students to make the day a success by being responsible for their own actions; but just as important were the planning and rehearsals that carefully framed the event. Teachers pointed out to me that the real educational merit of Sports Day lies in the opportunity to teach cooperation in large groups.

Students were responsible for the planning, and clearly they sought to please. The distinguished visitors from the parent-teacher organization and the city Board of Education were shepherded by students assigned to them, and a staff of students was in charge of coordinating activities. So seriously did they take their tasks that they kept statistics on minor injuries and other problems so that each year they could improve the event. A week later, a summary report detailing which events had been accompanied by falls and who had fallen was published with suggestions for improving the safety of Sports Day. Large activities like this obviously carry a significant level of risk for teachers because orderliness is put in jeopardy, but the risk is thoroughly understood and generally well managed.

Sports Day, the Culture Festival, and the class trip are exciting and fun. They stand in stark contrast to the usual daily grind of classes. They are holidays, but holidays organized under school auspices and given educational rationales. After sitting through hours of classes and feeling at times quite depressed about the spirit of education in Japanese high schools, I was delighted by these separate moments in the school year, when enthusiasm, humor, and imagination flowed from the usually silent and passive students. Even many of the teachers proved to be lovable and entertaining, despite their otherwise serious demeanor. But the major concern of teachers was the fact that order was in jeopardy. Well-trained, well-behaved students evidence the socialization that parents and officials expect.

The level of risk in these events varies greatly from school to school. Nada's teachers hardly participate, so certain are they that their students will be reliable. At Yama, however, achieving a good showing is quite difficult, and there is much tension and anxiety among the faculty around these events. Some pull their homerooms out of the Culture Festival if they are not doing a good job of preparing, and others drill for weeks in advance to guarantee a praiseworthy presentation.

Full participation is another important value taught by school events. This has already been seen as the cornerstone of the long homeroom discussion. Teachers and students discuss how pleased they are that not one homeroom member missed Sports Day, or that special funds have been found so that no one will miss the class trip. When students or faculty do not participate, this is taken as a sign of alienation or the failure of group relations to have developed a sense of commonality and purpose. Teachers work to bring nonparticipating students back into the fold, as in the instance of Tamura's homeroom. Participating in groups is assumed to be natural, healthy, and proper. Nonparticipation, it is assumed, is accompanied by loss of self-confidence and self-worth. To pull back is an act of protest, but also a cry for help. Restitution to the group is often a process akin to psychotherapeutic acceptance. It usually requires a painful process of reflection and reform for the individual and the group, and yet, given the group basis of organizational life, it is necessary and even cathartic. The concern with full participation in Japanese high schools is a concern with maintaining the basis of community spirit.

Occasionally, teachers undertake radical efforts to improve the quality of social behavior in their schools. Given the political differences within many faculties and the lack of interest on the part of *salariman* teachers, however, such efforts are rather uncommon.

Just as I was leaving Kobe in spring 1975, the Yama faculty decided to tackle the problems of delinquency and lack of academic motivation in their school.[12] When I returned three years later I was surprised to learn the extent of the changes made. As a start, the faculty

---

12. This tightening of discipline came amid a number of other shifts in Japanese education that marked a swing of opinion to the right. The Japan Communist Party moved toward embracing many traditional Japanese virtues and against extreme leftist disruptions. In the leading intellectual journals, educational critics continued to condemn the entrance exam situation but called for a sturdier form of education. In what was virtually a manifesto, Shimizu Kitaro (1974), a respected authority, criticized the educational thought of the left as no longer appropriate and called for an end to the age of excuses. And Kawai Hayao (1975) attacked the excessively protectionist attitudes of parents and teachers. Most recently, Miura Shūmon (1982) has praised the accomplishments of Japanese education, using international comparisons.

guidance section had decided that students exhibiting bad behavior and those not performing up to the standards for their grade level would be held back for a year. To prove their resolve, as many as 10 percent of some homeroom students were told they could not advance to the next grade. Although the school average was not nearly this high, there were homerooms with three or four students held back in the first year the policy was instituted. In subsequent years, thanks to the sobering effects of this approach, few students were forced to repeat a grade. Though in the long run this approach was effective, it received much initial opposition, as it is virtually unheard of for students to be held back in Japanese public schools, and few teachers wanted to teach those held back.

Following this initial and spectacular tightening up, the guidance section established methods of closer supervision aimed at curtailing unacceptable student conduct. Section members came to school early to stand at the school entrance, saying "good morning" to arriving students and apprehending the latecomers. Teachers began to check systematically which students were taking their books home, and those who brought comics and bad literature to school were taken aside and warned. Teachers did not hesitate to stop students at the gate to look in their bookbags and ask what homework they had done. Anyone found carrying cigarettes or makeup was severely admonished.

A much stricter enforcement of the school's dress code was begun. Girls were told they could not come to school with permanent waves. Colored or striped sweaters were not permitted. Boys wearing uniforms cut in the fashionable zoot suit style were told to have them retailored. Repeated offenses led to telephone calls home and ultimately to temporary suspension. Gradually, the delinquent look so popular among students in lower status schools was eliminated. Yama students came to look almost as proper as the boys and girls going to Okada and Otani.

More serious punishments were aimed at boys who smoked. When the guidance teachers found a boy with cigarettes, they would pressure him to promise to quit, and friends were pressured to agree to quit together. As a result, some did stop, and smoking in and around school ended. On several occasions, boys who had promised to stop were given a nicotine test, in which their saliva was chemically tested to check their claims of fidelity. All the smokers were known and put under considerable pressure in this way. Posters of popular singers and movie stars came off the walls of the homerooms. Truant students were hounded until their behavior changed.

Within two years, the school's general atmosphere, and especially the behavior of the delinquent students, was radically changed. Teachers became more confident in asserting authority. Teachers say the number of police arrests of Yama students declined. The school's reputation improved. During 1977 and 1978 it enjoyed increases in the number of applications, which in turn allowed the admissions committee to weed out those least able academically and those likely to be discipline problems. The committee began surveying the applicants taking the school's entrance examination to spot obvious delinquents. Such students are now rejected. Some teachers objected to this procedure, but most have gone along with it because they are weary of dealing with problem students. The average test scores of entering classes have progressively improved, and the number of students entering from the city's problem junior high schools has declined. "As more students apply, our standards go up and fewer delinquent students are able to enter," said one teacher with obvious satisfaction.

Clearly, individual high schools, independent of national policies or local Office of Education direction, can effect significant reforms on their own. But sufficient will on the part of a faculty is rare, and in this case the Yama guidance section is recognized as having led a reluctant faculty. The accomplishments are appreciated, but the methods and demands on teachers were not popular. Students remained essentially docile in the face of the new measures, and no questions were raised about individual rights or the limits of teacher authority. Parents supported the new regime and cooperated by tightening up supervision at home. City educators praised the reform as going at the heart of Yama's problems.

One of the two heads of the guidance section provided clues to the reasoning behind the rather Draconian methods. Students of vocational schools, he explained, come from disadvantaged backgrounds and face lives as second-class citizens. This is a situation beyond the students' or the faculty's power to change. It must be accepted as a fact of life. What can be influenced is the training given vocational students to help them cope. Changing the curriculum or improving class size would not help prepare them emotionally for the hard road ahead. But the severity and discipline thus instituted would help students learn to be strict with themselves and better able to endure and succeed in adverse circumstances.

Order and community are universal organizational values desired by American as well as Japanese teachers. The cultural differences are more subtle. In Japanese high schools, it is not expected that community will arise from the voluntary action of students; it is created by teachers who set examples and assert authority. Once order is established, the necessity for overt teacher control declines, but it is always fundamental all the same. There is no propensity toward a liberal management of school affairs in which individual choice plays a significant role. Students are not young adults given (or having taken from them) the right to prove that they are deserving of full citizenship, as is the inclination in the United States. American parents expect teachers to be friendly guides, not formidable disciplinarians, and our cultural heritage encourages us to sponsor democratic processes involving students as co-decision makers. Where strict controls are put in effect, they are generally legal in character and enforcement divides students and faculty. A regime such as the one effected at Yama would improve conduct but ruin morale, in the American view. When an overriding ideal of freedom is present, discipline and authority are seen as natural enemies, and order is properly achieved only through voluntary processes.

In Japan, too, order must be based on compliance, but the responsibility for shaping the context rests within a recognized, legitimate hierarchy. Ideally, discipline should not be necessary, and in the face of problems, the proper first step should center on teacher examples and self-sacrifice. Nevertheless, the assumption is of thorough control by teachers, especially in response to serious problems. The difference is between a management approach, in which hierarchy is legitimate, and a democratic approach in which it is ambiguous, between a moral order founded on productive efficiency and one founded on choice leading to individual growth.

## Summary

The notion of school organization as a miniature society has not proved to be as simple as it sounds. Japanese high schools contain a number of dissimilar activities and social groupings. The dominant organizational principles seem to be: 1) a strong emphasis on faculty supervision; 2) the organization of individuals into small groups; 3) an emphasis on a few long-term group memberships rather than on choice and fluidity; 4) an absence of formal reward and control systems to steer teacher behavior; and 5) a heavy dependence on peer pressure and faculty leadership to motivate and guide conduct. The organization does indeed center on small groups, as do so many Japanese organizations, and this makes morale, leadership, and participation into crucial managerial concerns, for they are critical to the effectiveness of a group-based approach.

A considerable variety of group experiences is available in school. Some clubs are autocratic, whereas others are quite casually run; some depend heavily on teacher support, but a few are autonomous. Homerooms vary in the quality of their teacher leadership. Even more significant, however, is the place of group activities in the school routine. Most of the day, students are not interacting with one another, but are sitting passively listening to lectures as they prepare for the very individual competition to enter universities. Small groups play no direct role in this overriding concern, except insofar as the homeroom is an environment for instruction. What they do provide is peer contact, excitement, and opportunities for the expression of nonacademic interests. This is important, and it certainly makes group activities more pleasant and satisfying than the lonely pursuit of test-taking capacity.

Space, time, and social organization leave little room for peer society to develop among students in the independent form it has achieved in the United States. Japanese students are not surrounded by a peer group world as complex, as animated, or as full of status-producing and -reducing events as are their American counterparts. Tight schedules and spatial arrangements in Japan are joined by persistent supervision, a stability of social place, and a weightier flow of coursework. The social environment provides well-defined roles and asks for performance. The American school tends to leave part of the job of defining things up to each student and to unsupervised peer group processes. Japanese students learn to adjust to social "givens" with no illusion that they could help generate a society partly of their own making.

Faculty-student relations resemble the parent-child relationship. Three things are particularly indicative of the parallels: close supervision, little student choice, and teacher responsibility for student behavior away from school. This is perfectly consistent with Confucian tradition, in which the teacher's authority is legitimate and he is revered. The issue in contemporary Japan is not authority, but lack of sufficient dedication and love on the teachers' part to fulfill the spirit of the traditional role: *salariman* teachers threaten to undermine this cultural approach.

On the other hand, students of Japan will naturally wonder about the significance of school relations to the general observation that Japan is a society based essentially on personalized vertical relationships.[13] The ideal teacher-student and the senior-junior relationships do illustrate such a pattern; yet, in fact, teacher-student ties in high school are rarely very close, and only in the context of the well-organized clubs do both sets of relationships assume notable influence. There is, in other words, a significant gap between the cultural ideals and the actual practices involved. School organization is not a collection of personalized cliques centering on teachers or senior students, but a bureaucratic organization with a strong inclination to a group rather than an individual basis. When close teacher-student relations develop, education is undoubtedly enriched and an ideal is realized, but until other educational goals supersede exam preparation such ties are not likely to become central.

In fact, neither the vertical or horizontal dimensions nor the democratic versus authoritarian qualities are what is most notable. The distinguishing trait is that organizational routines hold the high ground without apologies to any higher ideal. Lacking any overwhelming ideological imperative, Japanese educators are not obliged to play the peculiar game of continually jumping back and forth between the competing requirements of a set of ideals and the organizational order. The highest explicit moral concerns essentially reinforce that order. The costs of disorder are clear. Order means an efficient environment for the pursuit of individual goals related to the examinations.

The association of students with teachers and with one another is relatively brief. No great common purposes unite students with other students. Exam success rates do serve as a measure to compare high schools, but individual exam goals are much more central even to teachers. In academic high schools this reality is indeed shared.

13. Nakane (1970).

Most Japanese high schools produce impressive levels of orderly behavior, but one wonders whether the causes for this are not largely the private ambitions of students for exam success. The exceptions, the vocational schools, seem to prove the rule that where exam expectations are low, order is a problem.

Japanese high schools are not training grounds for democracy, Japanese traditional values, or a new egalitarian order. Rather, they are best understood as shaping generations of disciplined workers for a technomeritocratic system that requires highly socialized individuals capable of performing reliably in a rigorous, hierarchical, and finely tuned organizational environment.

# 7

## Politics

Education is a weapon, whose effects depend on who holds
it in his hands and at whom it is aimed.

JOSEPH STALIN

No Japanese institution in the postwar period has experienced
more political conflict than public education.[1] The machinery
of educational policy making has witnessed intense and persistent
conflict between the Japan Teachers Union (JTU) and government
authorities, especially at the national level. Fist fights in the national legislature, teachers' strikes and sit-ins, mass arrests, and
legal suits have occurred regularly. Hostility, distrust, and acrimony
have often divided faculties and paralyzed schools.

This situation raises many questions about the actual political
control of high schools and the influence of political conflict on high
school life. The JTU and the Ministry of Education both exercise
greater influence over education than do comparable entities in the
United States, but, ironically, ideological indoctrination is rarely encountered in high schools, and students are even more politically ap-
athetic than their American counterparts.

### The National Context

Since the occupation, Japan has been divided into two opposing political camps as far as public policy issues are concerned: a conserva-

1. See Duke (1973), Thurston (1973), Pempel (1975), and Park (manuscript) for

. If the left points to the egalitarian aspects of the Chinese revo-
for example, the conservatives are not hesitant to reveal their
tion for the new spirit of diligence and social responsibil-
re. The Ministry of Education has avoided a public examina-
educational opportunity, and the union has not come up with
ious proposals for solving youthful malaise. The conserva-
ew structural differentiation as an inevitable aspect of a com-
onomy. To them, efficiency must have the higher priority. In
t, the left views the alienation of the young as a product of
, discrimination, and lack of opportunity. What is needed is
social reform. Moral education forced from above by govern-
not the answer, but is symptomatic of the problem.

debate is one familiar in most advanced democracies, but
'comes to earth" in the politics of Japanese education is the
of the rather unique postwar administrative situation.

the war, teachers were viewed as public servants with a
serve the nation. They were expected to epitomize loyalty.
activity on their part was deemed improper, and criticism
rity was condemned. The JTU naturally objects to this con-
of teaching. To the union, a teacher is a particular kind of
ne with responsibilities to students, but not to the estab-
. The occupation's legacy here is confused. The Americans
istinction between the classroom, where a teacher should
rtisan, and private life, where a teacher should be a con-
itizen. Furthermore, although the legacy followed United
al practice in outlawing strikes by national public servants,
was intended to be an effective force in a pluralistic so-
vily dependent on legal means of control, the ministry has
force the law prohibiting political activity by employees,
mpts to penalize union leaders who call strikes. The union
insists that, in or out of the classroom, teachers should be
and the union should be free to strike.

rewar system, teaching was described as a sacred profes-
ying an unusually high level of dedication and self-sacrifice
the respect and gratitude of the nation. Such a legacy, of
ts union demands for better wages and working conditions
ad light. The label "sacred" has therefore been rejected by
in favor of the term "educational laborer." Compounding
the fact the public views the profession's responsibilities

tive element that has held national power and an opposing element
of leftist parties. The JTU is a key element in the opposition camp.
The Ministry of Education, of course, belongs to the government of
the ruling conservative camp.[2] Figure 2 illustrates this arrangement,
showing how the political parties reach into the schools where each
has a representative.

On the face of it, an analogy between political conflict in Japanese
education and the kind of warfare waged between the entrenched
German and Allied forces in World War I is suggested, for many
years of heated but indecisive battles have led to a stalemate but no
general truce. Ad hoc cease-fires in some localities, skirmishing in
others, and the everpresent possibility of general hostilities characterize the present situation.[3]

Recall that the occupation permitted the unionization of teachers,
which resulted in the creation of a powerful counterforce to official
authority.[4] Second, it stripped the Ministry of Education of some of
its former powers and distributed them to prefectural, city, and local
administrations, thus partly dismantling education's highly centralized character. Third, new and quite different educational goals aimed
at reinforcing a democratic system were introduced. Prewar education had been a powerful instrument of political legitimation; the
occupation sought to undermine such a connection by creating an
educational outlook that was adamantly independent and politically
neutral.

The Americans succeeded in changing many things, yet the new
system of dispersed authority was far from complete, lacked sufficient resources, and did not gain the understanding and complete acceptance of parents, administrators, and teachers. The Americans
succeeded in sweeping away the old, but what they introduced was
not stable, based as it was on principles and social values that were
partly alien to Japanese experience. A battleground between left and
right was inadvertently created. The institutional shakedown had

overviews of the politics of Japanese education. There have been no studies of politics
at the school level, however, and Japanese writing on the subject is almost entirely
partisan in nature.

2. Duke (1973), Pempel (1975), and Yung H. Park, "Education Policy-Making in
Contemporary Japan: A Study of the Liberal Democratic Party in the Ministry of Education" (manuscript).

3. Rohlen, in Krauss, Rohlen, and Steinhoff, eds. (manuscript), discusses the complex character of this conflict as it varies by time and place across the nation.

4. See Gayn (1948), Kawai (1960), Anderson (1975), and Duke (1973).

**Figure 2**
Relations of Educational Institutions and National Politics in Japan

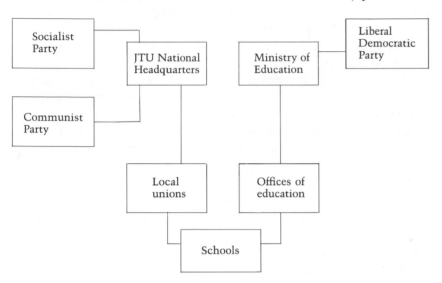

hardly begun before the Americans were gone. The teachers' union had embraced the purpose and goals of making education democratic and vigorously pushed for continued reform at all levels of education. The effort was twofold: to take power from official administrators and give it to teachers, and to increase the progressive or leftist content of education. The conservative government, on the other hand, viewed the occupation's reforms as excessive and in need of reorganization and nativization. The ideological and political lines were thus drawn, and both political camps viewed the struggle to shape education as vitally important.

At issue was both political power and the cultural character of Japan. American-inspired education stressed individualism, social criticism, and personal development in a liberal atmosphere. The status quo was put in jeopardy, and this naturally appealed to the opposition camp. Prewar schools had emphasized polite conduct, a sense of duty to society, and respect for authority. Older Japanese, witnessing rising juvenile crime, ethical confusion, motivational stagnation, and finally student protest, readily laid the blame on the new school system. The union's voice, on the other hand, called for

education to be more egalitarian, more in[ ] and more politically progressive in conten[ ]

Initiative rested with the conservatives, [ ] ically launched national drives to gain gre[ ] and to reestablish the teaching of ethics [ ] posed such moves, accusing them of bein[ ] at the reestablishment of "fascism."

Rarely do partisans of either side avoid [ ] ceived evils in education to social proble[ ] selected as crucial have been significan[ ] heart of the political struggle is control [ ] ideological debate is what is wrong w[ ] Japan's most serious problems in socia[ ] trialization, and Japan's defense treaty [ ] conservatives find them primarily in sp[ ] of the younger generation.[5] Just becau[ ] are quite predictable does not mean th[ ] both sides hold them as articles of fai[ ] nese people, who are not consistently [ ] spective, take great interest in both in[ ]

Being Socialist-led, the national JT[ ] ist structure of Japanese society a ba[ ] form of authority maintained by a r[ ] big business, conservative politician[ ] Public education is a tool used by th[ ] the masses, as well as an integral pa[ ] social structure. The union, for exam[ ] introduction of vocational courses af[ ] that this created a two-track system [ ] portunity. Minorities, the entranc[ ] high schools, and so forth are all is[ ] light of social structural problems.[ ]

The conservatives, on the other [ ] education's failure to maintain th[ ] work, and willingness to sacrifice[ ]

5. Friedman (1977); also such statemen[ ] Jiyūminshutō Seisaku Chosakai (1977) ar[ ] the JTU like Hyōgo-ken Kōtō Gakkō Kyō[ ] partisan books on education such as Inaz[ ]

natio[ ]
lution[ ]
admira[ ]
ity the[ ]
tion of[ ]
any se[ ]
tives v[ ]
plex ed[ ]
contras[ ]
poverty[ ]
general[ ]
ment is[ ]

This [ ]
how it [ ]
product[ ]

Befor[ ]
duty to[ ]
Political[ ]
of autho[ ]
ception [ ]
laborer,[ ]
lishmen[ ]
made a [ ]
be nonp[ ]
cerned c[ ]
States leg[ ]
the unio[ ]
ciety. He[ ]
tried to e[ ]
and it att[ ]
naturally [ ]
free acto[ ]

In the [ ]
sion, imp[ ]
repaid by[ ]
course, p[ ]
in a very [ ]
the union [ ]
the issue i[ ]

to children as sacred. Political activities, strikes, and anything that disrupts teacher devotion are inappropriate in the popular mind. Infighting between administrators and the union becomes more subtle and convoluted as a result.

The changes quickly and naïvely introduced by the Americans created a greatly altered field of authority and power within education, but they certainly did not succeed in separating education from politics. Quite the contrary. Rather than becoming a pliant institution readily used by the government, education turned into a highly politicized institution, and Ministry of Education attempts to reshape it have met with concerted opposition at the school level wherever the union is well entrenched. School-level decision making has determined the success or failure of many policy moves by the national government. On the other hand, many political disputes arise within particular school faculties as the result of union-administration tensions. Both kinds of conflicts deserve our attention.

## *The Administration*

The School Board in Kobe is a set of citizens, appointed by the mayor, who are distinguished for social service or cultural accomplishments.[6] It has some influence in decision making, but no one I spoke with regarded its role in politics as central. Its members symbolize citizen control and theoretically prevent the misuse of administrative authority, but the real power and initiative lie in the Office of Education, the administrative arm of the School Board. Personnel matters, policy proposals, and the supervision of schools are all responsibilities of this office. Although my study did not focus on this level of administration, some general observations are in order.

Offices of education in prefectures and large cities are semi-autonomous entities operating within the framework established by the various national laws regulating education. They are guided by the Ministry of Education, which finances part of public education, enforces the laws, establishes the standards, sets the curriculum, attempts to improve pedagogy, and approves the textbooks for the nation's schools. For high schools, the local Office of Education is re-

---

6. School boards were locally elected for a brief time during and after the American occupation, and the JTU gained some seats through organized campaigning, which in turn caused the ministry to push through a law ending such elections.

sponsible for districting, entrance examinations, school expansion, the quality of instruction, relations with the local union, personnel development, and special problems such as delinquency. Offices of education do not generate significant innovation in areas where the Ministry of Education has primary authority, yet they have considerable autonomy in local matters. A further complication arises in educational policies wherever elected local government belongs to the opposing camp rather than to the conservatives. Kobe's mayor gained office supported by a coalition of leftist parties including the Socialists and Communists. His appointments to the School Board and to the Office of Education have been aimed at reducing conflict with the JTU. The fact remains, however, that Kobe's Office of Education administers the laws and policies set by the national government and is therefore an accomplice, sometimes an unwilling one, in the conservatives' efforts to control education from above. To retain its own authority, moreover, an Office of Education must counter the union's moves to gain power over school decisions.

The people who occupy responsible positions in the Kobe Office of Education are part of the elite of the teacher corps.[7] Virtually all have come up the ranks of teaching, and after some years serving in the central administration they will return to positions in the schools. These are men in the prime of their careers who are known for loyal hard work during years of service. Typically, they are neither supporters of the union nor among its outspoken critics. Besides being respected and hard-working, they are usually quite politically shrewd. They fit the administration's need for effective pragmatists who can navigate the tricky waters of school politics and keep the many ships of the educational fleet afloat and together.

Although there is no doubt that individuals with such talent are spotted early in their careers by senior educators, they are not actually transferred to offices of education until they are in their early forties. No one is hired from outside the teacher corps, and there is no alternative track into administration. Five to ten years of service in an office of education exposes those who are selected to the nature of administrative problems and authority and ties them into the

---

7. I did not focus my study on the Kobe Office of Education. I know its activities from friendships with several of its administrators and from what high school teachers told me. I have not found any published materials on the subject of its operations and organizations.

informal network of communication and influence among teachers. Having been on the inside of administration, many are then on track for promotion to vice-principal and principal jobs. Some are promoted to leadership within the Office of Education itself.

In effect, then, the Office of Education is the center for the recruitment and training of an elite cadre of educational administrators. These individuals work to maintain and direct the school system. They deal with the city and prefectural union leaders, men like themselves who have risen from the teacher ranks. The two groups are very different in their politics, their personalities, and even in their styles of dress, but they are destined to face one another across the negotiating table.

No heavy hand of authority is visible in the conduct of the Office of Education. School supervisors circulate almost daily to listen, observe, and consult. They learn a remarkable amount about what is going on, particularly as it reflects the political situation of the school. But they do not publicize their knowledge, and they are usually careful to wait for the appropriate time and place to take any corrective action. Their major concerns—that all should run smoothly and that quality should improve—are best attended to through maintaining a low profile but persistently managing small problems. They use the established chains of command in schools when they feel change is needed, asking the principal or the head of some committee to take up a question or proposal with his subordinates.

What they hope to avoid is union opposition to their influence and plans. Suspicion on both sides is often strong. Past confrontations encourage continuing suspicion. At times, the union's power in a school is truly threatened. Because in many schools the union actively opposes the administration's leadership, the union is viewed as obstructing the practical needs of education.

Personnel management is often the critical means of preventing union opposition to administration plans. In hiring new teachers, there is a concern to avoid employing those who might be union activists. No direct political questions can be put to applicants, but personnel officials attempt to gauge attitudes on the basis of less direct evidence. Transfers and promotions are more critical. Through judicious use of transfers, the Office of Education can work to establish control over various faculties. It can weaken union leadership in particular schools by shifting teachers in and out. In some cases, it may decide to give the union one or more schools where it is already strong, regularly granting the request of union activists to join the faculties of these schools. In thus creating "union castles," the administration reduces union influence from other schools. Yama is a union castle.

Administrative rules and regulations are also created to circumscribe union activities. But the agents of the Office of Education are rarely dynamic leaders; and the principals' and vice-principals' ability to enforce rules against the will of a faculty is limited. Many principals try to avoid the troubles and headaches of battling with an independent and sometimes politically antagonistic faculty. I was told on several occasions that being a high school principal shortens one's life. "Just look at the fact that one annually dies in office," remarked a friend in the Office of Education.

Nor does administrative authority in Japanese education benefit from control mechanisms common to most modern organizations. Tenure is automatic from the first day. Teachers cannot be fired for anything short of gross or illegal misconduct. There is almost no discretion in the wage system, and there are no promotions to manipulate. The Office of Education can penalize teachers through salary deductions and even suspension from active duty, but these punishments are limited almost entirely to strike activities, which are illegal, and to cases of student injury due to teacher misconduct.

Until the end of the war, a school principal was a powerful figure, greatly respected in the local community and capable of shaping the character of his school in significant ways. Principals had tremendous authority over their teachers, and many reportedly were greatly admired by their subordinates for the way they personified the ideals of education. In general, these men were confident, dedicated, and energetic. Social expectations and political circumstances encouraged these qualities. The principal was to be keenly interested in his teachers and by a mixture of fatherly concern and stern discipline was to shape them to a particular mold that emphasized dedication, skill, and firmness, the very qualities the principal represented.

In a democratic age, such a regime appears authoritarian. After the war, teachers, imbued with new ideals, naturally found the principals' authority a major barrier to change. The union, representing this reform impulse, came regularly into direct confrontation with principals who stood for different aspirations. That confrontation persists in many schools, and it has greatly lowered the stature of principals.

Regardless of political preference, the principal today must seek to retain authority. He is responsible for the school and must see that teachers abide by the laws and administrative rulings of the nation and locality. To build a unified, supportive atmosphere among the faculty and to assure that the basic tasks are accomplished, principals must be conservative. They cannot afford to be patient with notions of the school that view it as an agent of protest and social reform. Their task is to improve what exists, whereas the union seeks to change the basics. The principal must accept the limits of finance, law, and custom; the union may find these insignificant. The principal's major worry is the school, whereas the union leaders focus primarily on larger social issues. The principal must acknowledge the wishes of parents for discipline and exam preparation; the union can label such concerns authoritarian. Finally, and most significantly, the principal must strive to get the most work possible from teachers, but the union must attract teachers to its own activities by offering to protect them from such demands. The contest for faculty time and loyalty is indeed broad and complex.

Contests with the union are themselves evidence of decreased authority. The lives of many principals have become lonely and thankless. Once regarded as the crowning reward of an outstanding career, the job is now considered undesirable by most teachers. Of the four public high school principals I observed firsthand, three seemed resigned to a passive, bureaucratic role. They seldom emerged from their offices to talk with teachers and spent much of their time away from their schools. Recently assigned to their jobs and having arrived as outsiders, they did not know their teachers well. Their accomplishments belonged to another time and place.

In essence, high school teachers cooperate with the administration and extend themselves in their work primarily on the basis of voluntary compliance. To keep their jobs they must perform in the classroom and do a modicum of support work; but beyond that, nothing official can stop them from ignoring students, quasi-administrative responsibilities, and even their fellow faculty members. Some teachers do the minimum, but most offer more. The reasons for this lie in their professional identity and in the school itself.

The principal's position has leverage only when its occupant has the skill and stomach for political maneuver. Consider this example. In 1969, Mr. Tanabe was director of personnel for the Kobe Office of Education. In the early fifties, he helped organize and lead the union, but later his commitment waned because the union "put politics above education." In 1969, during a period of university campus unrest throughout Japan, small numbers of radical students "occupied" several academic schools in Kobe in imitation of what was happening in universities.[8] For several months, the occupied high schools experienced a paralysis of education. General meetings were held in which the virtues and ideals espoused by the students were contrasted with the obvious chaos and loss of study time that such tactics imposed on the entire student body. The union was caught in a particularly awkward position; it could neither condone nor support the student radicals. The reputations of the occupied schools declined in the eyes of parents. Promising applicants chose more stable academic environments. Almost constant faculty meetings could not resolve matters. Tempers were short, and much faculty disunity developed.

Tanabe was at the pinnacle of his career within the administration. Witnessing the chaos, he asked to be made principal of Otani, one of the occupied schools. It was clearly a very sensitive and volatile assignment. The faculty was quite senior, quite independent, and strongly influenced by a set of union leaders hostile to the administration. The faculty did not support the students, but they had refused to consider firm efforts to cope with the occupation of the school.

Within a short time, Tanabe had gathered the necessary support of parents and faculty to expel the students and end their occupation. Expulsion was virtually unheard of at the time; but in retrospect most see it as the proper course. A less severe policy in Kobe's other occupied high school greatly prolonged its troubles and left the faculty in shambles. Ten years later that school had still not fully recovered, and its reputation kept it at the bottom of the ranking of public academic high schools.

Tanabe stayed at Otani, determined to administer it with the same firm resolve. He saw the teachers as largely arrogant and unrespon-

8. One Kobe school gained notoriety when a handful of the occupying radicals hijacked a Japan Air Lines jet and went to North Korea, where they remain today. Sometime later at the same school a student burned himself to death in protest.

sive to the needs of students. They were too willing to ignore minor infractions of the rules. They went home early, paying little attention to after-school activities. They took pride in their abilities as academic specialists, but they hid behind the union when it came to doing their share of the hard work of supervising extracurricular activities. They were, he said, *salariman* teachers working by the clock.

To correct this situation, Tanabe began a personal recruiting effort aimed at drawing to his school the best of each crop of new teachers hired by the city. To him, the "best" meant young people of strong will, dedicated to being excellent teachers who would sympathize with his outlook. Over five years he succeeded in adding six young teachers of his own selection while transferring out some less desirable teachers. This was enough to tip the scales back toward a balance between union and administration strength in the school. Balance in this case meant that neither side could comfortably count on winning a majority of the faculty in any conflict. Tanabe proceeded to push for greater faculty supervision of students and greater responsiveness to student needs. When I visited Otani in the year of Tanabe's retirement, many of those in his camp regularly remarked on how the place had improved because of his administrative talents. His unusually strong character was the key. Elderly and old-fashioned, yet more energetic than the middle-age *salariman* teachers he disliked, Tanabe remains a very memorable, but not a typical high school principal.

## The Union

Every public high school in Kobe has a JTU local (*bunkai*), and virtually all public high school teachers belong to the union.[9] There is a separate union for private high school teachers, but because Nada's teachers are not involved I learned very little about it. At the city level, the union is led by officers who are sympathetic to, or are members of, the Japan Communist Party. They see local issues— even matters pertaining to just one school—as tied to national politics. The Communist Party draws electoral support from less than 10 percent of the voters, and even in the JTU its members are a minority faction.

9. Thurston (1973) offers a more complete portrait of the JTU organization.

The city- and national-level union organizations depend greatly on the participation of the thousands of school locals. When national strikes are called, for example, each local decides whether to participate. The union's ability to block major policy moves by the national government thus rests on its capacity to mobilize school-level support. Besides contributing monthly dues, some of which go to the national union and its political campaigns, the locals recruit teachers to spend time attending union meetings and demonstrations, preparing studies, and otherwise supporting union efforts. Some union activities take teachers quite far afield, for the JTU attempts to aid other labor efforts and has extended its interests to anti-establishment efforts from the anti-war movement to environmental protests. The union's actions are coordinated with a wide network of leftist organizations. School locals are thus regularly asked to supply volunteers to work for other causes. A minority of teachers, perhaps 10–20 percent, view these campaigns and activities sympathetically and willingly give their time, but a larger group are reluctant, some for lack of time and energy and others out of political repugnance. The enthusiastic union participants are inevitably a rather distinct group within the teacher corps.

Active participation in citywide union activities is, however, but one measure of teacher commitment. The majority of teachers do appreciate the union 1) for obtaining improved wages, benefits, and working conditions and 2) for serving as a counterweight to right-wing influences and governmental authority. Even among those who find the union's politics offensive, there is general agreement with these points. If one were to ask how a union whose leadership represents a political minority can remain so effective, the answer would be through the broad support given to these two aspects of its role in education. Most teachers are relatively liberal in their social opinions but rather conservative in their preference for orderly, smoothly run schools. They may, with the union, disapprove of the examination hell and its inequitable results, but as a rule they find the predictability of the instructional process comfortable. There are some dedicated teachers at every point across the political spectrum—no group has a monopoly of virtue. Nevertheless, it is the union that seeks an easing of the rules and requirements aimed at greater teacher output. Strikes are an extreme example, but in many less obvious ways the JTU protects teachers from having to behave in a dedicated manner, and teachers divide rather evenly over this facet of union policy. In sum, the great majority of teachers have quite ambiguous feelings about their union, and their support varies greatly from issue to issue.

The union's tiny regular staff in Kobe can accomplish little without volunteers. If activist teachers could not leave their schools when classes are over, the JTU would be seriously crippled. Realizing this, it is the administration's position that, by law, teachers owe the school eight hours each day. The union responds by asserting that teaching duties are limited to classes. The union has long been demanding special stipends for after-class extracurricular work. Neither money nor the "laborer" versus "sacred trust" notions of teaching is the central issue. The struggle is over control of teachers' time. Educational politics is grounded in the competing realities of mobilizing a mass organization and running schools.

Most teachers are not keen participants in union affairs, but many do have second jobs or other private interests in the late afternoon and for this reason are happy to support the union's position. Those teachers who regularly stay after school are the flies in the ointment, according to the union. Administrators and some teachers, on the other hand, view the union's appeal for stipends as a clever excuse to avoid fulfilling what they see as the natural and proper responsibilities of a good teacher.

To gain a firm understanding of educational politics in any city, one must learn the circumstances school by school. Enthusiastic unionists are a majority in only a few of Kobe's high schools. Year after year these leftists succeed in electing their colleagues to leadership of the union's headquarters. Why should a highly politicized but small minority retain power so easily? The answer lies in the fact that the majority of teachers do not unite politically and have no interest in taking control of the union, leaving the field open to the activists. If a contest for control were to occur, it would take place between two organized minorities: followers of the Communist Party and followers of the Socialist Party.

Each school local is a crucial link between the leadership minority of political activists and the mass of teachers who are only mildly committed to the union. The leader of each local must be a sensitive broker between the teachers of his school and JTU city headquarters. He must arbitrate between the ambitious programs and demands of the headquarters staff and the far less committed, school-centered, and reluctant membership of his local. As viewed from headquarters, the successful leader of a local is one who keeps union morale high, recruits volunteers, and mobilizes support for sit-ins, work stoppages, and strikes that accompany bargaining and national campaigns. Viewed from the typical member's perspective, however, the successful local leader is one who does not demand too much of teachers, but uses union power to manage the principal and the rules. Teachers assume that the city headquarters staff will success-fully negotiate better wages and concessions from the Office of Edu-cation. In this respect, the union is well entrenched.

In Kobe, locals range in character from those of high commitment to those offering empty gestures of support. Faculties unanimously for or against union activism are rare; they symbolize the extreme outcomes of a political power struggle that has not been decided in most schools. Occupying the middle ground are locals engaged in a constant game of balancing and redefinition that neither denies nor fully submits to the leadership of either union headquarters or the administration.

The annual faculty election of its union leadership is an event that can reveal much about a school's political situation. That elections are rarely contested does not mean that considerable deliberation is not involved. Existing leaders typically nominate their own replace-ments. Who they consult in this process is most revealing. If the opinions of a broad group of senior teachers are considered, then the nominations reflect a general consensus, and the local is likely to be moderate in its politics. On the other hand, if an entrenched and highly partisan leadership chooses its own successors without con-sulting opponents on the faculty, the union is either safely in control or destined to serious conflict. In a school with a tradition of no more than pro forma union membership, leftist teachers themselves will be excluded from the nominating process. Schools tend to re-main in political character for many years as the nominating process perpetuates the existing pattern. The proposal of opposition slates is a sure sign of considerable internal conflict.

Most high school teachers find the prospect of working as a union leader as unappealing as becoming a principal. The job is sought only by keen unionists. Ironically, only in schools where the tradi-tion is one of union activism are these teachers certain to play active union roles. In centrist schools, activism can disrupt faculty bipartisanship, and activists are often bypassed in the selection process. Union loyalists therefore often seek transfers to the few schools controlled by the JTU, the union castles.

Any discussion of the union activists of a school must begin with the character of the local in terms of the foregoing simple typology. The leadership of union castles generates many partisan activities and stands ready to wage war against any principal who ignores its power. Middle-ground locals seldom push hard for participation in union matters and are ready to compromise with principals. Dormant locals are mere formalities. The character of union affairs in several of our five schools will help illustrate the differences.

Yama is the leading union castle within the city system. Activist teachers abound there. About one-third of the entire faculty always supports the leadership of the local—one which, incidentally, has produced a number of leading figures in the citywide union organization. One Yama teacher, in fact, had just resigned to become a Communist Party candidate for the prefectural assembly. A number of other Yama teachers have also gone on to higher union and party work. The local, or at least its leaders, is thus strongly tied to the wider leftist movement. Yama's activities in such matters as minority (Burakumin and Korean) rights, the introduction of social issues into the classroom, and opposition to Ministry of Education changes are widely acclaimed at citywide union meetings. It is a model union school, and less active locals are urged to follow its example.

The Yama union is strong enough that it encounters little resistance in using some of the teachers' room wall space for election posters supporting the Communist Party, and during my visit there were frequent announcements over the public address system in the room urging teachers to attend political meetings, to pass out handbills, and to contribute funds to the party. Yet it was made quite clear to me privately that many teachers did not support the party. Some strongly resented the political invasion of the teachers' room, but only a few ever spoke up at faculty meetings.

The local has succeeded in silencing opposition from the principal and vice-principal on most issues. At Yama there is notably less administrative pressure than in other public schools to perform administrative or extracurricular duties. Most teachers at Yama, as a matter of course, take off their weekly "study day" (*kenshubi*). If teachers in any school have no classes scheduled on a particular day, they may stay home to study by agreement between the union and the Office of Education, but the incidence varies considerably. At Yama it was especially high. It would be incorrect to say that union activists are any less dedicated classroom teachers. Some devote themselves to students, but the weakness of the administration permits teachers much latitude, and as a result the school's discipline and morale were quite low at the time of my visit.

As evidence of union power, consider an incident that occurred here in the early 1970s. The principal at that time made the final selection of applicants with approximately the same entrance scores. It happened that among the applicants just at the cutoff point were several Korean students. The principal ruled against them in favor of Japanese applicants. This final selection process was not public, but the Yama local investigated, proved that the principal had discriminated, published the evidence, and finally forced him to resign. Ethically, the union's leaders were perfectly correct; yet by older Japanese standards, they had transgressed the principle of keeping school problems within the school and had shown no concern for the position of the principal. No teachers said the union was wrong, but many in Kobe education point to the incident as an illustration of how union activists will not hesitate to disrupt school unity in the pursuit of their goals.

Yama's present principal is a former union leader. He deals with the union without causing confrontation; some say he was appointed with union approval. His leadership appears weak, but his appointment is regarded by the Office of Education as successful because the school is now relatively quiet.

The Yama local, for all its power and accomplishments, periodically must contend with serious resistance from a minority of teachers who oppose its radicalism. In the absence of a strong principal, some teachers have learned to argue and contest with the union as their leftist opponents protest when they are out of power. In one instance, a thief had entered the school one night, and the next morning it was discovered that a few teachers had lost money and articles of minor value. The police, called to investigate, checked the premises and interviewed some of the teachers and staff. They found no leads, and later that day they called saying they would like to check the teachers' room for fingerprints.

This seemingly innocent proposal from the police was met with immediate strong opposition from the union. The law against public school teachers engaging in political activities is not strictly enforced, largely because there are so many teachers active in politics. Yet Yama's union leaders felt vulnerable around the matter of fingerprints and insisted that the police not be allowed back in the teachers' room, arguing that this would be an invasion of academic freedom by a known instrument of political oppression.

A meeting of the teachers was hastily called for the lunch hour. The principal said the decision had to be made by the faculty. While some sat at their desks correcting papers and nibbling their box lunches, the union's leaders presented their case in a forceful manner, insisting that the police would use the fingerprints against them. Then one of the gym teachers stepped to the microphone to argue against the union's position. I was startled that there would be such open conflict. He said that the money the teachers had lost should be recovered, and that the fear of being fingerprinted was the union leaders' problem. He and many of the other teachers had nothing to fear from the police. He added that collecting fingerprints is a normal practice, and that the union's suspicions reflected its paranoia about the police. As this man spoke there were angry calls of protest from union supporters, and he progressively raised his voice. The shouting did not stop when he finished, and a union spokesman took the microphone to counter his arguments. Many teachers appeared quite bothered by the show of temper and bent their heads to concentrate on their lunches or the papers on their desks. The whole episode was over within fifteen minutes because only two other speakers seconded the arguments of the gym teacher, each in a more conciliatory tone. A vote was called for by the union, and by a small margin the police were kept out. Many teachers abstained.

The Otani local is quite a different matter. About eight teachers are regarded as union people and year after year they rotate among themselves the key union positions in the school. Elections are held, of course, but no other candidates step forward. Occasionally the union leaders can gather a majority of the faculty to their position, but just as often their voices fall on deaf ears. Many teachers hope to remain neutral and many are simply disinterested. All of the younger teachers, the four gym teachers, and perhaps ten of the older teachers are opposed to the particular union people in their school, but

not necessarily to the union itself. One of them had been a moderate
union leader in the high school he had taught at before. Otani's principal, the Mr. Tanabe mentioned earlier, had the respect of most of
the faculty for his outstanding character and dedicated service to education. The union leadership could not regularly move against him
and be certain of faculty backing.

There are no political posters in Otani's faculty room, and requests for volunteers for outside union activities generally fall on
deaf ears. The union leaders are firmly committed to their cause, and
among their number are perhaps five dedicated Communist Party
members, but their influence over the rest of the teachers has been
on the wane. An assertive stance often isolates them, yet they persist in their work and at times succeed in gaining influence for their
ideas. Adept at public argument, they are ideologically committed
and convinced that conflict is necessary if they are to persist.

Schools that select centrist union leaders are not interested primarily in opposing the union, but in staying at a safe distance from
its extremist tendencies. Sakura has such a union. There are several
activists in the school, but they are not allowed to gain leadership of
the union. They participate at the city level. Sakura chose as its
union leader a mature, respected teacher with political acumen.
Union activities in the school are minimal, but the head of the local
is busy attending citywide meetings and conveying requests for support to his school. Periodically he will state that he must have faculty support for some union activity because his credibility or the
school's credibility is getting low with union headquarters.

Sakura wants to seem cooperative because along with other night
schools it is campaigning through the offices of union headquarters
to kill an Office of Education proposal to consolidate all night schools
as a result of declining enrollments. Indifferent to many political
issues but keenly interested in this matter, the faculty participates
in union activities at the city level to gain points. One evening, I was
shocked to hear that the students were all being taken to see the
movie *Mary Poppins*. Why this complete change in program? Because Sakura's teachers were going to City Hall to join a sit-in at the
Office of Education. Many said the issue did not interest them, but
they wanted to appear supportive in order to preserve their school's
place in union deliberations. It should be noted that night schools
and vocational schools are ranked lower than academic schools as

workplaces by teachers. Such schools more regularly have complaints with the administration and are therefore more in need of union leverage.

Elite schools generally have the least active union locals. Nada has no union at all. In several of the top prefectural public schools there is virtually no union activity. Assignment to an elite school is typically a reward for long, loyal service as a teacher, and such schools give teachers less to complain about. The injustices of society seem remote. If anything, union reform efforts threaten the busy order of elite schools.

Among Kobe's many high schools, there are four or five union castles and about as many dormant locals. The majority resemble either the Sakura case of cautious nonpartisanship or the Otani case of unresolved but limited conflict.

As a mass movement, the JTU in Kobe and elsewhere is considerably weaker than its near universal enrollments would indicate, yet its leadership is aggressive, well-organized, dedicated, and experienced. Its presence is of enormous consequence to most public high schools. The union highlights the political choices before teachers and counterbalances administrative authority. With its presence a large element of instability and intrigue is added to faculty relations.

## The Faculty's Role

Confrontation between administrations and unions in many schools has given faculties a central role in decision making and in resolving deadlocks. The faculty meeting is the central forum where differences are aired and decisions made. In this respect, public high school faculties are indeed democratic in practice as well as in theory. The presence of union opposition has established this situation.

Open conflict resolved by a majority vote is uncomfortable to Japanese, however, for it activates friction and animosity, and it creates winners and losers within a group that must work together.[10] Although national political mechanisms have been democratic since 1945, small-group and institutional decision making in Japan has been conducted principally by other processes that seek to put a har-

10. The characterization of Japanese decision making as consensual has various exceptions, but it does point to an ideal that is important.

monious face on the formal moments when decisions are made. For Americans, democracy began and still thrives best at the grass roots level; but for the Japanese the procedure of voting to settle issues is an uncomfortable, foreign practice in face-to-face situations. Voting to settle conflicts in schools occurs as a last resort. It signifies that prior consultation, consensus building, compromise, and established authority have not worked well enough to give a unified face to faculty meetings. Democratic processes are not idealized, and though not directly to blame for conflict, they appear to some teachers to encourage political division. Majority rule is sometimes relied upon, but its application is taken as a sign of internal strife. The fact that it is resorted to at all distinguishes decision making in high schools from most other group situations in contemporary Japan.

The weekly faculty meeting can be limited to information exchange and general coordination. Teachers are normally circumspect in offering opinions. The logic of an opinion is important, but so is the social logic of mutuality. In Japanese groups the ideal of mutuality in decision making is as follows: senior authority figures take a low posture until all opinions are coaxed from the group, and only then do they articulate the essence of the group's composite view and their own opinions. If consensus has not been reached, more meetings, some off the record, are held until it is achieved. Such a process depends on restraint, trust, patience, flexibility, and mutuality. It means that a minority (even one person) holds a powerful veto. Discussions conducted in this manner are primary indications that, by traditional Japanese standards, the group is united and healthy. Contrast this ideal with a process characterized by little prior consultation, inflexible public argument, the leadership taking sides, and resolution attained by vote. Winners and losers are produced. This is what occurred in the Yama fingerprint episode, and it is the pattern in cases where faculties are openly divided. The actual range of decision-making processes among schools is very wide.

The ultimate focus of school-level power is nevertheless the weekly teachers' meeting. If the teachers are supportive, the principal runs the school. If the union leadership is aggressive and supported by the majority of teachers, it can control the school. If neither side has a clear mandate, then faculty meetings can become arenas of considerable maneuvering. Both the administration and the union leadership must submit proposals and try to gain support among the faculty at large. Behind-the-scenes scheming, lobbying, and politicking then become active.

Neither side can sustain significant power if its margin of victory is persistently small because the alienation of the losing "near majority" causes great problems of compliance of goodwill and cooperation. Over time, simple majority rule is not sufficient to keep schools functioning well. Even hard-nosed Japanese teachers do not take well to the repeated application of a majority rule principle. Votes must regularly be followed by efforts at compromise and fence mending if schools are to work well.

More to the point, however, is the fact that in most high schools neither the union nor the administration commands any great or extensive faculty loyalty. In such schools, the faculty response to particular issues is often unpredictable. Both the union and the administration can readily lose support by going too far. Principals are sometimes willing to avoid implementing Office of Education policies that are not popular, and union leaders may do the same for union policies.

Centrist leadership often focuses attention from divisive political issues to matters of the school itself. A school-centered perspective puts education and students above politics, decries disunity among teachers, seeks a comfortable faculty atmosphere, protests the interference of outsiders (union and administration alike), and claims the uniqueness of the school's problems.[11] This is coupled to a goal of enhanced school autonomy. The reach of union and administration into school affairs is best limited by faculty leaders who seek to avoid internal polarization. Greater autonomy is a means of managing political conflict, the sources of which are largely outside the school and even education itself. Political neutrality and school independence are never absolute, however, but are matters of nuance.

Political party membership is not extensive among teachers. Their daily work environment also encourages a nonpartisan attitude because the order of the school requires cooperation within a varied faculty. Intensely held opinions should be kept private. The heated national debates about education seem rather abstract and simplistic when compared with the concrete realities of working relations in

11. Singleton (1967), e.g., reports the case of a teacher taking an office in the union local out of duty to the school, despite a personal repugnance for the union.

a school. In general, the lower levels of institutions have a sense that what is practical derives from shared, immediate experience in the work context. High level directives, administrative or union, seem intrusive and misguided, especially because they come down through politicized organizations.

Whatever the source of disagreement, the general and the particular usually become entangled in the labyrinth of faculty politics. A major disturbance among Otani teachers is a case in point.

The junior class trip is an ancient and venerable custom in Japanese high schools. Otani's junior class goes skiing, and the event is symbolically enriched by the fact that everyone, all the supervising teachers and second year students, participates. Ostensibly a voluntary matter, not participating is, in fact, tantamount to breaking the unity symbolized in the event. The fact that scholarships are provided to students who cannot afford the personal costs involved exemplifies the desire for full participation. Often the principal himself goes along.

A few weeks before Otani High School's junior class trip in 1975, the volleyball coach confronted the weekly teachers' meeting with the unusual request that the juniors on his team be excused from participating. His team had a chance to win the prefectural championships, he explained. But if his players went skiing, he feared they would lose condition, miss critical training sessions, and be exposed to the chance of accidents. He said team members themselves wanted to stay home and practice. The coach reminded his fellow teachers that the school rarely enjoys athletic success. A victory would boost school morale, especially as his players were already gaining respect as a Cinderella team because of their shortness.

Initially, no strong objections were raised. It was an unusual request, but so were the circumstances behind it. But then a member of the union's steering committee rose and expressed extreme opposition. A very bad precedent would be established, he thought. The team would simply have to do its best in the circumstances as they stood.

Many of the forty-odd teachers at the meeting were greatly surprised at this response. The propriety of the coach's plan, once questioned, did seem debatable; but then, among fellow teachers many debates are publicly avoided in the name of good relations and cooperation. The abstract issue of right and wrong may have been cloudy, but the social-structural relation of the parties to the emerging dispute was clear to all.

The union activists and the sports coaches are more regularly opposed than are any other groups on the faculty. Among the teachers who stay after school, gym teachers are the most notable. Their jobs require and encourage close contact with students in extracurricular activities. Even most of their weekends are tied up in school activities. They tend to be enthusiastic about school spirit, teamwork, and the idea of sharing more with students than just academic subject matter. In short, gym teachers personify a deep involvement with students, and in most schools they are hostile to the union. At Otani, a handful of academic teachers normally join them in staying after school. This total group is close to the principal, Tanabe, both personally and in terms of educational philosophy. This was the true rub.

The volleyball teacher, as part of this group (and as an avid skier to boot), is normally a keen supporter of the junior class trip. The members of the union steering committee, on the other hand, usually show little enthusiasm. But the antagonism felt between the two sides over the years apparently caused the union leadership to forget its usual stance on the issue of voluntary participation in extracurricular affairs. The irony was compounded by the fact that it was the union leaders who were strongly defending the importance of full participation—an ideal at the very heart of Japan's well-known proclivity to group solidarity, which under most circumstances leftists vehemently criticize as a buttress for conservatism.

Considered in the overall context of faculty relations, the union leaders' opposition was not only a reversal of their usual ideological stand. It was clearly a partisan act (rationalized in the name of faculty unity), and in this sense it was perfectly consistent with the persistent matter of antagonism within the faculty.

The volleyball coach continued to ask that his request be treated as exceptional. He urged a pragmatic approach, saying that if there was a principle involved, it was the good of school and the team, no more and no less. What was known of his daily commitment to students and extracurricular activities lent power to his request, just as the tendency of the union's leaders to partisan politics weakened their assertion of the principles of full participation and unity.

Many teachers at the meeting were not able to sort out all the an-

gles immediately, but political allies of both parties were quick to
see a fight, and among them the argument became heated. The principal avoided entering the dispute and adjourned the meeting before
any voting was called. Over the next week, teachers could speak of
little else. As the impasse became more and more apparent, the principal astutely offered to mediate. He proposed a private meeting in
his office between the coach and the head of the local. An open vote
would be too close to predict and too divisive to risk, he reasoned. In
proposing mediation, he acknowledged the good intentions of both
sides (a mild piece of managerial hypocrisy). Having thus allowed
the union to save face, he resolved the immediate issue in favor of
the coach, as was generally expected. But he accompanied his action
with a strong pronouncement supporting the union leadership's
point about the value of full participation in school activities. It was
this aspect of the total imbroglio that he was particularly interested
in from the start, and he wanted to get mileage out of the union's
mistake.

Political and ideological qualities of the school surfaced in this series of events. Note how political ideology, faculty animosities, school
norms, and the necessity for compromise and cooperation all inter-
sect and affect one another. In events like this we can see the way
the school context serves as a prism, transforming national issues
into outcomes that fit local conditions. This is a process of domestication, one that transforms the great ambitions of public life into
school-level compromises. The domestication of politics and ideology is a variable process responsive to the distinctive faculty relations within each school.

## Larger Conflicts

The incidents considered so far have been exclusively local in origin,
but periodically the entire national system is rocked by a power
struggle between the Ministry of Education and the JTU. Initiative
then has belonged primarily to the ministry, which has moved to
tighten administrative authority in various ways that threaten the
union. Aptitude testing, a teacher rating system, and the introduction of courses in morals have all been ministry-introduced changes
that were finally opposed by the union in school systems across the
land. Generally, in large cities, aggressive changes coming from the

conservative camp have failed or been transformed in the process of
execution due to a combination of school board caution and union
intransigence. That is, the changes were not pressed by local officials, and at the school level each faculty screened and redefined
them as they saw fit. Even nonthreatening ministry changes receive
differing receptions at the school level. When, for example, an hour
was set aside in the weekly curriculum for students to pursue a
hobby or leisure activity sponsored by teachers, the Yama faculty
voted to convert the hour to an extra long homeroom period; the
Okada faculty chose to generate primarily academic study topics
(such as foreign languages); and Otani teachers actually produced
leisure-oriented activities as the ministry had intended.

In 1976, after some years of relative quietude in the union-
government power struggle, the Ministry of Education introduced
an administrative change that opened old wounds and appeared to be
a new frontal assault on the JTU's position in each school. School
boards were directed to establish an intermediate supervisory level
in every school. This move, known as the *shūnin* system, would
shift the senior faculty to paid jobs in the administration, which in
turn would mean the loss of these teachers to the union. No new
responsibilities were created, but the union saw the *shūnin* system
as an attempt to extend administrative power deeper into the fabric
of school organization. The extension of salary benefits to the senior
teachers made them subject to administrative influence and challenged the notion that middle-level offices belong to the faculty. Administrative appointment would replace collegial election. Furthermore, despite the ministry's refusal to offer supplemental pay for
extracurricular work, in creating the *shūnin* system it established
a selective system of extra pay that would benefit only the older
teachers.

The ministry's justifications for this innovation were not unrea-
sonable. The number of middle-aged teachers had increased considerably in the seventies, but the number of openings for promotion to
principal and vice-principal had expanded very little. The traditional
capstone of a male teaching career, the public recognition and status of a principalship, was a receding possibility for many deserving
teachers. Their morale was down. The *shūnin* job was presented almost as a consolation to those unable to achieve the dignity and
status of a principal's position. It was also argued, again with justi-

fication, that the middle management level was weak, unpopular, and increasingly the source of inefficiency and friction in school organization.

Teachers with whom I spoke in Kobe confirmed both the union's fears and the ministry's rationale, and some added further observations. The real meaning of the change would depend primarily on the administration-union situation in each school. A de facto *shūnin* system was already in place in schools with a strong principal, whereas in schools where the union was strong, this innovation would not shift the balance of power. They also doubted that the high costs involved in political strife would justify the benefits of winning or losing to either side.

The pattern of opposition and implementation across the land was itself quite varied. For one thing, union strength is not the same everywhere. In seventeen prefectures, all largely rural, less than half of all public school teachers belong to the JTU. In these areas, offices of education are strong and closely aligned with conservative policies. The union is thoroughly entrenched in the nation's metropolitan areas, and many of these, like Kobe, had opposition camp mayors in the seventies at the time of the *shūnin* issue. Finally, there are prefectures where a strong JTU confronts an equally determined conservative board of education. These areas witness the greatest conflict. The point is that no one locality, Kobe or any other, can be treated as typical in the larger political conflicts in education.

Within days of the ministry directive, the *shūnin* system was confirmed and established in a few rural (conservative) prefectures. In others, where the union was strong, no progress had been made toward its institution even in 1979. Where school administrations sought relatively harmonious relations with strong unions (especially true in cities like Kobe), the offices of education worked out responses that essentially allow schools to avoid compliance with the ministry's directive. Tokyo, for example, announced it would establish the system only with the agreement of the union, which was, of course, not forthcoming. Hyōgo left the choice up to the individual schools, saying in effect that no change was necessary. Where strong unions and determined offices of education confronted one another, such as in Hokkaido, Fukuoka, and Kagoshima, a drawnout period of protests, strikes, punishments of strikers, and police raids on union headquarters punctuated the gradual setting up, school by school, of the *shūnin* system. Three years later, a handful of union castles were still holding out in these prefectures.

The dates and styles of school board decisions on this issue also varied. Most prepared the way by privately consulting with the union. Those that moved quickly to execute the ministry's directive, however, were offices of education that chose to challenge weak unions. The amount of time that elapsed between school board decisions and actual implementation at the school level also varied, presumably in relation to the degree of behind-the-scenes union resistance and the complexity of the compromise process. Strikes also differed in intensity, number, duration, and degree of teacher participation. In some cases, they seem to have been staged more for the benefit of national JTU headquarters than to stem the tide of change. The administrative punishments also varied greatly. In a few instances virtually all striking teachers received a penalty in their paychecks, but generally only leaders were penalized. In some places they were even arrested.

The *shūnin* crisis, the greatest conflict in education in a decade, ended up as one more stalemate. Ministry of Education initiatives varied so greatly that no winner could be declared. Prolonged conflict was limited to a small number of prefectures. Careful compromise, partially disguised by more aggressive public postures, was the outcome in other places, like Tokyo, Osaka, and Kobe. Only where the union was weakest did the new system go into place almost overnight. If we remind ourselves that the majority of teachers and students belong to urban areas in which such autonomous compromises are worked out, then we can conclude that the *shūnin* battle was indecisive.

## *Summary*

This chapter has sought to explain the overall political situation within high schools, a situation far more complex than the national polarity between left and right would lead us to think. Although the postwar political and ideological struggles for control of Japanese education have significantly affected the administration of schools and the quality of faculty relations, they have not transformed either instruction or the routines of high school education.[12] Several reasons for this can be cited. The political power struggle in Kobe and in Japan's other large cities is at a stalemate in education. It is an acrimonious stalemate, to be sure, but it is also increasingly tiresome to teachers. Neither the Ministry of Education nor the JTU has been able to resolve effectively the great policy problems of Japanese public education because neither can firmly implement its ideas in a majority of schools. The occupation's fear of a resurgent nationalism has not occurred, nor has the union's greatest worry about schools becoming autocratic. Union strength is the crucial reason for this outcome.

On the other hand, many high schools have regularly been thrown into turmoil by political squabbles, and as a result faculties have learned to make their own adjustments. The power of the faculty itself has increased under these conditions, and centrist leadership has emerged. The school versus "outside politics" has become a major issue, with the order and community of the school as values contrary to those espoused by outside political forces. Further, an emphasis on faculty compromise and cooperation works to soften the impact of hardened ideological positions. In stark contrast to national educational debates, faculties downplay ideology in their search for ways to retain school organizational integrity and autonomy.

Working as they do within one of Japan's most politically and ideologically divided institutions, most high school teachers have come to criticize both the Ministry of Education and the union. Some openly express nostalgia for the spirit of the harmonious traditional school, while a few cynics view education as a falsely glorified factory rather than as an institution creating any sort of political value.

The educational policy of the occupation was itself political. The Americans sought the development of independent citizens for a new Japanese democracy. Student-centered education, personality

---

12. I believe Cummings (1980) has seriously overemphasized the JTU's role in democratizing Japanese education because he credits it with a greater degree of local influence and teacher support than it actually has. Thurston (1973) and Duke (1973) evidence the same tendency. What is certain is that the union has succeeded in blocking or neutralizing most right-wing moves originating in either the Liberal Democratic Party or the ministry that are aimed at significantly altering the power balance or the ideological content of Japanese education.

development, education for democratic citizenship were key catch phrases; and independence was to be fostered by coeducation, school clubs, student government, classroom discussions, and learning by doing. The basic principles in the American approach were decentralization of authority and extension of greater independence and flexibility to teachers and students. It is worth noting that although Japan today is held up as the model of worker participation in industry, it was the Americans who were seeking an analogous kind of participatory schooling in Japanese education.

The union has certainly been in favor of administrative decentralization and greater independence from government authority. Yet it seeks to replace them with its own authority. The American ideal of political neutrality for schools proved terribly naïve. American education at the time was not unionized, and American unions were not as ideologically left of center as the Japan Teachers Union. Nor was the American model of democratic education oriented to major social change; rather, it was for the preservation of an institutional status quo in a satisfied democracy. But the same ideals of progressive education were virtually revolutionary in Japan in 1945.

The meaning of these ideals had been thoroughly reshaped in Japan by 1975. Political conflict had become routine. School faculties had learned to gain autonomy by playing left and right against each other. In doing so, they preserved their own well-developed democratic processes of decision making. School autonomy raises the value of community and order, the opposite of political squabbling, within schools. Individualism is not encouraged, however, and student democracy is altogether a separate matter. Good citizenship as a goal of instruction is clearly desirable, but it remains the duty of teachers to provide this through guidance and firm control. Efficient pedagogy in crowded classrooms requires that instruction center on the teacher, not on the students. Democracy is indeed a mercurial quality in such complex circumstances.

In political debates, the American model has been dismantled and used piecemeal to serve partisan ends that bear little relation to the conceptual foundations upon which it was constructed. To the degree that faculties achieve autonomy they establish the dominance of a different model, one that weds the traditional norms of schooling to exam-oriented efficiency. What we are facing, then, is a subtle and multilayered arrangement by which schools and students are buffered—mostly by the instructional practices of the faculty— from the direct impact of political influence. A relatively apolitical education is thus produced by a highly politicized environment.

# 8

## Instruction

The students I had before me this morning were clean, orderly, well dressed, with habits and methods of work which
would pass muster anywhere. Indeed, I might go further
and say that, in his eagerness to learn, the Japanese student
is ahead of his compeers in other lands. The only difficulty
in teaching him is that he does not know how to work by
himself, that he wants to be passive in the classroom rather
than active, receiving all from his teacher, as far as possible without mental exertion of his own, and that he has a
confidence in his notebook which ultimately ruins his
memory.

ARTHUR LLOYD
*Everyday Japan*
(London, 1909)

To Japanese students, sitting in class is the most basic experience of high school. And to their teachers, classroom instruction
is the essential responsibility and challenge of their profession.
What occurs in class, how teachers teach, what is taught, and the
implicit messages about knowledge and thought are all of great interest, especially in light of the other factors that shape high school
education. The ideologies and theories and pressures and intentions
of and for education affect students most directly in the mundane
realities of classes and coursework. Frankly, sitting in class day after
day I found it hard to believe that such a monochromatic and monotonous kind of reality could inspire so much intellectual fervor and
political heat.[1]

Wada, a young social studies teacher, was lecturing to his ethics
and society class at Okada one day about the Protestant Reformation. The following is a brief synopsis of his lecture, which lasted
the usual fifty minutes.

1. I spent over one hundred hours in classes during my field study. Descriptions of
Japanese high school instruction apparently do not exist in the literature on Japanese
education.

Japan had a "mini-renaissance" during the Warring States Period in such cities as Sakai, Hakata, and Kyoto, but we never had anything like the Protestant Reformation. The changes in Buddhism during the Kamura Period were not comparable. The Reformation was caused by the power struggle between Germany and the Roman Church. Church power was based on money, and as the power of various states grew in the fifteenth and sixteenth centuries, Rome's authority declined. France and England had unified governments, but Germany was divided into small territories. Rome borrowed heavily from the German merchants. These merchants made profits on inflation, as they always do. Rome also collected much money in Germany from the faithful by selling them promises that their sins would be forgiven. The Germans resented Rome.

Luther in his famous Ninety-five Articles wrote against the authority of Rome and for the authority of the Bible, which had been translated into the native German language and published by the Gutenberg Press. Luther emphasized belief, an internal feeling, and said external practice was less important. He said religion had nothing to do with a person's social status. He was a social revolutionary who fought feudalism. Work is an expression of God's "grace." This idea liberated individuals from feudalism. In the Middle Ages, people were subjected to outside authority, but Luther emphasized the individual's conscience and awareness. This is one basis of European individualism.

Religious faith is hard to understand. This religion relates to freedom. It is about freedom from feudalism. Now all of you sometimes wish you could avoid school or not wear your school uniform. You dream of a kind of freedom. At university, a friend said to me once, "When there's too much freedom, life is meaningless." He was referring to the absence of pressure on university students. The freedom of the Protestant Reformation was about the idea that external pressure was not good, but that freedom from outside authority was accompanied by internal desire and personal meaning. The individual was the source of authority. It is difficult for us Japanese to understand that religion is a crucial aspect of the European emphasis on freedom.

To get back to the historical situation, the farmers were suffering greatly from class and status oppression, and out of their desire for a better life, they followed Luther's ideas. Thus Protestantism became a weapon of class struggle, but Luther was more for religious revolution than social revolution. He thought God had made society so it was unnecessary to change it. The farmers were disappointed, because they wanted a change in the basis of productive relations.

During his lecture, Wada stopped once to call on two boys at the back of the room who were talking. Catching them by surprise, he asked them how Rome got money from Germany. Both stood up sheepishly with heads bowed. The first said, "They sold milk," and the other answered, "They squeezed contributions out of them."

Wada did not ask students any other questions during class, and although he wrote some historical terms on the blackboard, they were largely the same as in the textbook, and most students took few notes. In essence, he was telling them his understanding of this important but somewhat exotic event, and presumably they were going to listen and learn. Okada students were eager to be accepted at good universities.

Wada's mixture of Marxist history and comparative thought was intriguing, and I found his lectures among the most interesting I encountered during the year. Clearly, he was keenly interested in history and ideology and wanted to pass on to students what he had recently studied at university. I compared his presentation with the textbook treatment of the Protestant Reformation. The textbook gave the subject a page and a half, in which it mentioned Luther and Calvin, the sale of bans, the Ninety-five Articles, individual faith versus church authority, the Bible, direct faith, and work as "God-given"—and all this as the foundation of modern individualism and capitalism. Economic causes for the Reformation were not discussed, nor was the meaning of words like "freedom" considered.

Wada was clearly teaching with considerable independence from the text, and his lectures reflected his politics. In a course devised by the Ministry of Education to bolster the "moral" sense of students, Wada was offering a portrait of Protestantism as an event in the progressive history of European class struggle.

Examples of this kind of instructional independence are rare, not because senior teachers or administrators are breathing down the backs of teachers (at least not in Kobe), but because most teachers design their lectures with only entrance examinations in mind. Students in Wada's class were not taking many notes. They seemed to realize that his interpretations of history would not help them pass the exams, and they probably complained about this among themselves. What they wanted were facts to supplement those in the textbooks: the teacher's job is to supplement and clarify the basic material.[2] Wada actually was keeping pace with the textbook in his lectures. In academic high schools, only by recognizing the centrality of the textbook do teachers retain significant pedagogical authority.

Obviously, instruction is profoundly influenced by the related

2. Television, which serves this purpose and is a common part of elementary classroom instruction, is not used at the high school level.

textbooks. Teacher coordination, both within and between grade levels, depends on every instructor covering essentially the same material at the same accelerated pace: today the Renaissance, tomorrow the Reformation, and Friday Kepler, Copernicus, and Galileo. Such an encyclopedic survey approach would be extraordinarily burdensome on teachers without the vehicle of textbooks to present the key statements and the bulk of the information. Wada is unusual, also, in his willingness to prepare in detail an independent discourse.

Faculty diligence often takes other forms. Some teachers spend time researching past entrance exams to pinpoint the most common questions in order to better guide student preparation. Others study particular tangents. An extremely serious English teacher once blurted out to me when drinking together, "I know I can't speak English, and your presence in school embarrasses me, but I study the fine points of English grammar, and this is more helpful to my students. They can use it on the exams."

Keeping up with the textbook leaves little time for classroom debate, or for considering the contemporary relevance of a topic. Discussions are inherently inefficient if information loading is the central goal. Other factors, such as large class size and profound reluctance by most students to express their opinions before a group also inhibit discussion. Japanese students prefer the comfort of passive and relatively anonymous listening to active participation.

A number of Kobe teachers actually tried to hold discussions during my visits to their classes. The results were quite instructive. Typically, the teacher would ask a question and wait for volunteers; getting none, he would call on someone; the student would stand, make some stab at an answer, and then stand waiting, obviously relieved. If they could not answer, students would stand silently looking at the floor, in some cases for up to five minutes, while the teacher called on others until either an answer was found or the teacher gave up. Typically at this point the instructor would lecture the class on being prepared and on learning to speak out and express themselves.

Noting the discomfort, I made a point of asking after class whether discussions were a regular part of instruction. In every case teachers said they want more discussions, but that it is difficult because students are so reticent. My presence, they said, was the real reason for

the discussion, as it is well known that Americans have a high regard for this kind of teaching. I was reminded of painful times when
Japanese parents had forced their children to play the piano for the
foreign guest. But those children were trained to play, unlike high
school students, who are not trained to debate or to raise questions
or to score points by relating their interpretations. Making students
stand to answer, furthermore, is hardly the way to induce open discussions. The fact is that neither teachers nor their students are
used to the practice. Instruction almost entirely by lecture is a thoroughly entrenched pattern.

American teaching should not be idealized, but crucial differences
remain between Japan and the United States. The American ideal for
high school instruction is that it should stimulate the students' interest and cause them to think, to question, and to want to learn
more. Class discussions are an important part of our strategy to attain these goals. Discussions pull students into the subject, causing
them to reflect. To us, learning to express our own ideas is very important. Independence of thought and open discussion are, of course,
basic necessities of democracy as we understand it. Our stimulus-
response model of teaching also presumes a life-and-death struggle
against student boredom and disinterest. A teacher must be lively
and interesting to be effective because it takes a lot to get high
school students to pay attention to academic subject matter. Our
goal is the stimulated student (attentive, intelligent, and expressive)
who is developing critical judgment (a mark of independence). Discussions are the key technique. Naturally we need smaller classes
and a slower curricular pace to pursue these goals.

Japanese students facing entrance exams do not need as much
stimulation from instructors. They are not going to be examined on
expressive or critical skills, but on diligence in the mastery of facts.
In the Japanese view, expressive and critical skills generally emerge
later and progress gradually throughout adulthood.

In sum, the lecture format in Japanese high schools teaches patient listening. It underlines the authority of the teacher as the superior in learning. Even Wada was teaching about individual freedom
and social revolution through lectures. Lectures eliminate the spontaneous and the personal, but they fit the overall orderliness of Japanese education. Many American students would soon rebel against
this kind of instruction, and there is no doubt that Japanese students

*An English class at Yama Commercial High School*

The boy standing to recite is making mistakes, which the teacher humorously acknowledges. The student's short haircut indicates that he is on a sports team.

find their classes monotonous and largely uninspiring. They are motivated by entrance exams, however, and trained by parents to view learning as a necessary burden in preparation for adulthood. Japanese exchange high school students whom I have met in America, on the other hand, have expressed impatience with American high school instruction as slow and easily sidetracked. The conventional standards by which to judge instruction are indeed very different.

What Japanese students are learning in class besides the subject matter can be enumerated. They learn to sit still for long periods of time. They learn to have their own thoughts, but not to need to express them. They learn to care about details. They may resent the authority of teachers, but they learn to accept them and not to challenge authority. They learn that teachers retain dignity by being serious and by not lowering themselves to their subordinates or trying to be entertaining. Diligence (of the "working long hours" variety) is the most rewarded virtue, and it is strictly an individual matter. Respectfulness is the way to avoid trouble. All of these qualities are highly valued, both in school and in Japanese society in general.

Nor are they totally unfamiliar to Americans, but we have not consistently made them the highest priorities of education, whereas in Japan they are enshrined by tradition and the entrance exam system. The academic schools where students are best at sitting still possess a kind of moral superiority. Note that our top secondary schools are distinguished, on the other hand, by animation in class and individual latitude of interests. The model schools of the two countries, although similar in some respects, are vastly different in their fundamental pedagogical techniques and goals. Even the lively discussions at Nada are drills with exam preparation as the goal, and they come only after the national high school curriculum has been thoroughly digested.

Obviously, the text-centered lecture format has much less utility for students who are not going to college. Yet the one-third of all Japanese students who attend vocational schools must endure the same kind of instruction but without the sense of purpose or reward. With little reason to value such a study regime, their experience of class is one of frustration and boredom. Like so many American students, most vocational students simply endure until graduation. Nor has the pace of study been adequately adjusted for their level of ability. Teachers of academic subjects in vocational schools typically find that even the easiest approved text is too difficult. Required to finish in a year, they must push through the material faster than students can absorb it. The confusion and frustration increase with time. This is an alienating experience that encourages discipline problems. Teachers, too, become embittered. The better ones would like to adapt instruction to the priorities and realities of their students, but only the Ministry of Education, which controls textbooks and curriculum, can make such changes.

## The World According to the Social Studies Textbooks

Textbooks are the pacesetters, and the repositories of what should be memorized. Teachers rely on them, and students make them their bibles in preparation for entrance exams. They set the standards for the nation's high schools, and when university entrance exams are composed, they form the basis for the questions.[3] Further, textbooks, especially those in social studies, are instruments of political socialization.[4]

It is well known that the prewar nationalist government used textboks as major vehicles for indoctrination, and that in 1945 the Americans insisted on a thorough purge of all nationalist messages in them.[5] Since then, the teachers' union has been seeking to have the courts overturn the Ministry of Education's veto power over textbooks.[6] Short of this, the union scrutinizes and criticizes the officially approved textbooks on a regular basis in the way opposing navies shadow each other.

From a more removed, cross-cultural perspective, textbooks are also interesting for what they reveal about the Japanese mind. In format, in their manner of conceptualizing things like society, in their treatment of history and Japan's social problems, and in their logical ordering they reveal how Japanese are taught to think on social and political questions. Social studies by nature reflect the bedrock of civic culture, those basic understandings and national "truths" that lie below the debates and political dissension. They provide an official world view.

Who is responsible for the textbooks? This is an important question, given their centrality to instruction and the political sensitivities involved, yet the answer is far from simple. Several university professors usually serve as authors, and these individuals have typically delegated much of the work to assistants. Editors at commercial publishing houses play an active role in shaping the product from beginning to end.[7] And texts must have Ministry of Education approval. The ministry's veto power is rarely exercised, but this is because publishers are careful to produce textbooks that do not

3. It is useful to recall that all the commercially sold supplementary materials—practice tests, review books, etc.—also rest on the basic official textbooks.

4. Many brief studies and discussions of Japanese textbooks have been published in English, including Karasawa (1955), Adams (1960), Duke (1964, 1969), Miyauchi (1964), Bellah (1965), Sato (1968), Craiger (1968), and Wray (1973). A thorough discussion of the treatment of religion in Japanese textbooks appears in Bonet (1973). Mainichi Shimbunsha (1977) contains a fascinating account of the marketing side of the textbook business.

5. See esp. R. K. Hall (1949), Craiger (1968), and Wray (1973).

6. Bellah (1965), Dore (1970), and Beer (1975).

7. Many retired former Ministry of Education officials serve as advisers in the writing process so that this whole approval process runs smoothly. Mainichi Shimbunsha (1977).

cause offense. Editors select as authors scholars who will not cause problems, and they consult informally with ministry officials and advisors to further assure the eventual acceptance of their offerings. Although high school textbooks do not actually carry the strong imprint of official government attitudes, they have been purged of materials potentially critical of the government's position.[8] And in order to appeal to teachers and avoid the scorn of the union, textbooks avoid topics and style offensive to the left.[9] They are thus characterized by a bland neutrality on key social and political issues.

The variety among texts on the same subject hinges more on subtleties in their degree of difficulty than in differences of interpretive content—and most interpretive variation would be missed by high school students anyway, just as Wada's views of the Protestant Reformation largely escaped his students because they would not help in the entrance exams. All textbooks are competent and compact. Some, however, have a higher density of material, which is the basis for determining their grade of difficulty.[10] Authors also differ in the way they add touches of salt or pepper to subjects, but all avoid stronger spices. Often only the teachers who review the range of available texts, following their changes over time, can taste the subtle differences.

Textbooks are inexpensive paperbacks that students buy and keep. These books are not nearly as bulky and difficult to carry as American high school texts, but they are also considerably less handsome. They are characterized by the same Spartan qualities noted of Japanese school buildings. To keep the prices of books low, publishers avoid color illustrations, use very narrow margins, and strive in other ways to present as much material as possible in a fixed num-

8. One astute social studies teacher explained the changes he has seen in textbooks over the last decade: fewer socially critical observations, less on the war, and more on intellectual history. "Publishers are in business," he said. "They flow along with the ministry's little shifts. We are Japanese and cannot afford not to pull together. We are flexible. We adjust to the realities."

9. Mainichi Shimbunsha (1977) and explanations to me by teachers in Kobe.

10. There are generally at least five or six texts available on each subject every year. Their similarities stem from many common constraints, including price guidelines, set by the Ministry of Education; the approval process; the "traditional" subject content; and broad similarity of teacher expectations. The low fixed price means that specialized or unique texts will not be produced for lack of sufficient volume to recover costs. The small differentiation among publishers therefore centers on the degree of difficulty, the explanatory approach taken in such texts as ethics and society, and cosmetics like the illustrations and graphs selected.

ber of pages. Photographic illustrations appear on more than half the
pages of social studies texts, but they are matchbox small. Some anecdotal material, such as famous quotations and case illustrations,
appear in boxes beside the text, but they are very brief.

Noteworthy is the profusion of detailed maps, charts, and graphs.[11]
In a typical politics-economics text, I counted 93 charts and graphs
in 217 pages. One finds such sophisticated items as a graph showing
rates of expansion of industrial output over seventy years for the five
leading national economies; another illustrating the relation among
the rates of increase of consumer prices, wholesale prices, wage demands, and wage settlements from 1955 to 1970; and a table with
the changing proportion of world imports and exports of various industrial countries between 1950 and 1970. The density of facts is remarkable even in comparison with American university textbooks.
One geography text used by tenth graders has such astounding items
as a map showing the shift of cotton growing in the southern United
States between 1930 and 1960 and another indicating the sources of
iron ore and two varieties of coal for the various centers of steel production in Europe.

In style, the texts are straightforward and easy to follow. A section
on the Italian Renaissance in a world history textbook begins:

> Throughout the Middle Ages, Italy was divided politically, and the bat-
> tle between church and state was central. Struggles ensued, not only
> between cities, but also within them. Monopolizing trade with the
> East, cities like Florence began to flourish by the beginning of the four-
> teenth century due to development of the woolen trade and of finance.
> The prosperous class among the city dwellers began to push aside the
> older ruling aristocracy and assume leadership. In the midst of this eco-
> nomic and social change and political turmoil, the establishment and
> values upon which the authority of the church and the feudal aristoc-
> racy had been founded began to crumble, and new ways of thinking and
> living became possible. Italy was the birthplace of classical culture and
> the home of numerous scholars who had emigrated there following the
> fall of the Byzantine Empire. The culture and way of life based on hu-
> man freedom that had characterized the classical period appealed to
> the hearts of many people. In this way, the basic pattern of the "Renais-

11. The remainder of this section is based on my own reading and interpretation of
twenty-four high school social studies textbooks in various subjects that I found were
either in use, used for reference, or being considered for use in the five high schools. I
also consulted middle school social studies textbooks and those prepared for high
school courses on home economics and personal health.

sance" [this term appears in English] as a revival of Classicism began in Italy's cities.

Fourteenth-century Florence gave birth to Dante's (1265–1321) *Divine Comedy*, which in subject and style crushed the medieval pattern, and from that city emerged Petrarch (1304–1374), the poet who sang of "humanism," and the writer Boccaccio (1313–1375), whose *Decameron* undermined traditional authority.[12]

This passage occupies one page and is accompanied by a map of the political divisions of Renaissance Italy, as well as photographs of Leonardo da Vinci, Michelangelo's *David*, St. Peter's Church, and a madonna and child. In the three pages devoted to the Renaissance in Italy, no less than thirteen leading figures of the period are introduced, the War of 1521–1544 is explained, and the economic decline of the city states is mentioned. Much the same pace, style, and density of facts mark the text from its first page, where Australopithecus, Sinanthropus, and Neanderthal are mentioned, to its last, where Einstein's theory of relativity is touched upon.

The bland taste and encyclopedic quality does not alter the fact that, as with textbooks anywhere, a particular portrait of reality, a world view, is implicit in the recital of presumably objective facts. Unlike educational materials consciously concocted by unfettered authorities for the purpose of ideological indoctrination, textbooks in contemporary Japan evidence much less strident and less obvious sets of biases.

Social studies as a discipline presumes to teach about the real social world, and as such it is the most sensitive discipline politically. The first and most basic quality of Japanese social studies textbooks is their studious attempt to avoid explicit interpretations and evaluations. Extraordinary individuals like Gandhi and Stalin, great events like the atomic bombing of Hiroshima, and powerful movements like fascism or communism receive only passing mention as part of the march of events and historical details. Passions are absent. Judgments are missing. Students are introduced not to the uniqueness or vitality or clash of historical forces, only to a recital of their labels. Totalitarianism, capitalism, communism, and a host of other "isms," including freedom and democracy (which are both "isms" in Japanese), are mentioned but not examined in concrete detail. In the

12. *Sekai-shi* (Tokyo: Yamakawa Shuppansha, 1972). This book lists four Tokyo University professors as authors. (Quotation from p. 157.)

eleventh-grade course on modern politics and economics, the "isms" are explored as abstract ideals, but the comparison is much like one made of different world religions in a United Nations publication. No hard choices are presented, and failings are ignored.

No villains or heroes and no momentous moral or national imperatives emerge. History does not contain good and evil forces. Even the cold war emerges as tepid. The somewhat self-aggrandizing titles that socialist states have selected for themselves are used in literal translation. The writers avoid siding with one or another ideological movement. Given the strong leftist sentiment among Japanese historians, the rightist attitudes of the government, and the great mix of opinions among teachers and parents, the uncommitted and blindly neutral character of the texts reflects a political and commercial compromise for which no alternative exists.[13]

There are, however, certain emphases that have survived the homogenization process. Japan's place in world politics is presented in a light that vaguely favors certain widely accepted perceptions that buttress leftist arguments for a disarmed and neutral Japan. There is a clear implication that history is progressive, and that movements for national independence, popular rights, and democracy are progressive forces throughout the world. People's liberation movements in the Third World are treated as the natural result of modern trends following the end of imperialism. Japan is not allied with either superpower, and her commitments are to the peaceful resolution of problems created by other, more aggressive nations. Neither the United States nor the Soviet Union is labeled imperialistic. What Americans call the Hungarian "revolution" is labeled the Hungarian "riots." The authors, it appears, do not want even foreign countries to take offense.

Nevertheless, the portrait of the world shows many quarrels and clear right or wrong only in the case of colonies seeking independence. Japan's treaty of defense with the United States is mentioned, but this is neither rationalized nor credited with preserving Japan. America does not appear in an unfavorable light, but neither is this

---

13. Teachers' unions in some localities have produced their own supplementary materials, and offices of education sponsor staff and task force efforts to provide materials and other pedagogical aids to teaching like improved experiments for science. What is commercially sound and what in a limited local way is possible are two separate matters.

ally praised. A few texts mention the Soviet occupation of a number of islands claimed by Japan, but most even ignore the longstanding hostility between the two countries. One text says it is unfortunate that politics has prevented Japan from trading more with socialist countries. Foreign policy opinions in textbooks are far more liberal than those of conservative party leaders.

Modern Japan emerges as a benign country seeking good relations with all nations. The goal is peace, and the answer is not stronger alliances or power balances or more principled action: it is the United Nations. Nowhere in the world is the U.N. more popular or viewed with greater naïve optimism. This institution fits the need of Japanese public sentiment for a neutral banner upon which to focus hope. Pictures of U.N. headquarters and explanations of its founding and operations and of Japan's participation regularly appear in social studies textbooks. The U.N. has long been a part of Japan's postwar civic culture, for it helps justify a national sentiment that conveniently ignores or stands above the cold war and realpolitik in general.

If leftist neutralism is vaguely supported by interpretations of the world political situation, the conservative position gains support from the textbooks' portrait of Japan's economic position in the world. Her dependence on outside sources for food and raw materials is underlined. The world's, and especially Japan's, reliance on Middle Eastern oil and the recent problems this has caused are mentioned. Economic statistics are regularly comparative, showing how Japan's performance measures up against those of other industrial countries. The prevailing framework is again international, but in economics the point is reiterated that Japan must export to pay for her import of basic necessities. One gets the impression that export drives are both benign and essentially for self-preservation. By American high school standards, economics, particularly world economics, is given enormous attention. Japan's postwar prosperity, furthermore, is shown to have been achieved and enjoyed by the country as a whole. No special interest groups or classes have had an advantage. Good economic management, hard work, improvement of skills, and cooperation by all, by logical extension, are the essential ingredients of national success.

National pride in accomplishment is balanced with a sense of economic insecurity. Japan's place in the world is not to be taken for granted. The very fact that high school students take half a year of economics testifies to the strength of economic realism in public education. Although many basic concepts are taught, economics is not presented as essentially a set of abstract theories. Emphasis is on the concrete realities of Japan's experience and present situation.

This knowledge teaches the Japanese adolescent a sobriety that reinforces orderly behavior. Few American youths consider international economic issues significant to their own lives, whereas most young Japanese can outline the relation clearly. As I read the textbooks, I sensed an implied corollary: that politics is best subordinated to national economic concerns. A nation dependent on imports and exports cannot afford to allow ideological and political ambitions to rock the boat. Again, by implication, to challenge the conservative establishment that has led Japan to its present economic strength would threaten that prosperity.

One also senses under the surface the assumption that all Japanese share a common set of basic economic interests. National unity is no longer mystical or dependent on the emperor. The ties of tradition are underplayed compared with the prewar approach, but the clear underlying message is that all Japanese are in the same boat as far as the economy goes.

Japan's political system, social problems, and economic structure receive balanced but rather saccharine treatment. The formal workings of her democratic institutions are dutifully outlined. Neither the inside workings of political parties (cliques, financing, and so on) nor the way decisions are actually reached are discussed. Democracy is neat and clean. Working conditions, standards of living, unionization, the size of industrial firms, welfare systems, environmental and urban problems, and more are touched upon and accompanied by scores of graphs and tables, but with little sense of social tension. Certain problems such as pollution are acknowledged, a factual base is supplied, and the topic concludes with a brief comment to the effect that efforts are being made and improvements can be seen. "This is a serious problem for our nation" or "We must all strive to improve this situation" are phrases that alert the reader to those social problems the government has acknowledged and is mobilizing to correct. Other problems—such as the discrimination faced by minorities, the university entrance system, and political corruption— are not mentioned. In sum, the picture is one of a progressive society free of class (and other) conflict, acknowledging the importance of individual welfare. The heavy accompaniment of statistics leaves the impression that improvement is incremental and complex, rather than dependent on political pressure or ideological change. Japan's great economic growth since 1945 has in fact sponsored this kind of social progress, but the role of protest and popular pressure has been more significant than the textbooks imply.

Coping with difficult political issues by omission has its limits. One of the most delicate issues in Japanese history is the causes of World War II. Every textbook I have examined offers essentially the same account. It all began with the Great Depression, which destabilized many societies, including Japan. This led to militarism, which led, in turn, to the invasion of China. Japan's "advance" (not "imperialism") in China was not going well. The impending war between Germany and Russia provided an opportunity to sign a neutrality pact with Russia and thereby allow Japan to break the China impasse by a move to the south. When France fell, Japan seized her possessions in Indochina. The United States was angered by these moves and tried to pressure Japan to withdraw by cutting off oil. Japan could not long endure such economic sanctions and entered negotiations with the United States, but the American demand of total withdrawal from China precluded compromise. Both sides prepared for war, which began on December 7, 1941, when Japan bombed Pearl Harbor.[14]

This is certainly a different picture of the historical events from that held by Americans. Japanese accounts of the origins of World War II in Europe also differ greatly. Germany is portrayed as following a calculated and highly ambitious program of expansion. The implication is that Germany moved out of strength but Japan out of weakness. Pearl Harbor came as the result of an economic embargo applied by a larger and inflexible foreign power. Blame for the war is certainly not simply a question of militarism and ultranationalism, as Americans tend to believe. The portrait of a vulnerable nation reacting defensively to outside forces, especially economic ones, is a central theme in Japan's national self-image.

Japanese nationalism is not emphasized, however. The textbooks scrupulously avoid the language of prewar education. Yet, in the wealth of factual material, one encounters many assumptions long a

14. See also Duke (1969).

part of Japanese popular thought. Society stands before the individual, historically and morally. Civilization and learning are of profound value. Morality is based on a consciousness of social relations, an awareness of being interdependent.

Neither ideology nor law is emphasized as the foundation of social order or meaning. Democracy, national self-determination, and industrialization are recognized forces, but the world is certainly not marked by a great Manichean struggle of ideas or powers. It is, rather, in constant flux and evolution, to which Japan must constantly adapt.

The portrait of society that emerges in the textbooks is largely one of a complex mechanism. It is an engineering model, one with sets of factors interacting systematically to produce finely graded outcomes. The abundance of charts, graphs, statistical tables, and outlines of systems contributes to this impression. This is a society best run by technocrats who know how to adjust the gauges and valves to maintain the optimal mix. The management of society is an economic, not a political science.

As an element in the socialization of the Japanese citizenry, social science textbooks encourage the development of a high level of competence and sophistication both in the facts of civics, history, and geography and in the principles of economics. Most high school students can understand economic and social policy, and because their outlook has been made quite international, they readily grasp the interplay of domestic and external factors. Ironically, the profound insecurity the Japanese feel about their nation's economy, which has persisted despite postwar economic growth, rests on this internationalist foundation. The textbooks do not say that the rest of the world is unstable or fickle in relation to Japan, but it is foreign and beyond Japanese control.

The inspirational side of social studies is largely neglected. Few images of national heroics or social injustices are conjured in the minds of Japanese high school students. No Norman Rockwellesque town meetings are portrayed. Great historical figures stare out, expressionless, at the reader. The strongest and most recurrent images are of the destruction of war (especially Hiroshima), the emperor's announcement of the postwar constitution, industrial growth, and popular demonstrations by labor groups. Each is a fundamental aspect of postwar Japan, but none portrays a romantic ideal.

The final pages of each text contain a statement of common purpose in which a host of platitudes and catch phrases are bundled together. Inevitably, peace, international respect for Japan, prosperity, democracy, respect for the individual, and a rich culture are the goals listed. It is every individual's responsibility or duty to contribute to these ends through study and hard work. The statements typically begin with the phrase "we Japanese" (*ware ware*) and often make the point that the small contributions of many individuals added together bring about improvement. The message is: devote yourself to your assigned role and progress will occur.

The relative balance given various topics is also revealing. Unlike the recent trend in Western social science curricula, little or no attention is given to primitive societies and peoples. The "developing" world is distinguished by political and economic trends that are changing the world order, but the cultural diversity and fascination of South America, Africa, the Middle East, and most of Asia receives little mention. The world is not full of different cultures to be appreciated each in their own right. The West is Japan's preoccupation. The degree of detail that the better high school students must learn on such topics as Greek thought and European geography has been noted. In world history texts, more than half the pages are devoted to European and American history. China and East Asia are the next most significant areas. The rest of the world receives less than one-fifth of the space. It is interesting to note some shift in emphasis between textbooks published in 1972 and 1975. The later editions, published after the oil embargo of late 1973, show small but notable increases in the attention given the Middle East and Africa. Textbooks are regularly updated, so such adjustments are a sensisitve measure of the changing Japanese valuation of different parts of the world.

Textbooks for the ethics and society course have an even more marked weighting toward Western subjects. Typically, European ethical thought, from its Greek and Christian origins to its recent products—socialism, existentialism, pragmatism—receives by far the most attention. Buddhism, Confucianism, and a select group of Japanese thinkers are also emphasized, but no other religious or philosophical tradition receives any attention. The predominance of Western over Eastern thinkers seems very peculiar. Imagine American high school students being raised in public schools on a heavy diet of Sufism and Zen. Of course, the Japanese exist in a world dominated by Western ideas and modes of thought, but even few Westerners know anything about Hegel or Heidegger. The explanation lies in an excessive regard among Japanese academicians for the relatively obscure aspects of a foreign tradition that they regard as dominant. High school students, to be properly prepared for instruction under such teachers in unversities, are burdened with memorizing an impressive but unjustifiable catalogue of foreign thinkers and schools of thought.

There are places in the ethics and society textbooks that discuss open questions. Basic issues—What is a human being? How do we find value? Freedom and duty? God and man?—are raised and then quickly answered. Contemplating such questions does not help on the entrance examinations; and they are difficult to teach given the reluctance of Japanese students to join in classroom discussion. The ethics and society course turns out to be intellectual history.

The textbooks in this subject are interesting for their discussions of philosophical and value questions. Both traditional schooling and prewar Japanese education placed heavy emphasis on moral instruction, and, since the demise of prewar ethics (shūshin) courses under the occupation, the conservative government and much of the citizenry have favored the return of moral education to the curriculum. But union and leftist opposition has been strong in the fear that ethics courses are a wedge for nationalistic instruction.[15]

The social and attitudinal context for the controversy, however, is rather different from how we know it in the United States. Morality for us has been largely an aspect of religion and therefore a matter of personal conscience within the boundaries of law. As such, the family and religious institutions are the proper sources of moral education, especially in a nation that scrupulously separates matters of state from those of church. We also depend on private activities (scouting, summer camps, and Sunday schools) as sources for moral training. Japan has no such set of distinctions. Until 1945, the dominant traditional morality—Confucianism—was regularly and by intention intertwined with the state. Few Japanese religions offer formal moral instruction for the young, and few young Japanese are regularly enrolled in a religious organization. Rather, the schools

15. Adams (1960), Miyauchi (1964), Duke (1964), Sato (1968), and Friedman (1977).

have been a valued source of moral education and discipline upon which parents have habitually relied. This delegation of moral authority to schools, a Confucian pattern, is still the popular inclination in Japan. The occupation's purge of ethics therefore left a serious void, and the Ministry of Education has periodically attempted to revive moral education in a politically benign form.

No aspect of any high school textbook evidences greater variations from publisher to publisher. Nevertheless, no ethical system is presented, and no claims for the superiority of any system are made in any text. The major persuasive effort of the texts is aimed at establishing in the reader's mind the importance of ethics to the rise and perfection of human civilization. The first chapters of various texts attempt to accomplish this by considering a set of questions relating individual behavior and judgment to culture and society.

The language and insights are those of contemporary social science, but the underlying conclusions are at some variance from those typically drawn by social scientists. Here is an excerpt from one rather demanding text approved in 1972.

> What is human? It is said that we are simply animals. To a degree, this is true. We must eat to live, and we use tools and skills for this purpose. We call ourselves human, however, because we are especially different from other animals [a detailed comparison follows] . . . The crucial difference is that humans differ from other animals in the way they do things, in their "human-ness." The question "What is human?" remains.[16]

The tone of the discussion is matter-of-fact, balanced, and rather sophisticated. The Japanese have been leaders for some time in the study of primate behavior, and it would not be surprising to find the next edition mentioning primate sign language. On the other hand, the discussion has not led the student far toward the topic of ethics and society. Rather, the authority of objective science, not ideology, is established as the point of departure. In several earlier texts, the comparison to animals leads to a view of morality based in social psychology. In this one, cultural anthropology becomes the vehicle for establishing the scientific foundation of ethics.

> Where do the differences appear? If we generalize, we say they appear in culture. What we humans create—language, tools, and society—is our

16. Published by Kyōiku Shuppansha. I quote selectively from pp. 21–34 of the 1975 school year edition.

culture. We are each different, but we are not autonomous; we can see that the basis of our cultural existence is its historical development and the fact that we share it, that it is reciprocal and mutual. For example, without the shared cultural understandings of others, our thought and expression would be meaningless.

Such especially human things like scholarship, technology, art, religion, morality, aesthetics, law, and politics are all part of culture . . . What one individual creates becomes the possession of others, and in this manner culture is passed on and developed. At the heart of this process is education. Without education there can be no culture and no growth of humanness. Human beings are animals that receive education.

When we think of education, most of us think only of schools, but education also takes place in society and in families. Throughout life, you are part of the educational process of culture.

Culture is not just to be preserved and learned, it must be created. Schools have a significant role in advancing the growth of humanity (*ningen no seicho*). How should human beings live to best learn and advance culture? A most decisive part of the answer involves what we do in school.

The value of culture is asserted, not questioned; the focus is not on cultural relativity, but on culture in the singular sense, where it is equivalent to civilization. Culture is synonymous with humanity and the basis of prosperity, progress, and social order. It is indeed a good thing. All people presumably value culture for the same reasons and to the same degree that the Japanese do.

We must digress briefly here to underscore the importance of culture or civilization to the Japanese. Only when Japan began borrowing from Chinese civilization via Korea did it acquire its first system of writing. Largely through the medium of written texts faithfully copied and transported to Japan as treasured objects, Japan learned of the richness of Buddhist and Confucian thought, of the sophistication of Chinese imperial administration, and of the glories of the Chinese world. The written word is respected everywhere as the storehouse of knowledge, but especially so in Japan. Writing, texts, and civilization are of a single piece to the Japanese, and the single character for writing and literature (*bun*) expresses this critical relationship. Culture (*bunka*), civilization (*bunka* or *bunmei*), literature (*bungaku*), and learning and the liberal arts (*bungei* and *bundō*) are all linked together. The Ministry of Education is literally the "ministry of *bun*." Many of Japan's historical heroes were people of culture (*bunkajin*), and the government awards prestigious prizes to contemporary culture heroes in the arts and literature. In sum, the textbook's authors have moved the discussion from natural science to a focus on one of Japan's oldest and most elemental social values.

> However much our own thought is individualistic, its expression to our fellow human beings is always going to be part of a particular, historically shaped social context. This means that humans are historical, social animals, and human culture is historically and socially determined.

The discussion turns to the variety of cultures, ancient and contemporary, and the fact that they can only be known through broad study and exploration. The tone is not strident or dogmatic.

> For this exploration to be possible, every one of us living in one culture—as scholars, technicians, artists, politicians, lawyers, and citizens—must consciously focus our energies on the task. And thus to the limits of life itself, we are destined to explore the question of what is human.

This inspiration, based as it is on a vision of society as cooperative, meaningful endeavor, is not an uncommon one in Japan. All work is thus characterized as a form of civilizing pursuit. Just where cramming for entrance exams fits into all this is not clarified.

Undaunted, the authors step closer to questions of ethics and behavior in the next section, which begins with an observation that without the care and socialization of the family, humans would neither survive physically nor understand what is wrong or bad. It is in the family and in other small groups (*nakama*) that we first learn right from wrong. In such intimate relationships we experience the consequences of our behavior and that of others.

> All human beings are born and raised in societies. And they learn to distinguish good from bad, beauty from ugliness, and right from wrong according to the culture created by their particular society's traditions, scholarship, arts, and laws.

One might expect at this point an encouragement of respect for things Japanese, but it does not appear. The text is steering the reader to basic Japanese values without labeling them as such.

The topic shifts to the environment. Culture is defined as a response of human groups to the difficulties of living in a natural environment. Its adaptive value is stressed, and schools are mentioned as one kind of group function that provides adaptive stength. The authors balance the discussion by mentioning that there is much room for change and improvement in schools, and that it is individuals who create such improvements.

> Practices that people do not like about schools can be reformed. Without exception, what you are taught can be given new meaning and form according to your own imagination and your ability to reconstitute what you receive . . . Humans are made by culture, but so too is culture made by humans.

Social change, however, is a carefully restricted realm. Freedom is essentially internal: the freedom to think, feel, and digest ideas as one chooses. Expressing disagreement or acting according to individual conscience is not mentioned. Implicit here is a duty to improve the existing culture, not to challenge or undermine it. In essence, culture precedes and supersedes the individual.

The closest the authors come to cultural relativity and social difference is a brief paragraph on the variety of social units in the world. Students are told that different groups have different cultural characteristics, and that from these differences many problems arise. This rather insipid observation is followed by an equally insipid conclusion: "One most important element of the way humans live is the pattern of activities by which they resolve such problems."

After twelve pages of thus positioning the subject of ethics, the discussion becomes more concrete. Reiterating that groups, large and small, have developed the customs, rules, and laws of society, and that these enable groups to be well organized and orderly, the authors explain that the reason for following these customs and rules is that they contain and preserve the correct, the good, and the beautiful. In the course of a long history, humans have strived to preserve these values by making many customs and laws and by constantly improving them. Yet "whether we want to [follow the rules] or not (*jibun no ki ni iru ka*) also makes a great difference . . . and this depends on whether the customs and rules give people true happiness."

This observation, however vague, reminds one of the Chinese notion of the mandate of heaven, in which a particular dynasty enjoyed considerable authority until natural calamities and popular unrest indicated the mandate was lost. Happiness is the ultimate test of the authority of a particular set of customs and laws, and one presumes that its loss is proper justification for change. A politically neutral theory of cultural/ethical authority appears in embryonic form in these passages.

The question of freedom and responsibility is then addressed directly in several paragraphs containing quite complex sentences that offer with one hand what is taken away by the other.

> In addition to supporting human society as discussed above, there is one thing that cannot be omitted—freedom. Everyone desires to enjoy a happy, worry-free life without hardships. Yet a good social life cannot be established unless we preserve a deep respect for society and for all its members equally. What this means is that we must respect the freedom that provides happiness and removes hardships, and we must preserve the freedom to consider and debate what this freedom is.
>
> When people say that youth loves freedom, what they usually have in mind is an impulsive kind of freedom in which desires are willfully and mindlessly pursued. Yet if we looked closely, often we can also say that such impulsive behavior by youth is involved with a desire to protect the basic conditions of human happiness, namely, freedom. It follows that while recognizing the importance of such impulses, it is also necessary to scrutinize the fundamental situation and work to theoretically refine our understanding of freedom.
>
> We must not forget that the essential nature of some kinds of impulses is vulgar and destructive. The development of freedom must be built on a foundation that does not ignore responsibility to society.

This remarkable section ends with the observation that it is the search for truth, goodness, and beauty that is the basis of progress, and that all mankind is engaged in essentially the same pursuit of objective value. One is reminded of the convoluted balancing of opposing perspectives in Japanese newspaper editorials. What I find notable in this introduction to an ethics and society textbook are 1) the admixture of various sources of value in postwar Japan and 2) that science is the source of intellectual legitimacy.

Underlying these messages, I perceive an inclination that might be termed traditional. Confucian morality is inherently practical and preeminently concerned with the well-being of society. Its stress is on properly ordered relations, and its basic inclination is to a conservative valuation of tradition. This introduction is grounded not in abstract principles or axioms, but in the concrete historical nature of culture and society. Its highest value is civilization, that which expresses a nation's truth, goodness, and beauty. Freedom is not an end, but a means to improving civilization. The essence of civilization is proper social relations, including both respect for differences and respect for tradition. Socialization properly teaches people to be harmonious and cooperative. As members of the national group, furthermore, all should share in the socially generated happiness. Social ethics is grounded ultimately in something greater than the individual. It is not religion, but national tradition.

Yet the modern social framework implicit in this account is a mass society in which family, school, workplace, and nation each have separate functions and different kinds of authority. Individual relationships are fluid and loyalties partial. Social hierarchy, so central to Confucianism, is not discussed, and certainly it is not absolute. Here the ethical in social relations is abstract, rather than particular to the basic dyads of parent-child, husband-wife, and so forth. Democratic institutions can be integrated with others in this kind of society, but they have no prior or higher moral weight.

The various pieces are not assembled in a firm structure, and the manner of expression is more clinical than inspirational. Postwar Japan is rich in examples of the art of making meaning from an eclectic assemblage of insights. Modern science, anecdotal aspects of Western thought, democracy, socialism, watered-down Confucian insights, popular Shinto ideas, and even Christian doctrines have found their way into various institutional efforts to shape an explanation for moral conduct that suits the Japanese without appearing tainted by the excesses of prewar nationalism. The creation of explanatory systems has been much richer in private organizations than in the government for the obvious reason that any public formulation must satisfy a much wider constituency. This I believe explains the anemic quality of ethical thought in the schools today.

Since the war, Japan's official ideology has remained largely in the disassembled and lifeless state in which it was left by the traumas of defeat and occupation. The government has made little effort to resurrect idealism, and it has not sought to mobilize or motivate the people by inspirational leadership. Native values, though increasingly pursued and applauded privately, have not been enshrined by the administration for fear that they will seem anti-democratic or anachronistic. To outsiders and to many Japanese, the leadership of the last quarter century seems embarrassingly dry, pragmatic, and monotonous, the epitome of a secular regime. Under these conditions and with a hostile leftist opposition within education itself, a course in ethics and society such as we have just considered is not likely to have much intrinsic life or dynamic.

Added to this source of blandness is the emphasis that students and most teachers place on exam preparations, not on the broader education of the whole person. The moral thrust in Japanese social studies is therefore so weak as to be insignificant at the high school level.

## *Summary*

The Americans encouraged the growth of social studies in the Japanese curriculum as a key to democratic education. It has become something rather different. The mechanics of democracy and the technical skills of understanding modern social systems are indeed taught quite thoroughly in the textbooks, but the basic democratic values as Americans understand them—individual rights, grass roots initiative, freedom, and social justice—are not emphasized in class. Nor is student attention focused on the issues of Japanese society and the responsibility of citizens to make decisions individually on such issues. This isolation from ideological turmoil is part of a general pattern of classroom isolation from politics.

However politically divided some faculties have become, instruction has remained largely immune to these divisions. What transpires in the teachers' meetings rarely carries into the classroom, and although high school teachers are not strictly monitored in what they teach, those who teach their political views are not a major influence on students.

Students know of the political squabbles among teachers. They are not told about them regularly by their own teachers, but the newspapers regularly describe such problems and carry statements by citizens expressing regret that politics interferes with education. Most parents also criticize striking teachers and point out how irresponsible political squabbling is. Students thus learn to think of politics as rather unseemly and as interfering with getting a good education. In my questionnaire to students of the five high schools, I asked which party they intended to vote for, about their attitudes toward the legality of the Self Defense Forces, and about their general political leanings. None of the minor variations from school to school reflected the political inclinations of their faculties. For example, in spite of the strong Japan Communist Party contingent among their teachers, the Yama students showed no inclination in that direction. In fact, the highest Communist Party support came from Nada students. Despite the JTU position that the Self Defense Forces (Japan's military, limited to defense capabilities by the Constitution) are illegal, Yama students and students in general did not agree. The dominant impression from all five schools is political apathy, or at least student withdrawal from organized politics. Half said they would not join or support a party.

High school instruction turns on the drive shaft that runs between entrance exams at one end and textbooks at the other. Both of these and the overall curriculum are matters outside the control of teachers, faculties, or local offices of education. The Ministry of Education is unable to rule education directly through its domination of local school systems and loyal teachers, but it can in fact control exams and textbooks. The ambition to succeed in education is the ultimate source of discipline. Without the entrance exam competition, neither textbooks nor curricular requirements would be sufficient to keep instruction as strictly focused on the narrow path of encyclopedic learning as it now is.

This raises the question whether the Ministry of Education is sincere in its periodic reform efforts aimed at ending the entrance exam problem. I cannot answer this factually, but I suspect that both the government and the conservative party would shrink from effecting any reform that would permit a general loosening of the vise of competition in which students find themselves. The political right has reason to condemn the excessive studying in which students are sometimes engaged, but it has no alternative form of basic control. That the ministry's dominance is still limited is illustrated by other facts as well. The national flag and national anthem are still prohibited from most public high schools.[17] Indeed, our review of the textbooks indicates that the ideological content of education is best assessed in terms of the crucial omissions and creeping mild insertions to which teachers are sensitive but students oblivious.

17. As if to make their own personal statement in reaction to this, several prominent teachers displayed Japanese flags outside their homes at the time of inviting other teachers to parties during the New Year holidays in 1975.

Another question here is the character of instruction in vocational high schools, where the influence of entrance exams is not strong and where, in Kobe at least, many of the most politically active teachers are located. I could detect no difference in the ideological content of instruction in academic and vocational schools, and questionnaires that I gave students in both kinds of schools revealed no significant differences in their political attitudes. My impression is that classroom teaching in vocational schools is little more politically inspired than elsewhere. Because this contradicts the more general thesis that entrance exam pressures and textbooks shape instruction, further clarification is called for. First, textbooks and a rapidly paced curriculum are also present in vocational schools. Second, although many vocational school students come from the very social class that activists teachers seek to assist, and their lives reflect the discrimination decried by the union, students themselves do not indicate any great enthusiasm to study such issues in school. Further, nonpolitical teachers are inclined to favor improving survival skills over making vocational students ideologically self-conscious. The argument is "Don't compound their disadvantages." Finally, some vocational school students are trying to prepare to enter universities and need all the academic help they can get.

The encyclopedic nature of Japanese textbooks also deserves to be underscored. It colors classroom instruction, governs homework, and becomes the basis for the entrance exam questions. An encyclopedic approach to learning establishes a factual basis for further learning, is politically neutral, and has the virtue of turning out individuals who are relatively well acquainted with many subjects. I was regularly embarrassed to realize that Japanese high school students were learning more about the United States than even many American students learn, and a hundredfold more than we learn about Japan. Yet I also recalled my own high school teachers' comments that we were in school to learn to think, that we could always go to the library to get factual details. By implication, Japanese high school education provides no intellectual roots, it turns out students long on information and short on intellectual understanding.

The Japanese are not, however, a people short on understanding. It seems that school has a different place in the Japanese conception of personal development than it does in our own. We assume that once out of school the individual can collect and master the facts that are practical and necessary. Over and above the basic skills and a certain level of knowledge, it is the analytic ability that we hold most fundamental to schooling. By implication, the Japanese view education differently. Following graduation, sufficient time is available for thought and understanding to mature as a matter of experience.

The comparison involves the relative importance of logic. Logic is the intellectual search for consistency and meaning within verbal domains. Taught well, it sharpens insight and allows early maturation of thought. But Japanese schooling pays little attention to this possibility. Theoretical debates and logical dialogues are simply not part of the approach. Rather, the Japanese seem to confidently assume gradual intellectual maturation that is independent of formal schooling. The crucial source of this maturity is experience of the real working world, something schools cannot offer. We encounter here a basic cultural difference. Schooling in logic is as old as Western civilization itself. By contrast, the Japanese tradition is heavily dependent on mastering foreign subjects and languages. It has long emphasized memorization and imitation. The assumption has been that wisdom would come slowly. A further implication is that the Japanese aim at training good listeners; Westerners aim at creating people capable of independent expression. Certainly wisdom is the product of long observation; logic is the result of vigorous mental activity. Both are important, of course, but educational systems weigh them differently.

A second difference, then, is time. American expectations for nineteen-year-olds differ from those of the Japanese. The Western approach sets a tight schedule in order to produce individuals capable of social independence and critical thought. Our family system, the labor market, and the needs of a democracy all require such a timetable of formal schooling. The Japanese face the unalterable fact of exams, but they have no sense of urgency about independence and maturity of thought. Recall that high school students are still considered children. All of Japanese society is constructed around a slower and more graduated course of personal development. Responsibilities are given later. Independence comes more slowly. Adulthood is not a plateau, but a continuation of development based on experience. From schools, individuals enter companies where further education is a responsibility taken seriously by management.

Japanese high schools are not burdened with the necessity of turning out finished citizens.

This raises a third question: does the less inspired Japanese approach to school better fit the realities of the institution? Americans have had difficulty accepting limits for secondary schooling. We set out to do more than the Japanese. Our ideals and our ambitions encompass much more. We mix math and English with citizenship and driver's education. We favor teacher independence and student choice in a crowded environment. Our ambitions clash with the limitations of mass education processing, with the limits of student initiative and capacity, and with the limits of organization itself. By contrast, the Japanese have created a narrow educational approach with little risk. It seeks to produce high average results in very constricted channels of learning. An encyclopedic approach does not overburden the institution, only the students. Americans have produced the reverse kind of system. Our problems stem not from overworked students, but from confusion and tension over the goals of education. Our teachers are overburdened with a system of contradictory priorities and a student subculture that has not been brought into line. If the Japanese suffer from too much standardization and routine, American high schools suffer from lack of focus.

Finally, we should contrast the rote memorization practiced in the Confucian schools of old and the study habits of modern Japanese preparing for entrance exams. Both have sought to master set bodies of rather lifeless material. In both, the written word—the Confucian classics and the official textbooks—carries great authority. But teachers in the older approach had greater latitude and responsibility to interpret, coach, and exemplify. Their subject matter was moral and political philosophy, not strictly utilitarian facts. The best teachers were aware of the old Chinese saying mentioned in the Confucian analects, "He who learns but does not think is lost."

Important qualities have been lost in the modern approach. What seems unaltered from past to present is the emphasis on a disciplined apprenticeship in which, through arduous study, basic knowledge is memorized. The student is trained first to be a patient, persistent worker, a good listener, one preoccupied with details and correctness of form. Unlike many of their American counterparts, they do not learn a glibness that has little foundation in knowledge. But Japanese students learn to keep their thoughts largely to themselves, even as their minds mature. High school teachers know very well the great issues and contradictory theories of their respective disciplines, but they, too, follow the conventional format and keep matters uncomplicated. Teachers and students are, to borrow Masao Miyoshi's intriguing phrase, Accomplices of Silence.[18]

18. Miyoshi (1974).

# 9

## The Adolescent Pattern

If you would form the tree, do so while it is young.
A JAPANESE PROVERB

E DUCATION's most powerful influence is in the realm of the un-spectacular and the mundane. How schooling shapes the regular habits and life patterns of millions of people is of greater significance than what teachers say about political truth or even how much equal opportunity the system offers. We miss this point for many reasons. The patterning of daily behavior occurs generally below the level of conscious awareness and develops over many years of schooling. It is rarely quantified or even carefully measured, and few society-to-society comparisons of daily behavior are available to highlight what the real differences are. But if we stop to contemplate what teaching every child in a country of 100 million to sit still and concentrate just five more minutes per day would mean for both learning and adult output when multiplied out day after day, year after year for an entire population, we can begin to appreciate the significance of habitual conduct on the general, macro-level results that we categorize as economic or social or political.

In a manner akin to those developed in public health and mass marketing, we can attempt to draw a portrait of the habitual patterns of Japan's adolescent population, using what statistics are available. Fortunately, both Japan and the United States have compiled broad-based data on adolescent behavior in selected matters. What these

271

data boil down to in nearly all cases is either the percentage of an age group that do a particular thing (drink, date, earn money) or their average allocation of time among a variety of options. Comparing such data for two societies and comparing different subpopulations of the same society can be striking when they are put into a social context like the one we have now developed for the high school years.

School is but a major segment of the lives of adolescents. It greatly affects their activities and priorities, yet it is only part of a larger whole. To grasp the total picture, an understanding of adolescent conduct away from school must be added. How do Japanese adolescents spend what might be termed their discretionary time? Do Japanese teenagers have as much autonomy and much the same patterns of friendships, romance, and recreation as Americans do? If not, then what activities dominate their free time, and are the patterns different for the students of our five high schools?

In exploring this topic, we are pursuing insights into the important matters of how Japanese attitudes and behavioral patterns set priorities among such basic social categories as work, family, and leisure. We are also focusing on the social patterns that shape an entire nation. Our survey focuses, then, on the place of family, city, friends, part-time work, romance, and delinquency in the Japanese teenage experience.

## Family, School, and City

High schools fix parameters in the lives of students. At a minimum, Japanese teenagers must be in school thirty-six hours each week, and rarely can they commute from home by train or bus in less than thirty minutes. Discretionary time is thus restricted to several hours during the late afternoon, evenings, half of Saturday, and all of Sunday.

Three quite distinct worlds—family, school, and city—are linked in the lives of most Japanese adolescents. The patterns, priorities, and balances established among them are important determinants of adolescent experience in every country, and differences from school to school are major distinguishing marks of school subcultures.

The contemporary path of human maturation proceeds from family to school, then from school to an adult existence. The modern trend has prolonged schooling and extended the time spent as a ward of the family. As a student advances in school, the hours spent away from school and home gradually increase, and from high school on, time at large in the city increases. This is true in Japan as well as in the United States and Europe. Elementary school pupils generally go straight home, but by high school a significant degree of autonomy has developed. By college, students in Japan typically spend more time wandering in the city than in class, and many no longer live at home. A shifting balance along a continuum of this kind is a basic attribute of the maturation process in all developed societies, yet comparisons in the balance between home, school, and city for high school students reveal interesting national differences.

First, let us compare the general qualities of the three worlds. The family is a place of security and intimacy. So familiar is it that it cannot offer much that is new, unusual, or exciting. The support of parents is, of course, coupled to their authority. Space in Japanese homes is notably constricted. Mothers generally are very attentive, even to their teenagers, but as in most countries relationships carry a high potential for friction because they cannot be fully adjusted to the changing adolescent. The home is also the place where the hard work of preparing for exams takes place. The family sponsors academic achievement.

The city stands in marked contrast. Its streets are lined with interesting shops, movies, restaurants, and other attractions. Coffee houses and snack shops abound—places where friends can sit and talk for hours if they can afford the steep tariffs. If most homes are preoccupied with the student's future and the serious work of study, the city is geared to the immediate and the pleasurable. It is rich in choices, and it offers freedom from parents and teachers. The city provides the unusual—fashions, music, glamour, and excitement that contrast so sharply with the narrowness of home and the drab stoicism of school. But for students to join the throngs of consumers they require money and leisure time. Each morning they join the mass of commuters headed for offices and factories. The school is their factory. Except for homework, they don't need to work late. Many have time to perfect the habits of the urban consumer.

In the eyes of teachers and parents, the city is essentially a temptress seeking to steal the young before they are ready. The city's enticements threaten serious study and thus educational opportunity. Its influence confuses the values and authority taught by parents and teachers. This judgment is not absolute, there is no intention to cloister students, but Japanese parents and teachers certainly seek to limit exposure to the city.

Delinquency occurs largely in the city. Whether the city is the cause or simply the context for it is unclear, but to adult observers, the city spells trouble. The classic intergenerational tug-of-war over the rate at which social maturation is allowed to advance and the equally classic issue of living for the present or for the future are both evaluation frameworks by which to judge the proper balance of family, school, and city in the lives of high school students. Choices about pocket money, club membership, part-time work, *yobikō*, and friendship involve these basic considerations. Clearly, to do nothing but stay at home studying for exams is a long-term strategy that postpones maturation in the urbane pursuits. On the other hand, if an adolescent runs away, he or she is rejecting family and school for the city and seeking immediate satisfaction at long-term expense. Both examples are extreme; a balance is more typically struck in every student's life between the two. As would be expected, there are differences between Japan and the United States, as well as among our five schools, in this respect.

We have already noted that Japanese adolescents are in school sixty days more each year than are their American counterparts. Their weekends are shorter, and Friday nights are school nights. Even Japanese teenagers who are prone to cruising around the city have only one night a week to do so, and because of the short vacations, there are half as many free days and nights in the summer, too.

About 60 percent of the students in Kobe are members of after-school clubs. Some are busy every day in this activity; others only occasionally spend time after school.[1] A 1972 national survey of American high school student participation in extracurricular activities offers some comparative insight, although American students often join several activities on a nonexclusive basis.[2] This survey found that during a twelve-month period the pattern was as follows: 35 percent of American students were involved in some sport or other club; 13 percent were in cheerleading, pep clubs, and the like; 27 per-

1. This is according to my own research with a sample of over four hundred students in the five schools.
2. Fetters (1975).

cent enrolled in drama, debate, band, or chorus; 16 percent joined hobby clubs; and 15 percent worked on newspapers, yearbooks, and other journalistic activities. Although there is considerable redundancy of individual participation in the American figures, the Japanese appear at least as successful with the club idea as American high schools. My guess is that a smaller percentage of American students are regularly involved in after-school activities, but this must remain conjecture given the poor comparability of the two sets of statistics. Exam preparations, more homework, more class hours, and longer commuting time have not, that is, cut very deeply into club participation in Japan when measured against American experience.

There is less doubt about the different uses of time away from school. A 1973 national survey of the hourly allocation of time by sixteen- to nineteen-year-old Japanese for weekdays and Sundays presents a striking contrast to what we know of American adolescent patterns.[3] On a weekday, the average Japanese high school student spends an hour and a half commuting; two hours on homework (boys more and girls less); just over two hours watching television; half an hour listening to the radio; an hour helping at home (boys less and girls more); an hour reading casually; and less than half an hour in social relations with peers outside of school.

The average Sunday pattern for Japanese has the same proportions. On Sundays, Japanese teenagers sleep about two hours longer—a phenomenon familiar to all parents of teenagers. During the rest of the day, they study about an hour longer than on weekdays (three hours for boys and slightly less for girls). Television viewing increases to an average of four hours, and radio listening goes up a bit. Surprisingly, helping at home and casual reading remain unchanged. Leisure and exercise (including club activities, shopping, movies, sitting in a coffee shop, and so on), which account for an average of one hour each weekday, increase to two hours on Sunday. The average time spent in social relations on Sundays amounts to slightly less than one hour. Even if it is assumed that all leisure and exercise activities are with friends, the total time spent outside the house with one's peers on Sunday amounts to only about three hours for boys and two for girls. Homework and television viewing each account for considerably larger proportions of the students' time than do peer

3. Kyōiku Gyōsei Shiryō Chōsakai (1975), p. 35: report of the 1973 Nihon Hōsō Kyōkai survey of high school students' living patterns.

relations, and this is true all week. Total time spent in social relations (excluding exercise and leisure) is but five hours a week,
whereas television viewing accounts for sixteen and homework for
fifteen hours.

The portrait is clearly one of a home-centered existence during the
time not spent at school. Even if we go further and assume that the
commute to and from school is made with peers (this is often true),
we arrive at a division of time between peers, television, and homework that is approximately equal.

Americans, when they think of adolescence, think first of a virtual explosion of peer group activities. Parents expect that their adolescent sons and daughters will hardly be present after school and
during weekends. Parties, jobs, cars, romance, and just "hanging
out" are what we deem natural. Kids "need to get out of the house,"
causing parents to "need to know where they are and what they are
doing." Even on weeknights, our adolescents find ways of getting
out. A study of the teenagers in an Indiana city in 1977 revealed that
47 percent of the boys and 56 percent of the girls were out of the
house between dinner and bedtime at least five nights a week during
the school year. A survey of a larger sample of high school seniors
found 53 percent out on three or more nights a week for fun and recreation.[4] I recall a popular book for parents in my high school days
entitled *Where Did You Go? Out. What Did You Do? Nothing.* The
degree of independence acquired by American adolescents is remarkable by Japanese standards. Not only is the Japanese weekend
abbreviated and spent largely at home, but much after-school free
time in Japan is spent on public transportation. Without their own
cars, with little money to spend (in 1977 the average total weekly
expenditure by Japanese high school students was less that $5), and
with few unsupervised places to go, even those who seek privacy
and independence are not likely to find it.[5]

The time spent studying also contrasts sharply with the American
pattern. The Japanese average of two hours a night plus three hours
on Sunday compares with an American average of well under one
hour per night. Only one in twenty American students spends more

4. These surveys are in Bahr (1980) and Bachman et al. (1980), respectively.
5. Perhaps one in one hundred Japanese high school students has access to a car
and a driver's license. Half of all American high school seniors own a car. Bachman et
al. (1980), p. 174. For Japanese students' weekly expenditures, see Sōrifu (1977), p. 70.

than ten hours a week on homework, and 65 percent report doing fewer than five hours of study at home per week.[6] Our top 5 percent does less homework than the average Japanese!

Our youth spend their time in very different ways, but not necessarily in unproductive ways. Part-time jobs after school and employment during vacations is a hallmark of growing up in America. Only 18 percent of Japan's male high school students and 11 percent of the females have side jobs or work during summer vacations. A recent survey of sixteen thousand American high school seniors found 78 percent holding part-time jobs during the school year, with nearly 34 percent working twenty or more hours per week.[7] A number of American industries, such as fast-food chains, have been built on the assumption of readily available high school student labor, and during the summer our students pour out into many areas of the economy. The shorter Japanese summer vacation is certainly a restrictive factor here. The average duration of a summer job in Japan is just eighteen days.[8]

More significant to explaining these differences, however, are: 1) the Japanese preoccupation with entrance examinations and 2) the implication of low social status that part-time work carries. One-third of all Japanese students attend vocational high schools, yet more than half of all those with side jobs are vocational students. In the United States, middle- and upper-class students obtain jobs rather easily, and our acknowledged problem is finding summer jobs for inner-city and poor youth. Our government attempts to help here. Most American teenagers work for the money, but to middle-class parents it is the experience that is of greatest value. Part-time work teaches discipline, the value of money, and, it is hoped, a respect for labor. Summer jobs have provided the American elite with experiences of physical labor and drudge work that create lasting impressions for many. For all, the experience teaches the value of money and an interest in gaining greater earning power. In Japan, the government's concern is that student employment not interfere

6. Fetters (1975). The Japanese average of fifteen hours per week of homework is also reported by Sōrifu (1977), p. 183, in a larger 1976 sample.

7. Bachman et al. (1980).

8. Sōrifu (1979), p. 264. But this is not all of the story. Consider, e.g., the report in a national student newspaper that the average number of hours per day put in by seniors on exam preparation during the summer vacation was 7.5 (*Gakuen News*, July 15, 1978).

with studies, cause bad health, or open the possibility of moral corruption. Such jobs carry essentially negative connotations. Government efforts are directed at assuring that teachers do an adequate job of screening and supervising those who work. These differences are consistent with the different interpretations in each country of adolescent maturation and the importance of educational achievement. Working students are anomalous in Japan because they are mixing goals and allegiances and because they are spending too much time in the city.

Recreational time with one's peers is almost a residual category in the Japanese case. At the most, it averages about fifteen hours per week if commuting and club activities are included. In United States surveys, no inclusive category of peer group activities is used, therefore precise comparisons are not possible. Nevertheless, there is no question that a major difference between the two nations exists. Nearly half of all American seniors report going on at least one date weekly, and parties on weekends are commonplace in the lives of an even larger percentage.[9] Neither activity would engage as many as one in twenty Japanese adolescents in any week. American teenagers spend much weekend and vacation time together. They stay overnight regularly at homes of their friends. This rarely happens in Japan. I would estimate peer recreation time in the United States to average more than thirty hours a week, double the most liberal estimate for Japan.

These basic differences in the use of discretionary time reflect different priorities and differing cultural formulations of what adolescence is and should be. First, the Japanese do not dwell on adolescence as a distinct period in life as we do. They do not see it as a very peculiar point in time, when many of the prerogatives of adulthood are gained but few of the responsibilities are shouldered. Adolescence is not a period marked by much free time. Rather, it is the critical period before exams, the time when hard work is expected and rewarded across generations. Parents, teachers, and most students recognize the need to buckle down.

There is, indeed, a youth culture in Japan. It is distinguished by much the same fashion, music, and hero worship that Americans know. In fact, a great deal of it emanates from the United States, and

9. Bachman et al. (1980), p. 22.

homegrown additions follow the imported trends. The difference is the place of the youth culture in the lives of the young. Japanese students go to school in uniforms, not in school fashions. They listen to records at home and not at parties. Some go to rock concerts, but the music is imported, not the creation of their peers. Although they do most of the same things and share the same enthusiasms, they devote less time to such activities. The Japanese youth culture is a largely foreign-born dream world that is squeezed in among activities that do not sustain it.

To make their own youth culture work, Americans need money. They are very active consumers who pay with their own money. By age sixteen they are also quite mobile. Access to cars gives them the power of choice, autonomy, and privacy. They create many of their own fashions. They hold their own parties, fix up their own cars, and start new fads. They are constrained by family and school to a degree, yet compared with the Japanese they possess the resources for great independence of action. American adults, furthermore, are distinctly, painfully ambivalent about this independence and quite ineffectual in directing it. Our cultural values compel us to encourage our adolescent sons and daughters to view their lives as shaped by their own initiative. We fear too much freedom and know the price being paid in car accidents, drugs, disillusion, pregnancies, and all the rest, but we are neither well prepared nor coordinated to cope effectively given the cultural and institutional situation.

High school in America is a time of experimentation. In relationships, leisure, and work teenagers reach out for adulthood. Most try drinking, drugs, and sex. They learn about reality through summer jobs, adult reading, and travel. Learning by experience is part of growing up, and—there is no doubt about it—our young are much more experienced and mature than their Japanese counterparts. By Japanese standards Americans begin too early, move too fast, and lack adequate adult control. But our ideals have generally urged parents and teachers to give more freedom and choice—not less. The difference between the two cultures and between the two social conventions of adolescence is profound, and they are much farther apart than parental sentiments in the two cultures alone would indicate.

The economic and mechanical underpinnings of teenage autonomy—high standards of living, cars, telephones, and the like—will always be used as explanations for cross-cultural differences in adolescent social patterns. It is true that Japanese teenagers do not have cars, good places to meet, or sufficient pocket money. But this only confirms something deeper, for in spite of great economic prosperity, Japanese parents are slow to extend independence to their young. Material resources are part of the story, but other factors are more important.

The foundation of the American notion of maturation lies in its focus on experience, choice, and judgment. We make our own destinies and are responsible for our own choices, therefore our young need to practice making up their own minds. This requires freedom, but ironically, only maturation is a guarantee that freedom will be used wisely. Between childhood and adulthood, adolescents are seen as passing through a dangerous time of transition in which many pay a price for misusing freedom. But our general commitment to the cultural ideal of individualism makes this a price we are ready to pay.

In Japan, maturation centers on the process of integration into the larger society. Shifting first from the dependency and intimacy of infancy into family group membership and then to generalized social roles and group membership in school leads to adulthood, as defined by integration into work organizations and parenting roles. A second aspect of the course toward adulthood in both Japan and the United States is the mastery of requisite attitudes and skills. This rests squarely on the principles of adult guidance and youthful compliance. There is much less concern in Japan with selectively exposing adolescents to adult realities and freedoms, or with helping them find their own occupational path as part of a transition to ultimate individual autonomy. High schools in Japan rely on the last leg of the exam competition for discipline and leave to universities and workplaces the final responsibilities for deciding what additional skills are needed. The responsibilities and choices about maturation are less individual than institutional.

The striking differences involved in the allocation of time may cause Americans to wonder whether the Japanese adolescent enjoys this period of life. Our culture has long made a cult of youthfulness. We have idealized the time of youth for its energy, freedom, and romance, and we seem to have a strong disposition to see our youth epitomize the exuberant qualities of our young nation. Our cultural history, furthermore, has been marked by an expansion of this period to include the teens and twenties and into a vision of retirement as a second youth—illustrating just how central to our sense of well-being this idealized evocation of youthful freedom is. The relatively somber, work-filled, and dependent life of Japanese high school students thus causes us to react negatively to the Japanese situation. "Is there life before nineteen?" we might cynically ask.

There is no doubt about it. The time of youth in Japan seems narrow and unexciting by American standards. It is not a time of memorable opportunities, but a rigorous apprenticeship in which control belongs to adult society.

These comparisons of Japan and the United States must now be joined by comparisons among our five high schools regarding the allocation of time among different segments of the Japanese adolescent population. Academic rank correlates well with differences in activity patterns. The lower the rank of the school, the greater the time spent in the city; the higher the rank, the greater the time spent in school and at home. The normal American pattern of adolescence, in other words, resembles the lower status pattern in Japan. It is interesting to note that Japanese evaluating the conventions of American adolescence by their standards can easily find them rather uncivilized. Conversely, to an American like me, the lower status Japanese pattern has great appeal in its independence, social focus, and vitality.

Surprisingly, it is not club participation rates that illustrate the differences (see Table 8). The lower rate of participation for the night school students is explained by the fact that after-school club activities for them start late at night (about 9:30 or 10:00), and most have jobs that start early in the morning. I did not anticipate the high level of club participation at Nada. The Japanese media portrays education as so preoccupied with entrance exam preparation that it comes as a surprise to find club activity for boys about the same everywhere. The stereotype of the anemic, nearsighted, test-taking brain that is used to caricature those students aiming at Tokyo University is not substantiated here.

Girls are more involved in clubs than are boys, but this may not be significant because many more girls are members of cultural clubs that meet irregularly.

More vocational than academic students take part-time jobs. Few are college bound, and jobs do not interfere with their studies. Some

**Table 8**
Percentage of Students
Participating in a School Club,
Five Schools in Kobe, 1975

| | |
|---|---|
| Nada (male) | 61 |
| Okada | |
| Male | 57 |
| Female | 70 |
| Otani | |
| Male | 55 |
| Female | 77 |
| Yama | |
| Male | 63 |
| Female | 44 |
| Sakura (male) | 46 |

come from poor families and need the money. Others simply want more spending money. At the opposite pole are Nada students, who do not work at part-time jobs even in the summer. Their priorities are their studies, and economic pressures are not a factor. In the other academic high schools, Okada and Otani, a few students work after school and more take brief jobs at vacation time, but the percentage is considerably smaller than for Yama students. As with Nada students, there are strong reasons not to spend time working, and few need the money. A national survey confirms this school-rank related pattern.[10]

The number of hours spent at home doing homework is just the reverse (Table 9). The boys at Nada and Okada particularly put in more study time than Yama and Sakura students and more time than academic high school girls.[11] Many Nada students go to special advanced cram schools during summer vacations. Nearly one-fifth of the Okada boys attend cram schools (yobikō) in the afternoon in the school year.[12]

10. Sōrifu (1979), pp. 262–265.
11. The general tendency of boys to study more than girls is confirmed in all national surveys of time given to study for the high school age group; however, more refined investigations reveal that boys outstudy girls primarily in the college-bound group, but not at the lower academic levels (Kajita, 1976).
12. In an investigation of three academic high schools in and around Tokyo, Kajita (1976) found that hours of study correlate closely with school ranking. Whereas in the

**Table 9**
Study at Home in Number of Daily
Hours, Five Kobe High Schools,
1975

| | |
|---|---|
| Nada (male) | 2.86 |
| Okada | |
| Male | 2.89 |
| Female | 2.37 |
| Otani | |
| Male | 2.10 |
| Female | 2.25 |
| Yama | |
| Male | 1.54 |
| Female | 1.44 |
| Sakura (male) | .85 |

What about the students who are not in clubs and who do not have jobs after school? Here I can only report my impressions and those of the teachers in each school. Vocational school students go straight home less regularly. We know the family background differences for our five schools. Yama and Sakura households are more likely to be crowded and less economically well-off. Single parents and working mothers are more common. The great majority of unhappy home situations in the notes I took belong to vocational school students. Often there is no one at home in the afternoon, and in some cases parental supervision may not begin until late evening. Teachers worry about students who have no parent waiting at home, and national statistics confirm a considerably higher rate of delinquency among them. It should be no surprise that Yama teachers describe their students as inclined to loiter downtown in groups, to frequent snack shops, and to ride around on motorcycles after school. Especially the boys and the more wayward girls do not go home.

A surprising number of Nada, Okada, and Otani students, on the other hand, go directly home after school. They often proceed slowly and in the company of friends, stopping to look in bookstores or shop windows, but by four or five most who are not in a club are at

---

low-ranked rural school just over an hour was the average time for homework at night, the higher ranked schools averaged over three and four hours.

home starting homework or, in the case of girls, helping their mothers. One Nada student I befriended, for example, nervously talked with me in a coffee shop near his school and finally explained that it was bad form to be sitting around in such a place where he might be observed. The academic subculture makes snack shop loitering improper; the vocational one treats it as normal.

There is a significant difference between boys and girls in the matter of helping out at home (see Table 10). Fewer boys make their beds and clean their rooms. Few boys, but one-quarter of the girls, do their own laundry. None of these proportions show much variation from school to school with the exception of Nada, where the boys on all accounts are more cared for and less likely to do household tasks. Most high school students buy their own clothes, but less than half of the Nada boys do. It is in such details that one senses the different degrees of family mobilization for exam taking.

Truancy is another element of the picture of different balances struck between school, home, and city. Otani has just a few students who slip off campus at lunch, but truancy is an acknowledged problem at Yama. On any night about 20 percent or more of Sakura's students are absent; but it is hard to simply label their behavior as truancy because they work all day and may not have the stamina, or their boss's permission, to go on to school from work. The police said that truancy was a regular and serious problem for several of the city's lowest ranked private schools.

I do not have time diaries for students of the five schools, yet there is no question that in moving down the ranking from Nada to Sakura, and particularly as one passes the critical key watershed between academic and vocational schools, one finds the city occupying a larger role in the students' lives. Less time studying, more time away from home in the city, a likelihood of part-time or summer work—all are indications of the different emphases associated with school rank. Yama and Sakura students are closer to the American pattern in their interests and preoccupations, in their greater independence from family, and in their rather casual attitude toward school and homework.[13] But the high-status pattern is exemplified by the Nada boys, diligent in their studies and patiently cared for at home.

13. A most interesting attempt to track electronically the daily activities of American adolescents is reported in Csikszentnihalyi et al. (1977), but activity diaries are usually difficult to keep for adolescents, and their reliability is difficult to gauge.

**Table 10**
Percentage of Students Who Do Household Tasks, Five Kobe Schools, 1975

|  | Make Bed | Make Own Breakfast | Clean Own Room | Do Own Washing | Purchase Own Clothes |
|---|---|---|---|---|---|
| Nada (male) | 59 | 5 | 53 | 3 | 47 |
| Okada |  |  |  |  |  |
| Male | 66 | 20 | 61 | 9 | 70 |
| Female | 74 | 28 | 78 | 22 | 90 |
| Otani |  |  |  |  |  |
| Male | 43 | 11 | 47 |  | 63 |
| Female | 80 | 17 | 72 | 23 | 77 |
| Yama |  |  |  |  |  |
| Male | 68 | 20 | 62 | 8 | 84 |
| Female | 80 | 30 | 79 | 27 | 89 |
| Sakura (male) | 54 | 20 | 63 | 23 | 80 |

## Friends and "Lovers"

Friends are very important in Japan. Surveys consistently reveal that high school students (roughly 80 percent) are inclined to discuss their problems with their friends rather than seeking the advice of parents or teachers.[14] This certainly resembles the American pattern.

The crucial source of friends is school.[15] Neighborhoods are not the basis for high school enrollments, and friends from middle school days are often split up. High school is a time for making new friends. But starting afresh with a group of strangers is difficult. National surveys reveal that although almost all friends are made at school, about one-fifth of all Japanese high school students do not have a friend "to whom they can talk intimately." The lack of a close friend is strikingly more common among boys (29 percent) than among girls (15 percent).[16] My own questionnaire to second-year students confirmed this pattern and revealed some interesting differences among boys across the school ranking. Boys at academic high schools are less likely to have a close friend, and although most who

14. Sōrifu (1977), p. 205.
15. Ibid., p. 195.
16. Ibid., p. 194.

lack a friend express a desire to find one, more boys, and especially more boys at Nada, say they do not need friends. Again there is an apparent correlation with the importance of studies and academic achievement.

Despite the dominance of school and home in terms of time allocation, surveys reveal distance from teachers and parents in emotional and judgmental terms. Here Japan fits the classic portrait of adolescence in most cultures. A questionnaire given to Otani students, for example, shows few of them acknowledging respect for or reliance on teachers as a group. Asked if they would go along with their parents on an outing, most answered, "Only if I liked the idea." In answering these questions, boys showed more independence of adult influence than girls. Parents with whom I spoke expressed confusion with the sullenness and withdrawal of their teenage children. This emotional disharmony, well-known to American parents, is not accompanied by the same physical distancing as in America. Japanese youths are in the home much more and therefore are under closer parental supervision.

Like their American counterparts, Japanese adolescents glue themselves to the television or closet themselves in their rooms to listen to the radio. A kind of electronic peer world develops around such shows. Large numbers tune in to certain stations focused on their age group. The young disc jockeys are more congenial than is the society of their parents. Many students stay up late listening to programs offering the latest hits, study tips, and advice to the lovelorn. One in three boys and one in four girls are still up at midnight. Getting up for school is a big problem in Japan, as in the United States.

The fact remains that Japanese teenagers are not with friends as much as American teenagers are. Even on Saturday nights, most are at home. Many friends do not regularly visit each other's homes because they would have to travel far at night to do so. Besides, there is no private place in most Japanese homes for them to use. Thus, although they are moving toward greater emotional independence of their elders and more reliance on friends, Japanese adolescents do not move as completely or as rapidly as Americans to a friend-based social existence. Because peer activities are weakly developed, groups of more than three or four friends are rare (see Table 11). But friendships tend to be close and lasting. They have little if anything to do with cliques or popularity, and, given the low level of peer interac-

**Table 11**
Friendship Among Students of Five Kobe Schools by Percentage, 1975

| | Have Friend(s); Am Satisfied | Don't Need Friend(s) | Wish for Friend(s) | Classmates are Competitors, Not Friends |
|---|---|---|---|---|
| Nada (male) | 62 | 13 | 23 | 1 |
| Okada | | | | |
| Male | 68 | 5 | 22 | 6 |
| Female | 79 | 4 | 14 | 1 |
| Otani | | | | |
| Male | 61 | 3 | 17 | 5 |
| Female | 92 | | 10 | 1 |
| Yama | | | | |
| Male | 76 | 6 | 15 | 3 |
| Female | 83 | | 16 | 2 |
| Sakura (male) | 73 | 6 | 18 | 3 |

tion, the turnover rate among friends is low.[17] In other words, because opportunities to make close friendships are few, because friendships are not buffeted by a swirl of peer group activities, and because boy-girl relations are limited, friendships develop considerable intimacy.

There is no doubt, however, about the mutual interest between boys and girls. Girls talk about boys a lot, and their magazines are full of romance. Boys are interested in sex, particularly as expressed in the magazines and comics they read. Popular singers, movies made for teenagers, and aspects of the news media play upon strong romantic interests. By Western standards, however, the general tone remains largely platonic and dreamlike. It is indicative that, in Japanese movies and songs, love spurned or unexpressed is more prominent than love realized. Young Japanese, when asked, state almost categorically that they will find their own mates and make "love marriages," yet most are painfully shy and awkward in pursuing this

17. These statements are based solely on my own observations and interviews plus the observations of students of mine who have been exchange students in Japanese high schools.

*Typical lunch period scene in one homeroom*

All the girls eat and chat together on one side of the classroom, with the boys on the other side.

ideal. Only after high school do most begin dating. I would estimate that over one-third of all Japanese marry without having had a serious romantic involvement, even with their future spouses.

Consider the results of a 1977 survey of relations between the sexes among high school students. In response to the question "Do you have a friend of the opposite sex?" almost 7 percent said they had "a lover" (*koibito*); 19 percent said they had someone with whom they were close enough to talk to on a one-to-one basis; 18 percent said they had a friend of the opposite sex in some club or other group activity; and 55 percent said they did not have a friend of the opposite sex.[18] Through the distinctions it made, this survey achieved a degree of precision that most questionnaires on the subject do not. There is a general vagueness in Japan about the terms "lover" and "friend" (*tomodachi*). Boy and girl "friends" may rarely

18. Sōrifu (1977), p. 196. To put this in international perspective, the answer to the same question, "Do you have a friend of the opposite sex?" received negative replies from 11 percent of the American queried, 15 percent of the British, 10 percent of the French, and 5 percent of the Swedish.

see or talk with one another. "Lovers" may only hold hands and may rarely, if ever, go on a date at night. Or, they could have a sexual relationship. I recall one girl telling me that her *boifurendo* had moved to Tokyo several years before, adding that they had spoken on the telephone or exchanged letters once or twice since.

Coeducation in Japan would greatly accelerate interaction between the sexes, one might think, but by American standards this is not true. Homerooms and clubs are largely coeducational, but within both one finds considerable segregation. Each homeroom is responsible for a thorough cleaning when classes end, for example, and yet the boys typically disappear at cleanup time, leaving this domestic task to the girls. Teachers occasionally try to change this pattern, to no avail. At lunch breaks in the homeroom, any exchange that occurs between the sexes is in groups. Girls gather their desks together to eat, talk, and share homework, and boys do the same; boys *or* girls go off down the hall to find a friend or to stroll outside. But in the homeroom, boys and girls do joke together, and they talk over homework problems, ask to borrow things, and discuss serious matters facing the homeroom. All of this exchange is public and conducted with a degree of distance. No pairing off of any kind is discernible at school, and students leave school in groups of the same sex, sometimes exchanging comments back and forth as they loiter about the entrance. There is nothing to prevent girls from joining clubs with boys or vice versa, and many sports clubs are mixed, but boys and girls generally practice sports separately.

Compared with American high school hallways and schoolyards, sprinkled with flirtations and intense boy-girl discussion, the circumspection and reticence of Japanese students is striking. "Our youth are modest and naïve," I was told by a Japanese teacher who had visited American high schools for a year. Asked his opinion of American teenage relationships and pressed to be more than polite, he confided in being shocked and bewildered by the degree of open and active sexuality in American high schools. He said he had the uncomfortable feeling that he was witnessing something very primitive. Conversely, American exchange students in Japanese high schools find their counterparts "young" and "immature" in boy-girl relations.

Few students have dates (*deitto*) while in high school, and these are largely limited to sitting together in a park or coffee shop after school. Generally these meetings are surreptitious. The society's norms on high school dating are not clear. In the past several decades, more and more young couples are seen together in public, and the attitude that it is all right for high school students to date has advanced among teenagers. One poll in 1977 asked high school students what they would think if they saw a friend sitting with someone of the opposite sex in a park. Half said they would approve, one-third answered they would prefer "healthier" (*kenzen*) and "brighter" (*akarui*) behavior, and about 15 percent answered that they would feel the couple was "overdoing it" (*ikisugiru*).[19] The opinions of teachers and parents, we can assume, are considerably more critical on this subject. Hiding a meeting with someone of the other sex, however innocent the contact, is still the practice in Japanese high schools.

Accordingly, physical experience with the opposite sex is limited among Japanese adolescents. Several studies deserve our attention. The most careful one I have found was conducted in Tokyo among 466 academic high school students in the early 1970s.[20] It revealed that 34 percent of the boys and 25 percent of the girls had experienced kissing by their senior year of high school. To appreciate differences of terminology, it should be noted that more had a "lover" (*koibito*) than had experienced kissing! Nearly 20 percent of the boys but only 4 percent of the girls acknowledged some experience with petting. Among these nineteen-year-olds, 9 percent of the boys and 1 percent of the girls had had sexual intercourse. The partner for these experiences is not clear. My impression and that of teachers is that much of the more advanced activity does not occur between two students, but with an older adult. For boys, this means prostitutes, bathhouse attendants, and bar hostesses; for girls, it means older men. Teenagers are not experimenting together as regularly as in the United States.

The second study is the most extensive to date in Japan. Conducted in seven cities and involving over twenty thousand persons aged ten to twenty-one, this study offers data on both 1974 and 1981. Its more notable findings include the fact that there has been a marked increase in sexual experience among teenagers in this time-

19. Reported in the *Fukui Shimbun* (Fukui City), June 30, 1976, p. 7.
20. Naito (1974). But note that only academic high school students are involved. Presumably the figures for a wider sample would be higher.

span. In 1974, 14.2 percent of the boys and 6.7 percent of the girls over 18 reported having had sexual intercourse, whereas in 1981 the percentages were 26.0 and 17.1 respectively. Experience of petting also increased from 19.9 to 36.4 for the boys over 18, and from 11.1 to 30.9 for the girls. By 1981 nearly half of all eighteen-year-olds had experienced kissing.[21]

Compare this with what is known about sex among young Americans. Even in the late 1950s, Kinsey's surveys revealed that more than 20 percent of American women born after 1919 had had intercourse while in their teens.[22] A summary of the numerous surveys made across the country in the seventies indicated that 90 percent of both sexes had experienced "light" petting by age nineteen.[23] A majority had had their first experience with this before high school. At nineteen, nearly 50 percent of the females and about 70 percent of the males had experienced sexual intercourse.

Premarital sex among teenagers is connected to the much higher level of pregnancy and illegitimate births in the United States. The United States Department of Health and Human Services estimates that 10 percent of the females under twenty-one are pregnant each year.[24] Fully 17 percent of all registered live births are illegitimate, and the majority belong to mothers under age twenty. The rate of illegitimacy in Japan is under 1 percent of all live births, and only one in four involves a mother under age twenty-five.[25] The greater availability of abortion in Japan is a factor here, but the crucial difference is sexual activity among teenagers.

Kinsey found that early marriage followed early sexual activity, and here, too, the Japanese and American patterns are different. Ten percent of American high school seniors in 1977 were engaged, married, or divorced.[26] The few Japanese teenagers (mostly female) who marry have left school first.[27] Among women twenty to twenty-four

21. Reported in Soeda Yoshiya, "Seinen no Sei no Kaiho to Yokuatsu," *Juristo* (1982) 26:139–144.

22. Kinsey et al. (1953), p. 289.

23. "Light" means above the waist. Diepold and Young (1979). For a general treatment of adolescent sexuality, see Chilman (1980). This compares with an experience of light petting by 32 percent of Japanese high school senior boys surveyed and 10 percent of senior girls. Naito (1974).

24. Calhoun et al. (1980). The rate of pregnancy before marraige is much higher for black and much lower for white females.

25. Kōseishō (1978), p. 67.

26. Bachman et al. (1980), p. 17.

27. See Tamura (1974).

*Couple strolling on a weekend*

Both students wear altered school uniforms. The girl's skirt is too long. The boy has a permanent wave and slippers, and the rest of his clothing mocks school uniform propriety.

years old, about 60 percent of the Americans were married in 1970, whereas only 30 percent of the Japanese women that age were married in 1975. The average age at marriage is later in Japan than in any other developed nation.

These statistics document the simple fact that in romance and sexuality, as in the world of peer group relations and in the matter of independence from home and school, Japanese adolescents are behaving in distinctively different ways from their American counterparts.

Explanations for these differences must focus as much on the unusual qualities in the American pattern as in the Japanese. Certainly traditional culture cannot be invoked in a simplistic way. One hundred years ago, for example, the incidence of sexual experience among this age group was probably higher in Japan than in the United States. Prostitution was quite common, and in rural areas one or another form of premarital sex was widely accepted. Even in the immediate prewar period, young Japanese were more likely than Americans to be away from home before age twenty because of male conscription and the widespread practice of hiring farm girls for urban factories. America in the nineteenth century was still strongly influenced by religious morality, especially in rural areas.

The constriction of adolescent experience to family and school is a recent phenomenon in Japan, one that appears to have come about largely because of urbanization, the rapid increase in high school matriculation rates, and the growth in the proportion of adolescents focused on university entrance examinations. In short, prosperity and social progress in this century have created an adolescence that is decidedly old-fashioned by American standards. Although we often see the excesses and problems of our young as stemming from too much prosperity, and although Japanese adults shake their heads over the same presumed corruptive influences in Japan, it appears that the historical trends there have not made urbanization or prosperity causes for increased adolescent sexuality. In the West prosperity is associated with the decline of religious morality and the weakening of the moral nature of key institutions, particularly the family. Japanese morality never rested on a religious base, and sex was never prohibited on religious grounds. With secularization, Americans have found a new morality to suit our increasingly precocious individualism, whereas in Japan, urbanization, industrialization, and prosperity have drawn nearly the entire population into a middle-class pursuit of educational achievement. The postponement of independence and adult sexuality appears to be a by-product. Japan is not puritanical about sex, but it is very middle-class about getting ahead and very aware of propriety and status. Adolescent romance and sex are still improper. More and more Americans have also been joining the middle class and going to high school in this century, but the influence of education in their private lives has been notably different. Romance is a cultural ideal, and its pursuit is a gesture of individual independence.

Cross-national differences should not blind us to differences in the sexual conduct of students of different high schools in Japan. Teachers regularly note that girls attending lower status schools are more likely to become sexually involved. Each year several Yama girls become pregnant by older men and drop out of school, and there is a regular concern among Yama teachers about girls taking part-time jobs where they could be seduced by older male workers. Teachers at academic high schools voice much less concern, and no pregnancies were reported at Otani or Okada. On a number of occasions while passing low-status private girls' schools, I saw students in plain view of the school climb into cars with men and drive off. Certainly only a small fraction of the students were involved, but the schools' reputations were shaped by such occurrences. Unfortunately, no Japanese surveys examine school differences carefully in these matters, and impressions must suffice.

Newspaper accounts of teenage prostitution also draw attention to vocational and low-status private schools. The police arrest about two hundred fifty high school girls each year for this offense, and nearly all those arrested fit a particular pattern. The girls are low on the academic ladder, bored with school, and interested in pocket money. Typically, they are recruited in small groups by older men.

## Delinquency

The high school years are distinguished by a rising inclination toward and capacity for criminal activity on the part of a segment of each generation.[28] Whether legally classified as adults or not, high school students are certainly old enough to engage in many illegal adult activities. School officials must cope with this reality, and in some cases they must cope with criminal activities in the school itself.

Knowing what we do about Japanese society and education, we would predict the rate of juvenile delinquency to be relatively low compared with the United States. Japanese adolescents have less op-

28. The interested reader can turn to a number of articles on Japanese delinquency, including De Vos and Mizushima (1962), Makino (1970), De Vos and Wagatsuma (1972) and Wagatsuma (1973). The most useful sources of information in Japanese are the periodic white papers on crime and on youth that are published by the government.

portunity to get in trouble because they are at home or in school a greater proportion of the time. They are more closely supervised. The much lower levels of divorce, poverty, and discrimination mean, furthermore, that the family background factors that set the stage for juvenile crime in all countries are not as powerful in Japan. More Japanese than Americans remain in high school. And finally, the level of adult crime is much lower in Japan than in the United States. The Japanese context would not generate as much adolescent crime as the American for many reasons.

Comparative statistics strongly confirm our expectations; but first a note of caution. Comparisons of juvenile crime rates in the United States and Japan are made difficult by differences between the categorization and collection of crime statistics in the two countries. Obviously, because the age of the offenders is central to our interests here, we cannot rely on statistics of reported crimes because they do not reveal the criminal's age. Only arrest figures can be sorted by age. A major problem, then, is to assess the relative likelihood of arrest in the two countries. The Japanese police are generally viewed as more efficient than American police in apprehending criminals, and clearance rates (the percentage of reported crimes solved) for crimes are much higher in Japan.[29] How minor crimes involving juveniles are reported is another serious issue. In both countries there is undoubtedly a considerable amount of juvenile crime, particularly shoplifting and vandalism, that goes unreported. When police are not informed, no arrests or convictions are possible. One cannot even guess at the differences in juvenile crime reporting levels in the two countries. Laws affecting juveniles in the two countries also differ to some degree. Furthermore, American Federal Bureau of Investigation crime statistics generally use different age groups than the Japanese use, and often they do not cover the entire population. For all these reasons the following comparisons are necessarily rough, yet because the differences are substantial even such approximations are useful.

In 1976 in America, 3,259,174 persons under age twenty-one were arrested in police jurisdictions covering 175 million Americans for crimes other than traffic offenses.[30] In Japan (population 115 million)

29. Bayley (1976).
30. Kelley (1977).

during that year, 115,628 individuals under twenty were arrested.[31] The proportion of youth in the total population of both nations at the time was nearly identical (24 percent). Thus, the arrest rate per 1,000 young persons in America was 79, whereas in Japan it was 4. A difference this large is not surprising to anyone who knows the difference in either the youth culture or the levels of crime between the two countries.

Considering the kinds of crime for which juveniles are arrested in the two countries, further significant differences come to light. Seventy-five percent of the Japanese juveniles arrested in 1976 were taken in for theft. Shoplifting was the major offense (32 percent of all arrests), followed by the theft of motorcycles (11 percent) and bicycles (10 percent). In the United States, theft accounted for 17 percent of all arrests of persons under twenty-one, and burglary accounted for another 8 percent. Arrests of juveniles for all manner of violence or threat of violence in Japan constituted 12 percent of the total juvenile arrests. In the United States, homicide, manslaughter, rape, robbery, and assault accounted for 8 percent. The proportional weight of violence on the Japanese side should not disguise the fact that the rate of juvenile arrests for violent crimes in the United States is 6 per 1,000, whereas in Japan it is .5 per 1,000.

Drugs are much more available and widely used among young Americans. The Japanese police have virtually eliminated the availability of hard drugs, and few Japanese are arrested for drug use. In 1976, over a quarter of a million teenage Americans were arrested for breaking our narcotics laws,[32] and this was only the tip of the iceberg.[33] In Japan the analogous statistic is the 37,000 young Japanese arrested for sniffing glue and paint thinner.[34] Marijuana is virtually unavailable to teenagers in Japan, but one recent national survey estimates that in the United States about 10 percent of all high school students smoke it daily.[35] The consumption of alcohol by American teenagers is also high: 20 percent report they are drunk at least once

31. Kōseishō (1978).
32. U.S. Drug Enforcement Agency report, quoted in the CBS News Almanac. Maplewood, N.J.: Hammond Almanac Inc., (1978), p. 236.
33. Both Calhoun et al. (1980) and Bachman et al. (1980) report that over half of all high school students have tried marijuana and about 10 percent smoke at least once a week.
34. Kōseishō (1978), p. 432.
35. Johnston (1979).

a month.[36] In Japan one encounters so little adolescent drinking that it is not a social issue. The highest cause of death in the United States for this age group is motor vehicle accidents, a majority of which are related to drinking. As contributing factors in American delinquency and as indicators of the nature of peer group activities, drug and alcohol problems highlight the profound differences in adolescent social patterns in the two countries.

Total arrests of juveniles for prostitution amounted to 191 in Japan in 1976 and to over seventeen thousand in the United States.[37] This makes the American rate greater than thirty times the Japanese. Runaways are often involved in prostitution, and the Japanese police apprehended fifty-four thousand runaways in 1976, whereas it is estimated that six to seven hundred thousand young Americans run away (at least overnight) annually.[38] For many reasons, the police discovery rate for runaways in Japan is very high (85 percent), whereas in the United States it is thought to be between 15 and 20 percent.[39] The estimated runaway rate in the United States is about six times the rate in Japan.

These general comparisons illustrate the relative extent and character of delinquency in the two countries. Clearly, juvenile crime and the threat of it are far less significant in Japanese society.[40] This is also true of Japanese schools. The total number of assaults on teachers in Japan in 1976 amounted to 161, with 22 occurring in high schools.[41] In New York City alone in the first five months of the 1974–75 school year, there were 474 assaults on teachers.[42] A United States Senate study estimated that in 1974 there were 70,000 physical assaults on teachers nationwide.[43] By these measures, American

36. Calhoun et al. (1980).
37. Kōseishō (1978), p. 428, and Kelley (1977), p. 183. But Federal Bureau of Investigation uniform crime statistics combine prostitution and commercialized vice, so these numbers are only rough approximations. There is also considerable debate about whether many arrests of adolescents for prostitution are made for other reasons having to do with ease of processing.
38. Kōseishō (1978), pp. 436–437, and Brown (1979).
39. Ibid.
40. See Bayley (1976) for a general discussion of crime and police activity in Japan and the United States.
41. Sōrifu (1979), p. 278. The number had risen to 394 assaults on teachers by 1980, an alarming increase in the Japanese context. Most of the increase occurred in junior high schools. See "Japan's School Discipline Crumbles," *Christian Science Monitor*, March 18, 1981.
42. Subcommittee to Investigate Juvenile Delinquency, U.S. Senate (1977).
43. Ibid.

teachers are eighteen times more likely to experience school violence than are their Japanese counterparts. The Japanese police counted a total of 1,873 cases of fighting or other violence in schools in 1976, whereas it was estimated that American schools in 1974 witnessed 204,000 incidences of aggravated assault and 12,000 armed robberies.[44] Violence is fifty times more likely in American schools.

Yet Japanese adults will tell you their country is suffering a juvenile crime wave, and the police are very active in publicizing their concern. Juvenile crime, especially shoplifting and school violence, increased significantly in the 1970s. Teachers shake their heads about rising levels of delinquency and point out certain schools as virtual breeding grounds for juvenile delinquents. Newspapers carry shocking stories of teenage prostitution and violence in schools. The crime rate for adolescents is almost four times higher than the rate for adults: approximately one-third of all police arrests in Japan are of teenagers. There is good cause for concern among Japanese parents and teachers to whom the much higher crime rates in the United States are no consolation.

A closer look at the basic figures reveals that high schools are less affected than might be expected. Most of the increase in crime in the 1970s was the result of increased criminal activity among middle school students, and the 8 percent of the seventeen- to nineteen-year-olds who were not in school accounted for more than 25 percent of the crime in their age group. In sum, however disturbing the recent general trend, it does not mean that Japanese high schools are experiencing a juvenile crime wave comparable to that in America.

All the same, for some schools delinquency is a serious problem. In our sample of five schools, only at Yama and Sakura did the subject of student delinquent behavior arise regularly in my conversations with the faculty, and only at Yama did I see evidence of student vandalism. Delinquency is obviously correlated with school rank.

For proof of this statement, one must begin with police records, as most schools will not release their statistics on students. The police records for one of Kobe's large school districts (including three of our five schools) confirms our expectations (Table 12). High school students arrested or given police warnings (for such delinquent behavior as riding motorbikes, for hanging about in unsavory places, and

44. Ibid.

**Table 12**

Delinquency Rates in a Large School District in Kobe, 1974 (12 months)

| | Number of Schools | Arrests | Warnings | Total | Combined School Enrollments | Delinquency Rate |
|---|---|---|---|---|---|---|
| Top private, academic | 4 | 6 | 4 | 10 | 2,040 | .005 |
|   Boys | 2 | 3 | 3 | 6 | 1,200 | .005 |
|   Girls | 2 | 3 | 1 | 4 | 840 | .005 |
| Top public, academic (coeducational) | 2 | 6 | 43 | 49 | 2,220 | .022 |
| Average public, academic (coeducational) | 2 | 19 | 37 | 56 | 2,200 | .025 |
| Low-ranked private, girls (academic & vocational courses) | 2 | 51 | 75 | 126 | 2,100 | .060 |
| Public, vocational | 2 | 50 | 154 | 204 | 1,900 | .107 |
|   Technical (90% male) | 1 | 31 | 107 | 138 | 835 | .165 |
|   Commercial (70% female) | 1 | 19 | 47 | 68 | 1,065 | .063 |
| Public night schools | 2 | 11 | 52 | 63 | 670 | .094 |
|   Academic (80% male) | 1 | 6 | 33 | 39 | 460 | .085 |
|   Technical | 1 | 5 | 19 | 24 | 210 | .114 |

SOURCE: Data from Hyōgo Prefectural Police, Juvenile Section, unpublished records.

for behavior leading to criminal acts) come largely from vocational schools or low-ranked private schools. Apparently, about three-quarters of the delinquency in Kobe among seventeen- to nineteen-year-olds involves students attending schools in the bottom one-third of the school ranking. Translated into our five-school sample, this means that although perhaps one out of three hundred fifty boys at Nada and one out of every sixty at Okada and Otani is involved with the police any one year, the rate jumps to about one out of every sixteen at Yama and one out of every nine at Sakura.

Only a much closer study of this question could reveal how much recidivism is present. If recidivism is not assumed, then as many as one in every five or six Yama students is in trouble with the police at some point during his three years in high school. Obviously, there is a strong correlation between low academic achievement and delinquency. Delinquency, as we know from so many studies, is affected by background factors and by the character of a school's subculture. Relative social disadvantage, problems with school, and antisocial behavior are tied together in every advanced society. Japan is distinctive only in the small degree of its problem.

In Japan, delinquency is not a matter between only the police and parents, and it places a particular burden on vocational and low-status private schools. When they have a student in trouble with the police, homeroom teachers must talk to the family, the arresting officers, and the juvenile section of the police department, and they may accompany the student to apologize to the aggrieved party. This takes time and taxes a teacher's energy and patience. One young teacher told me that in his first month at Yama ten of his homeroom students had been temporarily expelled, and he was expected to work out their problems through consultations with their parents. Clearly, the academic ranking of schools correlates with differing patterns in the allocation of teachers' time between exam-oriented and social maintenance activities.

The busiest and most heavily burdened teachers at Yama are the two heads of the guidance section. It is their responsibility to see that the school copes with all disciplinary problems, whether they arise in or outside the school and whether or not the police are involved. Smoking in school is a problem because about one-quarter of the students are regular smokers (a very high average for a group of this age bracket in Japan). Minor vandalism is another problem. One day at lunch the head of Yama's guidance section rattled off for me his estimates of the kinds and numbers of cases of delinquency he handles in a year.

| | |
|---|---|
| Shoplifting | 5–6 cases involving 40 students |
| Family court cases | 10 cases |
| Sexual misconduct, prostitution, etc. | 2–3 cases |
| Smoking in school | 13–14 cases |
| Motorcycle riding | 24 cases |
| Knives, drugs, etc. | 3 cases |
| Traffic injuries | 2–3 cases |
| Dropouts | 10 students |

| Fights in school | 2 cases |
| Fights outside school | 5 cases |
| Truancy | "Very frequent" |

He observed that he is glad Yama students are mostly girls, as technical high schools with a preponderance of boys have greater problems.

Sakura has less preoccupation with delinquency than Yama, not because its students are less inclined to get into trouble, but because as night school students they have less free time. Police statistics reveal that night schools have somewhat lower arrest rates compared with daytime vocational and low-level private high schools. Dropouts from night schools are not counted in the figures, however, and this makes a significant difference, as those who quit night schools are much more open to the temptations and influences that cause delinquency. If the figures were aggregated to include night school dropouts, I would expect their arrest records to be higher or on a par with the figures for the worst private boys' schools. Sakura students, in spite of the motorcycle gang appearance of many of them, do not cause much trouble in school. They speak roughly to teachers and to one another, and there is much punching of shoulders and playing at fighting in the halls, but Sakura teachers have little reason to be afraid. Some newcomers are undoubtedly fearful, as I was the first few nights in the school, but one learns to look past the facade of toughness. There is something endearing in all the rough-tough poses of Sakura's students.

### Summary

It must be recognized that there is considerable difference in the experience of adolescence among Japanese. The accumulation of delinquency around low-ranked schools is just part of the fundamental pattern encountered throughout this book in which high school subcultures reflect hierarchical position. Entrance exams do the sorting, and family background factors explain much of the variation, but the process of student differentiation continues through three years of school.

By sixteen or seventeen years of age, most Japanese have a clear idea of what their place in society will be. Certainly the self-confidence and optimism of Nada students contrast sharply with the general aimlessness and pessimism found at Yama and Sakura. At Nada, students are given more free rein and are expected to show initiative. At Sakura, teachers have low expectations, and they spend long hours supervising. In this way future leaders and followers are created.

High school subcultures and their associated life-styles prepare students to take their destined social stations. To be powerful, efficient, and long-lasting, a social structure must be supported by a moral order, one that rationalizes inequalities and causes individuals to accept the structure. Identity formation in high school is an important aspect of this legitimizing process in Japan. The higher in the school hierarchy, the greater the discipline, rewards, and self-worth. Students who do poorly on entrance exams feel guilty as well as inadequate. They have let their parents down. Once in high school they find themselves defined by their school's reputation. Delinquency, even on the part of a few of their fellow students, tarnishes them. Academic weakness is thus linked to low morale and low social reputation. The order-filled, studious lives of academically successful students epitomizes a recognized moral superiority. In Japan, differences in school subcultures and adolescent experience largely accomplish the adjustment of individuals to their future places in the adult hierarchy. If, someday in the future, research on Japanese society develops to the point that it reveals some basic class differences in such matters as attitudes toward work, leisure, family, marriage, and so forth, it is likely that these differences will be consistent with the differences between the five schools considered here.

The general behavioral patterns of a whole age segment from the populations of two large nations have just been contrasted. The kind of activities considered, however mundane when they occur individually, make for profound differences in overall social outcomes when they occur en masse. That is, the daily micro-level conduct of millions of people makes for significant results at the macro level, where social efficiency and economic achievement are measured. Because high school is the central institution of adolescence, it has been used as a vehicle to make this comparison between the two national populations. At no subsequent point in the life cycle is such a comparison as readily made because employment, marriage, and many other factors enter to greatly complicate the picture.

The major discovery here is that school and home have a much greater influence in the lives of Japanese than American adolescents. Behavioral differences bifurcate neatly along the line between activities that occur in these two institutions and the more autonomous realms of adolescent activity, where peer influence is greater and adult supervision less. Undoubtedly, Japanese high school students are more regularly and closely supervised, more sheltered from the world, and more restricted by circumstances than their American counterparts. They spend notably less time socializing together, creating their own world, or exploring the adult one. They get into trouble less. American teenagers do not work nearly as hard on their studies. They have more time for leisure, friendship, and romance. When they work hard, it is likely to be at part-time (probably unskilled) jobs. They begin sexual relations much earlier. Both national populations assume that their own pattern is natural, and they take for granted the basic priorities and assumptions it contains. In the experience of adolescence, national culture is being formed.

It is common knowledge, for example, that, compared with Americans, Japanese employees work longer hours, take fewer vacation days per year, and change jobs less frequently. This is especially true of employees of larger firms in Japan. It is also a characteristic of the Japanese ideal that employees are loyal and devoted to their companies, meaning that men put their jobs at the center of their lives. In terms of time allocation, this means giving more to work and less to home, leisure, and friendship. The high school experience socializes male students in this direction. It rewards the habit of giving much time to work. Leisure, romance, and peer activities, on the other hand, appear peripheral to serious, high-status conduct. Americans, by comparison, have a higher preference for friendships and leisure activities, particularly those separate from work responsibilities. One popular way we calculate the meaning and value of work, for example, is to enumerate how it provides the money and time for personal enjoyment.

Japanese women, on the other hand, do not generally devote themselves to employment; rather, upon marriage, they devote themselves to the role of homemaker with the same intensity men give to their companies. We have noted how, during high school, a gap develops between boys and girls, with a much greater proportion of boys seeking to enter four-year universities. Females study for comparatively long hours by American standards, but they study less than Japanese males. They spend as much of their time at home as do the boys, but more of it is spent helping their mothers. They are no more oriented to an active peer group than the boys are. The pattern is already largely in place by high school.

The division of labor between husband and wife in Japan is quite developed. Married couples spend much less time together there than do couples in the United States, and this, too, is consistent with the adolescent pattern of little social contact between the sexes. Even if dating begins in earnest after high school, the experience and standard practices of courtship in Japan are relatively constrained. Young people remain shy and awkward, by and large, and one-third still marry by parental arrangement. Conjugal relations carry a much lighter load of expectations than for Americans. The low Japanese divorce rate reflects these much lower expectations, and this pattern also reflects the habits initiated during adolescence.

Couples and families are less often together for leisure activity in Japan. Couples do not socialize much with other couples, unlike the situation in the United States. Friendships are most frequent within three social spheres: schoolmates, co-workers, and family. Adults in both countries generally continue friendship patterns begun in their adolescent years; Americans make much of leisure-oriented relationships and male-female social interaction, whereas the Japanese are less focused on such activities but more inclined to tie them to work or family, and they are more inclined to the same sex socially. By the broad comparisons used here, the American inclination toward private parties, long weekends, vacations, and leisure-oriented events of all kinds separated from work follow naturally from our orientation in high school to a rich peer-centered existence that rests on a separation of work and fun.

The young Japanese finds adolescence a time of final adaptation to and integration with the larger society, one that brings great pressure to perform academically. One's social status and life opportunities are rapidly being fixed. High school does not represent an opening up of choice, but a narrowing down of focus. The overwhelming reality is not one of growing independence, but of certain inescapable givens about the relation of studying to future social status. High school provides opportunities for ambition, but only in the context of accepting and adapting to a clear social reality. It is a tight regime that does not encourage personal dreams, experimentation, individual variety, or idealism. These remain largely unexpressed and private. Those who knuckle down are admired and rewarded for their self-control, dedication, and singularity of purpose. These are Japanese virtues of long standing that have found continued reinforcement in the modern institution of high school.

We Americans continue to see our lives as a galaxy of relationships and activities that center on us as individuals. By adolescence we are rapidly extricating ourselves from the social world of the family.[45] We become preoccupied with choosing careers, friends, romantic partners, hobbies, and pleasures. We realize we cannot easily undo these choices, so we try to keep our options open. Is this not the essence of the American pattern at high school time? It is our dream and our nightmare. Despite the similarities in formal educational institutions and in the advanced industrial status of these two societies, the concrete behavior patterns of adolescence clearly illustrate the emerging differences.

We are considering national differences that are also truly profound in regard to the issue of social efficiency. The Japanese are producing an average adult citizen who is remarkably well suited to four requirements of modern industrial society:

1) hard, efficient work in organizations
2) effective information processing
3) orderly private behavior
4) stable, devoted child rearing.

I doubt that there is another nation in peacetime history that has put nearly its entire population through such a rigorous institutional socialization. And the Japanese are not doing this with an ideological coloration or sense of national crisis. Social competition and traditional pedagogy have combined to create this educational pressure cooker.

45. In this regard, consider the results of a recent poll that found 71 percent of young Japanese, but only 23 percent of young Americans and 13 percent of young Germans, saying they would prefer to live with their parents in adulthood. *Gakunen News*, September 22, 1979: report of a survey published by the Prime Minister's Office (Seinen Taisaku Honbu), entitled *Shakai Shihan Chosa* (n.d.).

# Conclusion

THIS BOOK began with a set of broad questions about social equality, Japanese culture, and national efficiency. Chapter by chapter, elements of the answers have emerged, and an interplay between factors external to high schools and the character of the schools themselves has become clearer. The five schools considered here illustrate a pattern of differentiation that reveals much of the underlying dynamic that shapes secondary education in Japan. The final portrait of Japanese high schools that emerges properly contains much variation, and yet many basic conclusions are in order.

## *Education and Social Structure*

A fundamental social issue in education throughout the industrial world has been equality. Clearly, social equality in Japan has a lot to do with schooling.

To review the key elements of the story:

Until ninth grade nearly all Japanese children are enrolled in public schools based on residential criteria. Curricula, teaching facilities, resources, and student abilities across the spectrum of elementary and middle schools are far more uniform than in the United States or Western Europe, where tracking begins earlier. This establishes a solid base of relatively equal opportunity.

High school entrance exams then sort each age cohort into what amounts to an eight- to ten-tier high school ranking system. Future occupational and status levels (elite, managerial, blue-collar, and so forth) are closely equated to this ranking. Further, at the point of high school entrance the entire age cohort is divided into three largely immutable classificatory distinctions: those leaving school, those entering vocational ranks, and those going on to academic high schools. In Japan's cities, 95 percent of all students are advancing to high school and nearly as many are graduating, signifying the near demise of the high school degree as a mark of distinction. The type of high school and the status of one's university are the crucial measures.

At the end of high school, differentiation occurs once more. About half of the nation's young men are ranked at that time according to the calibrations of university stature. Their future employment and social identity will be significantly influenced by which university they attend.

The ranking of high schools conforms closely to such matters as rates of delinquency, patterns of adolescent behavior, and pace of learning. These are notable moral and qualitative correlates of the academic hierarchy.

The ranking of schools also corresponds closely to the socioeconomic background of students' families and the educational level of their parents.

Females do about as well as males in the high school entrance competition, and they receive almost as much supplementary training at *juku*, but a much smaller proportion goes on to four-year universities, and only one in five students at the top universities is female.

Within each school, a general egalitarianism prevails. No tracking occurs, and the homeroom system encourages a sense of togetherness. Among students one finds almost no outward indications of socioeconomic status: school uniforms are worn and personal possessions are not displayed. What is more, student cliques and informal hierarchies are not pronounced (by American standards) because of the fixed nature of roles and relationships anchored in homerooms and clubs and the low level of peer interaction outside school.

In sum, Japan's well-developed system of academic stratification begins late, rests on entrance exams, and occurs at transfer points between school levels. This is a crucial point if we are to see how hierarchy, group membership, and individual identity are shaped in the process of high school socialization. Entrance competition is basically impersonal. It occurs among large numbers. Within schools, direct competition and differentiation among students is limited and not encouraged by teachers. There is a sensitivity to other students as future competitors in getting into college, but the social organization of schools causes Japanese young people to spend their daily school lives closely tied to small groups in which competition, differentiation, and hierarchy are superseded by group-centered concerns. This coupled with a minimal amount of choice inhibits the growth of individual distinctiveness, compared with the encouragement of choice and display of individuality in American high schools. Furthermore, when individuals are differentiated by exams, the criteria are narrowly academic ones that reflect only intelligence and diligence in preparation. Japanese education does not differentiate individuals by the many other standards applied in American university entrance. As a result, Japanese students are not regularly exercised in the development and display of personal distinctiveness. Their sense of self-worth centers on exam preparation and performance; they are not put through a process focusing on the existential question: "Who am I?"

Differentiation by sex is another significant structural aspect of Japanese high schooling. With the exception of home economics for girls, the official curriculum and entrance procedures provide for strict formal equality of opportunity regardless of gender, but parental attitudes, informal patterns of interaction in school, and the marked sex differentiation of adult roles all contribute to very different results for boys and girls in the period following high school. Girls, and their parents for them, choose different futures, it seems. They avoid technical schools in preference to commercial schools, for example, and a large proportion aim to enter junior colleges rather than universities. The powerful influence of career expectations can be seen in these tendencies. Few high school girls enroll in yobikō, and although one in four boys presently does a year of rōnin to better his university chances, only about one in fifty girls does so. Most significantly, more than 50 percent of all male high school seniors apply to a four-year university, but the rate for females is less than 20 percent. The great disproportion of males in the better universities is largely a product of this different orientation, one that arises during adolescence, but it is not because of discrimination in high school. The different ambitions of boys and girls at this age suggest that the goal of general equality between the sexes in Japanese work organizations is remote. Educational results in effect fix a cultural expectation that is contrary to the norm of sexual equality in employment.

From high school on, Japanese experience a progressively sharper differentiation and hierarchy within generations. One's awareness of one's place in a larger social world increases, and with the approaching entry to adult society, competition intensifies and opportunities narrow. A base of intimate relations is retained in the family, in school clubs and homerooms, and with close friends. Small groups become important refuges from the impersonal and hierarchical qualities of the general social context. This pattern continues in the adult Japanese tendency to turn to companies, and especially company work groups, as sources of intimate relations. A particularly Japanese pattern of competition and intimacy is the result.

Consciousness of social class in postwar Japan is often said to be weak. Classes in industrial society are large groups, each with a distinct role in the economic system—manual laborers, farmers, managers, capitalists, intelligentsia, technologists, professionals, office workers, and small entrepreneurs. Each distinct element has its own interests, attitudes, life-styles, and ways of interrelating with other classes. Typically, these relations are hierarchically organized, and classes thus become large horizontal segments of society. In a strongly class-dominated society, education replicates this structure by socializing and tracking in a manner that causes most children to remain in the same social class as their parents and to feel very different from other classes even in such areas as language use, values, and aesthetic preferences.

Nakane Chie offers a cogent portrait of Japanese social structure as hierarchical but not based primarily on economic classes. She begins with Japanese small groups, noting their characteristic capacity for cohesiveness and their internal rank ordering of status and role. She goes on to explain that Japan is not a class society for two related reasons: 1) loyalty to and solidarity within work institutions (which cut across class lines) constitute a more powerful form of basic allegiance than class affiliations, and 2) the general hierarchy of social rank (generated by age and sex as well as by education and employment) is much more dominant and elaborate than class distinctions alone. One is left with the sense that social hierarchy in Japan is subordinate to various forms of solidarity and is generated primarily if not solely by biological (age and sex) and ability criteria.

On the other hand, those stressing the importance of social classes point out the fundamental inequalities of resources and economic returns that exist in Japanese society. Very significant differences exist between employment in Japan's large firms and in her small subcontractors, between the salaries of her professional and managerial elite and the wages of day tradesmen, manual workers in small enterprises, shopkeepers, poor farmers, and women who return to work after raising families. In fact, Nakane's model works well only for certain kinds of workers and organizations, namely the male permanent employees of companies with five hundred or more workers. For them the company focus and the organizational hierarchy of status and role do generally predominate, but for the rest of the working population institutional ties are not particularly strong, and small group loyalties tend to be within, not between, economic classes.

It is important to relate what has been learned here about high schools to the question of social class in Japan. We have seen that the ranking of high schools in Kobe is strongly correlated with 1) family socioeconomic background factors; 2) future employment prospects; and 3) different school subcultures. Life-style, self-confidence, and self-worth are differentiated. All of this is certainly consistent with a class-based society, and nowhere is the structure so distinctly revealed as in the high schools.

A form of class consciousness is undoubtedly created by the hierarchy of schools, but it is not involved with the symbols and traditions commonly associated with capitalism. It is a merit-based class consciousness. Nada students are not sons of propertied fathers, nor are they destined to lead a capitalistic class. Their fathers are mostly managers and professionals, and the sons, too, are headed into leadership of public and private bureaucracies and into the professions. The fathers of vocational school students are largely manual laborers and small entrepreneurs, and their children will mostly take low-level clerical and factory positions. Their aspiration is to enter large companies where, as permanent employees, they will enjoy the rewards of membership in a prosperous and secure organization. As Japan has developed economically, the result has been that more and more of the sons and daughters of disenfranchised workers have found positions in the organizations Nakane points to as eclipsing a class orientation.

The meritocratic qualities of Japan's exam-based system offer a powerful legitimation of the prevailing bureaucratic hierarchies and help socialize individuals to accept their future roles within them. In sum, social inequalities persist with the complicity of education, but as the Japanese economy has evolved, the relevance of a classical approach to social class has diminished.

But now the meritocratic principle is threatened. The rise to pre-eminence of a set of private schools like Nada marks a significant change in which money appears increasingly significant to the purchase of educational advantage. Nada's ability to compete so effectively is partly the result of its freedom from both official and union constraints and, more important, the result of attracting talented students away from the public system. Elite private schools have grown strong wherever the best public high schools have been weakened. Reforms that have attempted to make entrance to public schools less competitive or to reorient schools away from a preoccupation with entrance exams have actually caused the decline of top public schools. The most notable example is in Tokyo, where in the late sixties a major drive to end the stratification of public high schools only led to a strengthening of the city's private schools. The best intentions of progressive reformers were thoroughly distorted by the more powerful ambitions and instincts for self-preservation of many parents, who quickly shifted focus to the private route. *Juku* attendance in Tokyo for elementary school children is the highest in the nation because private junior high schools are so important. This parallels the "backlash" response of American parents to school integration. Both illustrate the limitations on using public education for basic social reform in affluent liberal societies.

Of great concern to those who value equality of opportunity is the fact that with the rise of elite private schools a costly but effective route to Japan's top schools has been opened. Early supplementary tutoring and tuition costs are sufficiently higher along this route so that at least a significant part of the population is excluded for financial reasons alone. True, the outflow of top students to the private schools in Tokyo made room for larger numbers of average students in the public academic high schools, saving money for their presumably lower income parents. But have the pluses outweighed the minuses?

I doubt it. To the degree that elite education is tied to money, educational opportunity is distorted, and the legitimating power of the merit principle declines. At issue is confidence in public institutions and faith in the justness of society. Japan still offers an admirable degree of equal opportunity in education, but the rise of private schools, *juku*, and commercial study aids is a trend that could, if it continues, alienate many Japanese and raise class consciousness. The fact that in 1982 more than half of Tokyo University freshmen came from private schools will not go unnoticed. It means that money is playing a large role. It is noteworthy that efforts aimed at reforming high school hierarchies have come to a near standstill recently, as officials realize how they have encouraged parents to support elite private schools. The merit principle and hierarchical differentiation are inseparable in public education, a point reformers readily forget.

Compare this with the American pattern. We start with greater initial social inequality, and even in early elementary school partial tracking is necessary to cope with differences of reading and other abilities. We do not, however, have any kind of broad exam-based differentiation except for the gifted and those entering first-class private schools. We wait to formally sort the population at the time of college entrance. Nevertheless, by that time socioeconomic differences, the impact of residential segregation, and other factors have already sorted our population of students more drastically than the Japanese high school system sorts students there. On the one hand, our system results in a much larger flotsam (dropouts, functional illiterates, and so forth), and it suffers proportionally more troubled high schools with greater degrees of trouble than Sakura and Yama. On the other hand, we encourage our brightest minds and offer the top students (perhaps 5 percent) an excellent education, different but qualitatively equal to that which Nada students receive. Access to this opportunity, however, is even more closely tied to income. The sorting process in the United States is characterized by much less that is above-board, calculable, or based on objective measures. And despite our greater national attention and efforts to use education to overcome social inequalities, the greater magnitude of the initial problem in the United States and the autonomy of independent school districts have prevented us from meeting Japanese standards. Our school system preserves the greater social disparities of our society.

Throughout the course of education, furthermore, American students are given increments of independence from adult and curricular authority that lead them to create their own social world. Our individualism is an attempt to deny social structure itself.

## Japanese Culture

Imagine some hypothetical tribe of the kind that anthropologists typically study. An account of such a tribe would explain its social order and patterns of behavior by reference to its culture, a system of underlying meaning presumably shared by the members of the tribe. A cultural interpretation is most helpful in illuminating the unusual or inexplicable aspects of tribal conduct—from the observers' perspective. The study of culture is thus strongly inclined to dwell on what is different between the tribe's assumptions and understandings of the world and the observers' own. Once the distinctive perceptual and conceptual axioms are set forth, the logic of such elements as the tribe's religion, etiquette, social relations, art, and so forth becomes more comprehensible, and the culture assumes a clarity for outsiders that it would not otherwise have. Such a hypothetical tribal culture is as simple as it is foreign, for its assumptions are presumably shared, coherent, and unquestioned by the tribe's members.

Japanese high school education does not fit this model. It is part of a complex society in which social practices are regularly open to scrutiny, reinterpretation, and reevaluation. Historical legacies of many kinds remain. Many separate perspectives exist. Foreign ideas, political ideologies, and new educational theories provide a confusing mélange of basic values and assumptions. It would be misleading to pretend that Japanese high schools have a single pristine, coherent culture.

Nor is our problem that meaning is hard to decipher; education is an arena of modern life preoccupied with meaning. Value-consciousness among teachers is high, especially when political conflict is involved, and their interpretations of school events, as we have seen, are far from uniform. In sum, the surface or conscious level of school culture can be stunningly complex, or "thick," to borrow a phrase from Clifford Geertz.

All the same, there is much that is culturally Japanese about high schools. The teachers, students, parents, and officials all share the same general tradition, speak the same language, and are concerned with doing well in the same society. They do not necessarily agree about what should be, but they know what is.

We can also perceive a solid and somewhat coherent base culture underlying the surface diversity. The categories of time, space, and social organization order daily routines and serve as a grammar for the institution. Exams, textbooks, and even ideological disagreement are permanent and assumed by all. The basic cultural character of Japanese high schools can best be located in such qualities, taken for granted as they are.

Outsiders to the system can gain insight by making general comparisons about the implicit learning in Japanese and American high schools. We have noted an assumption of socially fixed goals, activities, and proper role behavior that leaves precious little room for individual choice. Japanese students choose how hard they will work. They choose a club and a few electives. They are not surrounded, as Americans are, by a regular flow of choices. Japanese students are not expected to find themselves through a process of choice, experimentation, and individual discovery. They find themselves presumably by learning to meet the challenge of exams. In the United States, we make the discovery of personal inclinations and desires a key to progress toward adult independence and adjustment. Through the experience of academic and social choice, part-time jobs, career counseling, and so forth, our young are expected to find their own way, one that they are personally committed to. Without that commitment, choice is empty and motivation shallow. Young Americans set out like pioneers to create an independent existence, one in which the orientation is to self-fulfillment, not to some institution. Personal preference is held a central value in all matters.

The Japanese high school years are defined by a fixed set of uncontestable realities centering on the exam system. The path is straight and narrow. Students stick more closely to family and school. Choosing not to study hard is severely penalized. A culture of diligence results in acceptance rather than experimentation and is oriented to external, not internal realities. Diligence means outward conformity to the system, persistence in the pursuit of its goals, and significant self-denial. To Japanese, these are crucial aspects of maturity. Dewey, one assumes, would be disappointed.

Japanese schools teach a buttoned-down sense of time and space not unlike what one finds in the military. Compared with American schools, there is less free time each school day, less vacation time, and more homework. Compared with our high schools, there is much less informality and spontaneity. Students have less per capita space, and decoration is sparse at best. Student uniforms are as simple and plain as the schools themselves. Expectations and standards for leisure, entertainment, and aesthetic satisfaction are low.

The goals of instruction are also quite different. Exam-oriented Japanese students become virtual information junkies, drinking in as many facts as possible. They learn to listen well and to think quickly, but not to express their ideas. Neither speaking nor writing is encouraged. Speculation, controversy, and interpretive relativism do not enter the classroom. Thought is weighted in favor of memory and objective problem solving with little official curricular interest in creativity of a humanistic or artistic kind. The pedagogy may seem Confucian, but the real explanation is the matter of passing entrance exams.

The avowed goals of American teachers are radically different. Although we, too, have lectures and facts to memorize in high school, they are just part of the story. Classroom instruction in the United States ideally includes discussions, digressions, and personal opinions. In our better schools it means essays and research projects and debates. Considerably less well-informed than his Japanese counterpart, the American student is much better prepared to express a personal opinion and to think of a question as having more than one answer. Previously, I cited the Chinese proverb "He who learns but does not think is lost" as a warning for Japanese educators, but Confucius' own comment on this proverb is one that Americans need to remember. He said, "He who thinks but does not learn is in great danger," implying, according to Arthur Waley, that chaos arises from opinions not anchored in learning.[1]

1. Waley (1938), p. 91.

Diligence and compliance are favored by all institutions, and high schools in both countries reward students who work hard and follow directions. But the standards are higher in Japanese schools. Very little in Japanese high schools stands in contradiction to orderly behavior and hard work. Peer culture is not strong, and the school/society boundary holds well. The school's organization is streamlined to maintain order, and there is little institutional encouragement of conflicting, potentially disruptive values.

The democratic ideals of the American occupation have obviously not taken significant root in the culture of Japanese high schools. They are not comprehensive, democratic in process, or aimed at producing individual independence of mind. The teachers' union has been a significant factor in shielding the schools from right-wing tendencies, but the political stalemate has resulted in an essentially amoral, apolitical kind of education. Only faculty meetings model democracy, but their acrimony is seen as an embarrassment, and students are kept uninformed. In this sense, politics in schools appears unsightly.

Japan's postwar civil religion is certainly anemic by prewar standards. Its principal elements—democracy, a peaceful Japan, international cooperation, and economic growth—receive considerable attention in the textbooks but are not enshrined in the daily conduct of high schools. The daily routines teach courtesy, not blind discipline, and hard work is taught as in the interest of the individual, not just the nation. A citizen's duties are to behave properly and to vote. But American-style grass roots democracy encourages citizens to scrutinize and criticize government and to initiate political change. In fact, Japanese democracy differs greatly from American democracy. The popular base of most Japanese political parties is narrow, and the degree of participation in local decision making is limited. Ironically, one of the most active local political organizations in what might be termed "popular politics" is the teachers' union. All in all, high schools do not encourage grass roots politics or citizen activism, but the union wishes they would.

The university entrance exam is the dark engine driving high school culture. One wonders whether academic high schools could remain as orderly and serious if this pressure were absent. Without exams there would be less compliance with conventions and fewer limits on political squabbles and reform efforts. School systems and

individual teachers would be more innovative and more independent of the Ministry of Education, and education itself would become more colorful and chaotic. I doubt that most Japanese would
find such a development comfortable.

But, to be fair, the seeds of American cultural ideals of democracy
and individualism have had great difficulty growing in the soil of our
own high schools. Schools are institutions of mass processing and
socialization, and they do not easily fit these values. Our educators
are deeply frustrated by the simple tasks of merely controlling students and motivating them to fulfill basic requirements. The responsibility to teach our sacred cultural ideals, especially when these ideals are intrinsically anti-institutional, creates terrific opportunities
for education's critics but complicates the job of teaching. Our search
for freedom and individualism in the inherently bureaucratic school
context has led to innumerable experiments (schools without walls,
schools within schools, work-study programs, minischools, alternative schools, flextime, open entrance-exit systems, and so forth), but
never to an admission of fundamental incompatibility. The Japanese, lacking such a cultural imperative, have not been driven to pursue such contrary goals. Organizational rationality and pedagogical
consistency, whatever we may think of their product, reinforce each
other. The occupation made Japanese education less exclusive but
(with the exception of faculty meetings) not more American.

This is not to say that the Japanese high school is without cultural
problems. A basic contradiction exists between the fundamental assumptions that underlie exam preparation and those that give significance to virtually every other aspect of education. Because the
Japanese do little to correct this contradiction does not mean they
are not acutely aware of it. When the Japanese state was virtuous and
Japan needed new skills, exam preparation could be equated with
service to the nation. Today that is a remote connection. Students
are motivated by personal ambition. Elite private schools like Nada
are characterized in the media as morally deficient. Perhaps this criticism is unfair, but as a way of condemning the entire secondary system's preoccupation with exams, of which Nada is the symbol, it
makes sense. Schools subordinate group processes and other educational goals to the task of cramming individual minds with information. Progress and will are so narrowly channeled when the focus is
entrance exams that the inspirational side of instruction shrinks to

insignificance. Many aspects of human potential are not challenged in Japanese high schools, making for lopsided results. Yet the exams are at the center of a system that maintains high standards in science, math, and factual knowledge, that teaches the habits of hard work, persistence, and mastery of detail.

Vocational schools are affected differently by this contradiction. Where there is little or no prospect of taking or doing well on university exams, schools can easily fall into anomie, for alone they possess little inspiration or legitimacy. Teachers in vocational schools surprised me with the intensity of their search for meaning. The tightening of discipline at Yama is just one example of a general effort in vocational schools to find a charter that fits their students' true situation. The political activism of many vocational school teachers is evidence of this, as is the growing attention to the high school as a moral community.

Outside expectations of public education are not being satisfied. The Left holds a vision of socialist values being taught, whereas the Right would like to revitalize traditional norms and nationalist glories. Parents want hardier, more joyful adolescents coming home from school. There is much talk about the need for more moral education to teach respect and responsibility. In essence, there is a general yearning in Japan for more idealism and less cramming. There is support for even greater discipline over adolescent conduct, but this is coupled with a somewhat reduced curricular pace and a clearer mandate for vocational schools. What is striking about the public commentary on education is the general uncertainty about the cultural direction of the nation itself.

Public education must preserve and pass on public values, for it is one repository of a nation's identity and spirit. Modern education has a role analogous to the place of religion. Its mission is to teach the nation's ideals. But in contemporary Japan, which values should dominate is a question that has not been settled.

In more nationalistic times, the technomeritocratic was part of the inspirational, but contemporary Japanese high school education suffers an imbalance between the two. Efficiency is high but inspiration is low. Contributions to the economic ledger and to the functioning of the social system are notable, and no one suggests a retreat from them, but education should do more for the human spirit. Some teachers stand out as exceptions, but the imperative of exam preparation and the debilitation of political stalemate mean that few dreams are born. Students learn to be cooperative and polite with others, but not to sacrifice for them. They learn to recite the achievements of great men, but not to emulate them. Japanese adolescents are capable of creative exuberance, but the public high schools they attend are fundamentally dull. Efficiency comes at a heavy price.

Routinized efficiency, moreover, may not prove to be sufficient for Japan as she achieves prosperity and assumes a leadership role in the world. That future role will certainly require new skills and talents. Innovation will be very important. Japan will have to be more open and international in practice as well as principle. Her leaders will have to take greater risks and be more flexible. And moral convictions will be needed to guide her in international dealings. The present high educational standards will, of course, remain important, but new qualities not now found in education will have to be cultivated.

On one occasion, following a lecture on the merits of Japanese education, I was asked abruptly whether I would like my children to be educated in a Japanese high school. I unhesitatingly said no, adding defensively that I would say the same about most American high schools. Reflecting on my answer later, I realized that my response to high schooling in Japan was in part a reflection of my own very American sense of independence, which does not abide the constraints and rigors I encountered in Japan. But it also reflected my feeling that Japanese high schools represent but a small part of that country's humanistic tradition, a tradition rich in beauty, sensitivity, and spirit. At present this tradition survives, even thrives in places, without significant support from public education. Here lies my own ultimate squabble with Japan's high schools. The well-intended teachers and well-behaved students put their efforts to purposes that are ultimately shallow and uninspired. The nation benefits economically. Society is well run. But it is a system without much heart.

## National Efficiency

Both Japan and America have traditionally valued efficiency, but clearly the Japanese have surpassed us in their achievement of efficient schooling. This is a sobering fact, given the shrinking world of economic competition.

In the United States, we spend 7–8 percent of our gross national product on education. The Japanese spend 5–6 percent.[2] Student-teacher ratios in high schools of the two nations are roughly comparable. The total costs (including new construction and debt service) per high school student are not remarkably different. At the 1974 exchange of 290 yen to the dollar, Japan's expenditures on high school education were approximately $850 per student ($675 for private and $950 for public schools), whereas in the United States in 1973–74 the per capita figure for all elementary and secondary schools was $1,350.[3] High schools cost more per student than elementary schools, so the American figure must be adjusted upward somewhat. But the yen-dollar exchange at the time may have undervalued the yen, in which case the figure would have to be adjusted a bit the other way.[4] The impression remains of a rough comparability of resources expended on high school education.

The Japanese get much better results for their money. A higher percentage of students graduates from high school. One in ten young Japanese, but one in four Americans, does not finish high school. Equal proportions of students now go on to higher education, but a considerably higher proportion of males is taking a bachelor's degree in Japan than in the United States. More important, the skills and achievements of the average Japanese student are far greater for all levels up through twelfth grade. The Japanese go to school one-third more time than do Americans every year; over twelve years, they have had four more years of school. They can accommodate a more accelerated curriculum. They don't lose, during long summer vacations, half of what they have learned the previous year. Elementary education takes them farther in the basics, as well as in art and music, compared with our schools. In high school all students have more required courses in math, sciences, foreign languages, and social studies. The result, I estimate, is that the average Japanese high school graduate has the equivalent basic knowledge of the average American college graduate. The Japanese clearly cannot speak English well, but their knowledge of written English is certainly better

2. U.S. Department of Health, Education and Welfare (HEW), *Digest of Education Statistics, 1979* (Washington, D.C.: U.S. Government Printing Office); and Mombushō (1975).

3. Mombushō (1975), p. 296; HEW, *Digest of Education Statistics, 1979*.

4. At 225 yen to the dollar, the Japanese expenditure on high school per student in 1973 would have been about $1,100, still somewhat lower than in the United States.

than the average foreign language ability of our college graduates. It is not surprising that the Japanese do well in international tests of math and science, or that they now produce twice the number of engineers per capita as we do, or that Japanese literacy as measured by per capita newspaper circulation is higher.[5] If we were to recalculate the costs of education up to twelfth grade, comparing them with the results, there is no doubt that the Japanese system would come out at least several times more efficient than our own.

The great accomplishment of Japanese primary and secondary education lies not in its creation of a brilliant elite (Western industrial nations do better with their top students), but in its generation of such a high average level of capability. The profoundly impressive fact is that it is shaping a whole population, workers as well as managers, to a standard inconceivable in the United States, where we are still trying to implement high school graduation competency tests that measure only minimal reading and computing skills.

Visitors to Japan rarely fail to note that the average Japanese is a model of good conduct. Here, too, it is the high average that is notable. Orderliness and care in attending to details are qualities of the general population that are regularly remarked upon by foreign visitors. Comparative statistics of all kinds—from crime rates to life expectancies—confirm the impression that the average conduct of Japanese is highly socialized and under control. Any number of general efficiencies accrue from such widespread good conduct. The public costs of managing the population and of remedying antisocial behavior are low. The social overhead spent on unproductive people is less. Health care costs are reduced.

Japanese parenting, greatly influenced by level of education, is notably nurturing and stable. The Japanese criticize themselves regularly for being too attentive and preoccupied with their children's education. Yet, all in all, the result is highly commendable.

Another consequence of the high average level of education is that public communication in Japan is more sophisticated in content and more effective as a means of implementing public policy than in the United States. The news in Japan, for example, assumes a higher average educational level for its audience. When there is a general need for change in individual behavior, for example, in energy con-

5. Japanese households in 1974 were subscribing to an average of two daily papers, and circulation per capita was the highest in the world. Sōrifu, Tokei Kyoku (1974).

servation, the communication is picked up by a larger part of the population more quickly, and the level of compliance to reasoned proposals seems to me higher in Japan. No documentation of this assertion exists, but it follows logically from all that is considered here.

Most important, however, is the impressively high level of skills and good work habits exhibited by the average Japanese in the workplace. I have been in contact with many people involved in Japanese-American industrial joint ventures. Those who look closely at comparable production processes in the two nations regularly remark on the capacity of the Japanese to do somewhat better with the same equipment and constraints. The reasons become clear only on close examination of how average workers perform their jobs. Better familiarity with equipment, greater cleanliness, quicker anticipation, and more attention to detail are mentioned most often.

What is true of industrial processes is also true of office work, agriculture, and other forms of production. Much has been made of Japanese management, and indeed, well-managed companies train and encourage high levels of average behavior. But it must be remembered that, before assuming adult responsibilities, young Japanese have undergone a socialization process that is the crucial source of much that we attribute to Japanese management techniques. This socialization teaches careful, intelligent work habits aimed at reducing routine mistakes. Another crucial ingredient is a capacity to remain alert and to find repetitive work interesting. Japanese workers generally accept organizations as allies and are responsive to their requirements—including, for example, working late to solve problems. Organizational discipline is high, as is the capacity of small work groups to sustain motivation and serve as the conduit for worker participation. All these qualities can be traced back to the learning and experience given young Japanese. High school has been the example here, but family, primary education, and company training are all involved.

Japan is shifting rapidly toward high technology. She has demonstrated swiftness and competence that properly worry her competitors in the international race to create and reshape industries using the microprocessor, robotics, and biotechnology. In this race, a basic technological breakthrough provides a temporary advantage; over a longer period, the broad capacity of a society to learn and to apply the new technology becomes of central importance. A work force capable of moving up the ladder of technology, a work force able to realize the achievements of innovative leaders, establishes the basic value of new knowledge for a society. Thousands of special skills are needed in production, and the entire population must learn the rudimentary applications of today's emerging technology. Just as it takes a literate public to utilize an invention such as printing, so an educated population is fundamental to realize the potential of each new breakthrough. Technological literacy is going to be a distinct advantage to Japan in the evolving competition. Japan produces more than twice as many engineers per capita as the United States, and the average Japanese worker has learned much more math and science in school. The new skills will come easily to a population prepared to move with the times. In the rapidly evolving, expanding areas of an economy, a shortage of skills is a predictable barrier to growth. This barrier is significantly lower in Japan due to education.

The connections between average abilities and the general efficiency of whole societies are not easily traced and documented with empirical precision. Particular connections are clear, and experience in every kind of social institution tells us that the level of competence of individual participants affects the overall institutional outcome. Yet linking the quality of human capital to micro-level behavior and linking this to macro-level economic and social results require an international comparative approach to whole societies, something we do not yet have. So many variables can affect the linkages that we shy away from comparisons of this sort. But when it comes to Japan, common sense insists that the whole issue be taken very seriously. The human capital contribution to overall efficiency is in evidence in many aspects of Japanese social life; and now Japan's international competitive prowess has raised the issue for other nations that must compete with her standards of efficiency.

The United States has benefited from abundant opportunity and a genius for innovation. We tapped the talents of immigrants and the ambitious by laissez-faire social policies. Until recently, that sufficed. In comparison, Japan has always seen human resources as fundamental. As a resource-poor late developer, she had no choice. The recent minister of education, Nagai Michio, once said to me, "When I was Minister I always had one overriding goal—the independence of the Japanese nation." He meant that he viewed education primarily as a critical factor in the defense and prosperity of his country.

What makes Japanese high schools notably efficient besides the longer school year? First, teachers conduct large classes, and with the time saved they administer the school. This, of course, is possible only because students are well-behaved, because they are grouped by academic ability, and because they are all intent on the same goal of entrance exams. Second, progress in the conventional subjects is rapid because the university race creates great momentum. The competitive realities of education are widely appreciated by parents. High school rank ordering and entrance exams bring this reality into the early years of schooling. Third, vacations are short, tangential issues are avoided, and learning time is narrowly concentrated. The curriculum is focused on basics and is nearly free of compromise. The school physical plant is simple to maintain. Fourth, the entire system is coordinated nationally by the high standards set by the Ministry of Education. Finally, the tightly run organization of the school reduces confusion and leaves little room for a student counterculture.

Would adopting components of this scheme help solve the problems of American secondary education? Japanese high schools can be a mirror but not a model for Americans. The profound fact is that the results of American high schooling are largely a reflection of our culture and the present state of our society. We begin with a very different population, a different university system, a different pedagogical tradition, and even a different sense of organization. The attitudes and habits of our young have not been learned only in schools and will not be changed by simply rearranging them. The root of our problem in failing to better develop our human resources is our failure to acknowledge that goal as our highest priority. I believe the Japanese challenge will change this. New international standards for the average citizen have been quietly set by the Japanese in an age when access to technology, capital, and raw materials is increasingly equal. We should not try to emulate Japanese institutions, but we must recognize and try to match their accomplishments.

To do this is to reverse our retreat from the responsibilities of child rearing, to end our casual, laissez-faire approach to pedagogy, and to enshrine excellence in the academic fundamentals. These are basic challenges. We may also have to set national standards and acknowledge the value of tracking by ability in secondary education. All this may seem to represent a retreat into traditionalism, but I prefer to see it as confirming two basic articles of faith: that life rests on social interdependence, and that the achievement of human potential is a fundamental social good. Individualism and freedom in any other context are sad illusions, and progress toward social equality that cannot be integrated with the pursuit of general excellence has no long-term viability.

# Appendix:
# Exams, Schools, and Youth Suicides

CRITICS can, and invariably do, find in the problems and social ills of society evidence of the failure of public education. It is easy to suggest cause and effect relations between schooling and the lamentable aspects of society, and it is equally difficult to disprove them. Sweeping interpretations containing some answers appeal to the popular mind and are useful in campaigns to reform education. A case in point is the relation between Japan's exam system and juvenile suicide.

Images are often more powerful than factual complexity; and the tragic image of a diligent student committing suicide upon failing to pass an entrance examination is one of the most powerful weapons in the armory of those in Japan and abroad who are critical of Japan's education system. Every year as examination time arrives, newspapers and magazines carry reports of student suicides. Typically, the suicide thus publicized is a middle-class boy who worked hard in school and became despondent about a coming examination, or guilty and depressed about having failed. During the rest of the year newspaper reports of juvenile suicide are rare. The general public thus receives the impression that the causal relation between exams and juvenile suicide is strong. Foreigners writing about post-World

327

War II Japanese education have echoed this theme.[1] The issue has not to my knowledge ever been investigated closely, but merely reviewing the available facts reveals a significantly different story.

In the early 1950s, the Japanese rate of juvenile suicide was spectacularly high by international standards, but it dropped dramatically after 1959 (Figure 3).[2] In the international rankings, Japan slipped from first place in 1955 to fourth in 1973 for the age group fifteen to twenty-four.[3] Moreover, by 1973 the rate for Japanese males fifteen to twenty-four years old was tied with Canada for ninth place, behind Finland, El Salvador, Czechoslovakia, Hungary, Iceland, Switzerland, Sweden, and West Germany. The rate for Japanese females that age remained the highest among industrial nations. After 1959 the high female suicide rate kept the overall Japanese juvenile rate near the top of international lists.[4]

The crucial point is that the juvenile suicide rate was dropping rapidly at the same time as matriculation rates to Japanese high schools and universities were rising. As the percentage of young Japanese involved in the pressures of the exam system increased, the suicide rate for their age group declined. Compared with 1955, 14 percent more of the age cohort were taking high school examinations in 1970, and 8 percent more were taking examinations to higher education, yet the suicide rate for fifteen- to nineteen-year-olds fell from 32 per 100,000 in 1955 to 9 per 100,000 in 1970.[5] If there is a relation between examinations and the suicide rate, it will not be discovered in correlations between the general trends in those two realms.

Japanese students do commit suicide, however, and there can be no doubt that a proportion of them do so in response to school problems, some in response to exams. Although anything short of direct case-by-case investigation will leave many questions unanswered, known statistics go far in sorting out the relationship. Seasonal vari-

1. Kobayashi (1963), Vogel (1977), Passin (1965), OECD (1977), and Reischauer (1977) are some of the writers (in English) who mention suicide in the context of a discussion of exam pressures.
2. Inamura (1978), p. 9.
3. World Health Organization figures, presented in ibid., p. 11.
4. See Iga et al. (1975).
5. Inamura (1978). In 1973 the suicide rate for Japanese males (fifteen to twenty-four years old) was 19.9 percent and for females 13.1 percent. For the United States that year, the male rate was 20.9 percent and the female rate 7.1 percent; Canada's male rate was 19.9 percent and the female rate 5.0 percent.

**Figure 3**
Suicide Rates per 100,000 Persons by Year and Age Group in Japan, 1947–1973

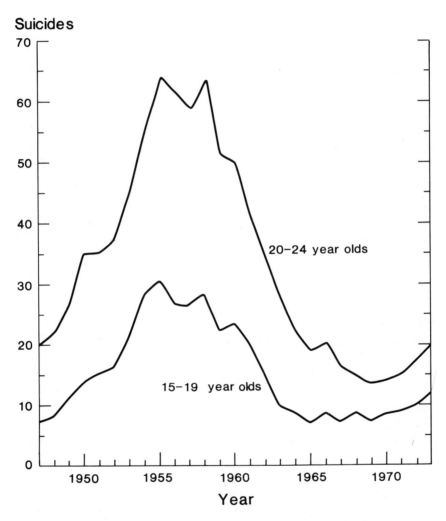

SOURCE: Data from Jisatsu Shibo Tokei, Koseishō, *Kosei Hakushō*, 1974.

**Table 13**

Motives for Suicides Among Persons Under Twenty-one in Japan, January to June 1977

| Motive | Number of Suicides | Percentage of Total | Male | Female |
|---|---|---|---|---|
| Family related | 54 | 13.6 | 37 | 17 |
| Illness related | 39 | 9.8 | 26 | 13 |
| Work related | 15 | 3.7 | 11 | 4 |
| Relations with opposite sex | 52 | 13.1 | 25 | 27 |
| School related | 106 | 26.6 | 72 | 34 |
| Other (including mental illness) | 132 | 33.2 | 96 | 36 |
| Total | 398 | | 267 | 131 |

SOURCE: Data from National Police Agency, Juvenile Section, as reported in Inamura (1978), p. 28.

NOTE: For each case only one cause or motive was labeled as primary for classification purposes.

ation in suicide rates should reflect critical events of the school calendar. The rates for middle and high school students are highest during the time just before and after the end of summer vacation.[6] The next highest period for both groups is the first three months of the school year (April, May, and June). This is a time when those who have failed entrance exams might become despondent. But the rates for February and March, when exam pressures are greatest and failures become known, are not high. This underlines the fact that Japanese newspapers report student suicides during that time to highlight an educational problem, not because there is a seasonal increase in the statistics. The question of seasons is further complicated by the fact that adult suicides in Japan, as in many countries of the northern hemisphere, also peak in April and May.[7] Only in the high rate at the end of summer vacation is the school-age pattern atypical. As we shall see, this will fit with other pieces of evidence pointing to maladjustment to school—not to pressures directly attributable to exams or high achievement—as the more powerful education-related factor affecting youth suicides in Japan.

6. Inamura (1978), p. 14.
7. Ibid., p. 15.

# Glossary

**bunkai**   school local of the Japan Teachers Union
**bunkasai**   annual high school Culture Festival
**Burakumin**   minority group of Japanese, distinguished by special
    low-status occupations until 1870
**deitto**   date (social engagement of a boy and girl)
**futsū kōkō**   literally, regular high school—one with an academic
    orientation designed to prepare students for higher education
**han** schools   fief schools
**homurūmu**   homeroom
**jishū**   self-directed study when teacher is absent
**juken jigoku**   literally, entrance examination hell
**juken sensō**   literally, entrance examination war
**juku**   tutoring or cram school
**kenshubi**   weekly day off for teachers to do research or preparation
**kodomo**   child
**koibito**   lover
**kurābu**   school extracurricular club
**kyōiku**   education
**Meiji**   the period 1868–1911
**mogi shiken**   practice entrance examination
**Mombushō**   Ministry of Education

**Nikkyōso**   Japan Teachers Union

**oyabun**   boss or patron

**rōnin**   literally, leaderless samurai; in this context, students who try again a year after failing to pass college entrance examinations

**salariman**   salaried employee of a company

**seishin**   spiritual, or pertaining to character strength

**sempai**   one's senior

**senmon gakkō**   higher vocational schools

**sensei**   teacher

**shūnin seido**   system in which head teachers are salaried administrators

**taiku taikai**   annual high school Sports Day

**Todai**   Tokyo University

**Tokugawa**   the period 1600–1868

**tomodachi**   friend

**tsukiai**   informal socializing

**yobikō**   supplementary preparatory schools at the secondary level

**zaibatsu**   large conglomerates of the pre-World War II era

# References

*English*

Adams, Donald.
  1960   "Rebirth of Moral Education in Japan." *Comparative Education Review* 4:1:61–64.
Anderson, Ronald S.
  1975   *Education in Japan; A Century of Modern Development.* U.S. Department of Health, Education and Welfare, Office of Education. Washington, D.C.: U.S. Government Printing Office.
Atsumi, Reiko.
  1975   "Personal Relations of Japanese White-Collar Company Employees." Ph.D. dissertation, University of Pittsburgh.
Bachman, Jerald G., et al.
  1980   *Monitoring the Future, 1978: Questionnaire Responses from the Nation's High School Seniors.* Ann Arbor: University of Michigan, Institute for Social Research.
Bahr, Howard M.
  1980   "Changes in Family Life in Middletown, 1924–1977." *Public Opinion Quarterly* 33:35–52.
Bayley, David H.
  1976   *Forces of Order: Police Behavior in Japan and the United States.* Berkeley and Los Angeles: University of California Press.
Beauchamp, Edward R.
  1976   *An American Teacher in Meiji Japan.* Honolulu: University Press of Hawaii.

1978 "Shiken Jigoku: The Problem of Entrance Examinations in Japan."
*Asian Profile* 6:6:543–560.

Beer, Lawrence W.
1975 "Education, Politics, and Freedom in Japan: The Ienaga Textbook
Review Cases." *Law in Japan: An Annual* 8:67–90.

Bellah, Robert N.
1957 *Tokugawa Religion.* Glencoe, Ill.: Free Press.
1965 "Ienaga Saburō and the Search for Meaning in Modern Japan." In
*Changing Japanese Attitudes Toward Modernization,* ed. Marius
Jansen. Princeton: Princeton University Press.

Bereday, George F., and Shigeo Masui.
1973 *American Education Through Japanese Eyes.* Honolulu: University Press of Hawaii.

Bidwell, Charles E.
1965 "The School as a Formal Organization." In *Handbook of Organizations,* ed. James G. March. Chicago: Rand McNally.

Bonet, Vicente M., ed.
1973 *Religion in the Japanese Textbooks.* 3 vols. Tokyo: Enderle Book
Co.

Bowman, Mary Jean.
1981 *Educational Choice and Labor Markets in Japan.* Chicago: University of Chicago Press.

Brameld, Theodore.
1968 *Japan: Culture, Education, and Change in Two Communities.*
New York: Holt, Rinehart & Winston.

Brett, Cecil Carter.
1954 "Japan's New Education Laws." *Far Eastern Review* 25:170–175.

Bronfenbrenner, Urie.
1970 *Two Worlds of Childhood: U.S. and U.S.S.R.* New York: Russell
Sage Foundation.

Brown, Marjorie L.
1979 "Teenage Prostitution." *Adolescence* 5:14:56:665–679.

Calhoun, John A., Edith A. Grotberg, and W. Ray Rickley.
1980 *The Status of Children, Youth, and Families, 1979.* Publication No.
80-30274. Washington, D.C.: U.S. Department of Health and Human Services.

Chilman, Catherine S.
1980 *Adolescent Sexuality in a Changing American Society.* Washington, D.C.: U.S. Department of Health, Education and Welfare.

Clark, Rodney.
1979 *The Japanese Company.* New Haven: Yale University Press.

Cole, Robert E.
1979 *Work, Mobility, and Participation: A Comparative Study of American and Japanese Industry.* Berkeley and Los Angeles: University
of California Press.

Coleman, James S.

1961 *The Adolescent Society: The Social Life of the Teenager and Its Impact on Education.* New York: Free Press.

Comber, L. C., and John P. Keeves.

1973 *Science Achievement in Nineteen Countries.* New York: John Wiley and Sons.

Craiger, J.

1968 "The Aims and Content of School Courses in Japanese History, 1872–1945." *Monumenta Nipponica,* 23:51–81.

Csikszentnihalyi, Mihaly, et al.

1977 "The Ecology of Adolescent Activity and Experience." *Journal of Youth and Adolescence* 6:3:281–294.

Cummings, William K.

1976 "The Problems and Prospects for Japanese Higher Education." In *The Paradox of Progress,* ed. Lewis Austin. New Haven: Yale University Press.

1977 "The Secret of Japanese Education: The Role of Education in Socioeconomic Achievement." Final Report to the United States National Institute of Education on Research.

1980 *Education and Equality in Japan.* Princeton: Princeton University Press.

Cusick, Philip A.

1973 *Inside High Schools: The Student's World.* New York: Holt, Rinehart & Winston.

Dearman, Nancy B., and Valena White Plisko.

1980 *The Condition of Education.* Washington, D.C.: National Center for Educational Statistics.

De Vos, George, and Keiichi Mizushima.

1962 "The School and Delinquency: Perspectives from Japan." *Teacher's College Record* 63:8:626–638.

De Vos, George, and Hiroshi Wagatsuma.

1972 "Family Life and Delinquency: Some Perspectives from Japanese Research." In *Transcultural Research in Mental Health,* ed. William P. Lebra. Honolulu: University Press of Hawaii.

De Vos, George, and Hiroshi Wagatsuma, eds.

1966 *Japan's Invisible Race: Caste in Culture and Personality.* Berkeley and Los Angeles: University of California Press.

Diepold, John, and Richard David Young.

1979 "Empirical Studies of Adolescent Sexual Behavior: A Critical Review." *Adolescence* 14:13:49–63.

Dore, Ronald P.

1964 "Education: Japan." In *Political Modernization in Japan and Turkey,* ed. Robert Ward and Dankwart A. Rustow. Princeton: Princeton University Press.

1965 *Education in Tokugawa Japan.* Berkeley and Los Angeles: University of California Press.

1967 "Mobility, Equality, and Individuation in Modern Japan." In *Aspects of Social Change in Modern Japan*. Princeton: Princeton University Press.

1970 "Textbook Censorship in Japan: The Ienaga Case." *Pacific Affairs* 43:4:548–556.

1973 *British Factory–Japanese Factory*. Berkeley and Los Angeles: University of California Press.

Duke, Benjamin C.

1964 "The New Guide for Teaching Moral Education in Japan." *Comparative Education Review* 8:2:186–190.

1969 "The Pacific War in Japanese and American High Schools: A Comparison of the Textbook Teachings." *Comparative Education* 5:1:73–82.

1973 *Japan's Militant Teachers*. Honolulu: University Press of Hawaii.

Fetters, William B.

1975 *National Longitudinal Study of High School Class of 1972*. Department of Health, Education and Welfare, National Center for Educational Statistics. Washington, D.C.: U.S. Government Printing Office.

Friedenberg, Edgar.

1965 *Coming of Age in America*. New York: Random House.

Friedman, Neil Kassell.

1977 "Education as a Political Issue in Japan." Ph.D. dissertation, Stanford University.

Fujita, Hidenori.

1978 "Education and Status Attainment in Modern Japan." Ph.D. dissertation, Stanford University.

Fukuzawa Yukichi.

1960 *The Autobiography of Fukuzawa Yukichi*. Translated by Eiichi Kiyooka. Tokyo: Hokuseido.

Gayn, Mark.

1948 *Japan Diary*. New York: William Sloane.

Hall, Ivan Parker.

1973 *Mori Arinori*. Cambridge, Mass.: Harvard University Press.

Hall, John Whitney.

1959 "The Confucian Teacher in Tokugawa Japan." In *Confucianism in Action*, ed. David S. Nivison and Arthur F. Wright. Stanford: Stanford University Press.

Hall, Robert King.

1949a *Education for a New Japan*. New Haven: Yale University Press.

1949b *Shūshin: Ethics of a Defeated Nation*. New York: Columbia University, Teachers College Press.

Hall, Robert King, ed.

1949 *Kokutai no Hongi*. Cambridge, Mass.: Harvard University Press.

Halsey, A. H., Jean Floud, and C. Arnold Anderson.
1961 *Education, Economy and Society: A Reader in the Sociology of Education.* New York: Free Press.
Hidaka, Daishiro.
1956 "The Aftermath of Educational Reform." *Annals of the American Academy of Political and Social Science,* vol. 308.
Husen, Torstein, ed.
1967 *International Study of Achievement in Mathematics: A Comparison of Twelve Countries.* Vol. 2. New York: John Wiley and Sons.
Ianni, Francis A., and Edward Storey.
1973 *Cultural Relevance and Educational Issues.* Boston: Little, Brown.
Iga, Mamoru, Joe Yamamoto, and Thomas Noguchi.
1975 "The Vulnerability of Young Japanese Women and Suicide." *Suicide* 5:4:207–222.
Ikutaro, Yoshihiro.
1963 "Entrance Examinations: A Challenge to Equal Opportunity in Education." *Journal of Social and Political Ideas in Japan* 1:3:88–93.
Jansen, Marius B.
1961 *Sakamoto Ryōma and the Meiji Restoration.* Princeton: Princeton University Press.
Johnston, Lloyd D.
1979 *Drugs and the Class of '78: Behaviors, Attitudes, and Recent National Trends.* Rockville, Md.: U.S. Department of Health, Education and Welfare, National Institute on Drug Abuse.
Kaigo, Tokiomi.
1968 *Japanese Education: Its Past and Present.* Tokyo: Kokusai Bunka Shinkokai.
Kajita, Eiichi.
1976 *Development of Self-Growth Attitudes and Habits in School Children.* Research Bulletin of the National Institute for Educational Research, no. 14.
Karasawa, Tomitarō.
1955 "Changes in Japanese Education as Revealed in Textbooks." *Japan Quarterly* 2:365–383.
Kato, Hiroki.
1978 "Is the Japanese Writing System Superior to the English System?" Manuscript. Honolulu: University of Hawaii, Department of East Asian Languages.
Kawai, Kazuo.
1960 *Japan's American Interlude.* Chicago: University of Chicago Press.
Kelley, Clarence M.
1977 *Crime in the United States, 1976: Uniform Crime Reports.* Washington, D.C.: U.S. Government Printing Office.
Khleif, Bud B.
1971 "The School as a Small Society." In *Anthropological Perspectives on Education,* ed. Murray L. Wax et al. New York: Basic Books.

Kinsey, Alfred C., et al.
   1953  *Sexual Behavior in the Human Female.* Philadelphia: W. B. Saunders.
Kobayashi, Tetsuya.
   1978  *Society, Schools, and Progress in Japan.* Oxford, Eng.: Pergamon Press.
Kobayashi, Victor.
   1963  "Japan's Examination Hell." *Education Forum* 28:19–23.
Kondō, Sumio.
   1974  "Off We Go to Our Lessons." *The Japan Interpreter* 9:1:15–24.
Koschmann, J. Victor.
   1974  "Tatemae to Honne." *The Japan Interpreter* 9:2:98–104.
Lee, Kenneth Bok.
   1974  "The Postwar Reforms and Educational Development in Japan, 1945–1970." Ph.D. dissertation, University of Southern California.
Long, T. Dixon.
   1969  "Policy and Politics in Japanese Science: The Persistence of Tradition." *Minerva* (Spring 1969).
Lortie, Dan C.
   1975  *Schoolteacher: A Sociological Study.* Chicago: University of Chicago Press.
Makino, Tatsumi.
   1970  "Juvenile Delinquency and Home Training." In *Families in East and West,* ed. Reuben Hill and Rene Konig. Paris: Mouton.
Makita, Kiyoshi.
   1968  "The Rarity of Reading Disability in Japanese Children." *American Journal of Orthopsychiatry* 38:599–614.
Maruyama, Masao.
   1963  *Thought and Behavior in Modern Japanese Politics.* London: Oxford University Press.
   1974  *Studies in the Intellectual History of Tokugawa Japan.* Translated by Mikio Hane. Tokyo: University of Tokyo Press.
Mitchell, Richard H.
   1967  *The Korean Minority in Japan.* Berkeley and Los Angeles: University of California Press.
Miyauchi, D. Y.
   1964  "Textbooks and the Search for a New National Ethics in Japan." *Japan Quarterly* 3:414–425.
Miyoshi, Masao.
   1974  *Accomplices of Silence: Aspects of the Modern Japanese Novel.* Berkeley and Los Angeles: University of California Press.
Murthy, P. A. Narashimha.
   1973  *The Rise of Modern Nationalism in Japan: An Historical Study of the Role of Education in the Making of Modern Japan.* Delhi: Ashajana K.

Nagai, Michio.
    1971 *Higher Education in Japan: Its Take-Off and Crash*. Tokyo: University of Tokyo Press.
Najita, Tetsuo.
    1974 *Japan: The Intellectual Foundations of Modern Politics*. Chicago: University of Chicago Press.
Najita, Tetsuo, and Irwin Scheiner.
    1978 *Japanese Thought in the Tokugawa Period: Methods and Metaphors*. Chicago: University of Chicago Press.
Nakane, Chie.
    1970 *Japanese Society*. Berkeley and Los Angeles: University of California Press.
National Center for Education Statistics.
    1980 *The Conditions of Education, 1980 Edition*. Washington, D.C.: U.S. Department of Education.
National Panel on High School and Adolescent Education.
    1976 *The Education of Adolescents*. Washington, D.C.: U.S. Government Printing Office.
Nishi, Toshio.
    1982 *Unconditional Democracy: Education and Politics in Occupied Japan, 1945–1952*. Stanford: Hoover Institution Press.
Nitobe, Inazo.
    1905 *Bushido: The Soul of Japan*. New York: G. P. Putnam's Sons.
Noguchi, Paul Hideyo.
    1974 "The 'One Railroad Family' of the Japanese National Railway: A Cultural Analysis of Japanese Industrial Familialism." Ph.D. dissertation, University of Pittsburgh.
Nordstrom, Carl, et al.
    1967 *Society's Children: A Study of Resentment in the Secondary School*. New York: Random House.
Okochi, K., et al., eds.
    1974 *Workers and Employers in Japan*. Princeton: Princeton University Press.
Ono, Susumu.
    1979 "The Japanese Language and Modernization in Japan." *Look Japan*, May 10, 1979.
Organization for Economic Cooperation and Development.
    1977 *Reviews of National Policies for Education: Japan*. Paris: Organization for Economic Cooperation and Development.
Osterndorf, Logan.
    1975 *Summary of Offerings and Enrollments in Public Secondary Schools, 1972–1973*. Publication No. 76-150. Washington, D.C.: U.S. Department of Health, Education and Welfare.
Passin, Herbert.
    1965 *Society and Education in Japan*. New York: Columbia University, Teachers College Press.

Pempel, T. J.
   1975   "The Politics of Higher Education in Japan." Ph.D. dissertation, Columbia University.
Pyle, Kenneth.
   1969   *The New Generation in Meiji Japan: Problems of Cultural Identity, 1885–1895.* Stanford: Stanford University Press.
Reischauer, Edwin O.
   1977   *The Japanese.* Cambridge, Mass.: Harvard University Press.
*Report of the White House Conference on Youth.*
   1971   Washington, D.C.: U.S. Government Printing Office.
Riggs, Lynne E.
   1977   "Ranjuku Jidai." *Japan Interpreter* 2:4:541–549.
Roberts, Joan I., and Sherrie K. Akinsanya.
   1976   *Schooling in the Cultural Context.* New York: David McKay.
Roden, Donald T.
   1980   *Schooldays in Imperial Japan: A Study of the Culture of a Student Elite.* Berkeley and Los Angeles: University of California Press.
Rohlen, Thomas P.
   1974   *For Harmony and Strength: Japanese White-Collar Organization in Anthropological Perspective.* Berkeley and Los Angeles: University of California Press.
   1975   "The Small Work Group." In *Modern Japanese Organization and Decision-Making*, ed. Ezra Vogel. Berkeley and Los Angeles: University of California Press.
   1976   "Violence at Yoka High School." *Asian Survey* 16:7:682–699.
   1977   "Is Japanese Education Becoming Less Egalitarian? Notes on High School Stratification and Reform." *Journal of Japanese Studies* 3:1:37–70.
   1980   "The Juku Phenomenon: An Exploratory Essay." *Journal of Japanese Studies* 6:2:207–242.
   1981   "The Education of Koreans in Japan." In *Koreans in Japan*, ed. Changsoo Lee and George De Vos. Berkeley and Los Angeles: University of California Press.
Forthcoming
         "Conflict in Japanese Education." In Ellis Krauss, Thomas Rohlen, and Patricia Steinhoff, eds., *Conflict in Contemporary Japan.*
Sato, Saburo.
   1968   "Image of an Ideal Japanese Person." *Educational Forum* 33:97–102.
Sawyer, Malcolm.
   1976   *Income Distribution in OECD Countries.* Paris: Organization for Economic Cooperation and Development Occasional Studies.
Shimahara, Nobuo.
   1971   *Burakumin: A Japanese Minority and Education.* The Hague: Martinus Nijhoff.

Shively, Donald H.
  1959 "Motoda Eifu: Confucian Lecturer to the Meiji Emperor." In *Confucianism in Action*, ed. David S. Nivison and Arthur F. Wright. Stanford: Stanford University Press.
Singleton, John.
  1967 *Nichū: A Japanese School*. New York: Holt, Rinehart & Winston.
Skinner, Kenneth Alan.
  1978 "The Japanese Salaryman in a Government Bureaucracy." Ph.D. dissertation, University of Minnesota.
Smith, Ernest A.
  1962 *American Youth Culture: Group Life in Teenage Society*. New York: Free Press.
Sommer, Robert.
  1974 *Tight Spaces: Hard Architecture and How to Humanize It*. Englewood Cliffs, N.J.: Prentice Hall.
Spaulding, Robert M.
  1967 *Imperial Japan's Higher Civil Service Examinations*. Princeton: Princeton University Press.
Spindler, George D.
  1974 *Education and Cultural Process*. New York: Holt, Rinehart & Winston.
Stead, Alfred.
  1906 *Great Japan: A Study of National Efficiency*. London and New York: J. Lane.
Steiner, Kurt.
  1965 *Local Government in Japan*. Stanford: Stanford University Press.
Sumiya, Mikio.
  1967 "The Function and Social Structure of Education: Schools and Japanese Society." *Journal of Social and Political Ideas in Japan* 5:2−3:117−138.
Supreme Commander, Allied Powers: General Headquarters.
  1949 *Education in the New Japan*. Tokyo: Supreme Commander, Allied Powers: General Headquarters, Civil Information and Education Section.
Thompson, E. P.
  1967 "Time, Work-Discipline and Industrial Capitalism." *Past and Present* 36:56−97.
Thurston, David.
  1973 *Teachers and Politics in Japan*. Princeton: Princeton University Press.
Tominaga, Kenichi.
  1970 "Studies of Social Stratification and Social Mobility in Japan." *Rice University Studies* 56:133−149.
United States Department of Health and Human Services.
  1980 *The Status of Children, Youth, and Families*. Washington, D.C.: U.S. Government Printing Office.

United States Senate Committee on the Judiciary: Subcommittee to Investigate Juvenile Delinquency.

1977 *Challenge for the Third Century: Education in a Safe Environment. Hearings on the Nature and Prevention of School Violence and Vandalism.* Washington, D.C.: U.S. Government Printing Office.

Vogel, Ezra.

1977 *Japan as Number One.* Cambridge, Mass.: Harvard University Press.

Waley, Arthur, trans.

1938 *The Analects of Confucius.* London: George Allen and Unwin.

Waller, Willard.

1932 *The Sociology of Teaching.* New York: John Wiley and Sons.

Wax, Murray L., Stanley Diamond, and Fred O. Gearing.

1971 *Anthropological Perspectives on Education.* New York: Basic Books.

Wray, H. J.

1973 "A Study in Contrasts: Japanese School Textbooks in 1903 and 1941–1945." *Monumenta Nipponica* 28:63–78.

Yamamura, Kozo, and Susan B. Hanley.

1975 "Ichi hime, ni Tarō: Educational Aspirations and the Decline of Fertility in Postwar Japan." *Journal of Japanese Studies* 2:1:83–125.

Young, Michael.

1958 *The Rise of the Meritocracy.* London: Penguin.

## Japanese

Asō Makoto and Fujinaga Tamotsu, eds.

1975 *Nōryoku, Tekisei, Senbatsu to Kyōiku.* Tokyo. Daiichi Hōki.

Asō Makoto and Ushiogi Morikazu, eds.

1977 *Gakureki Kōyoron.* Tokyo: Yūhikaku.

Endo Toyokichi.

1975 *Gakushū Juku: Hontō no Kyōiku to wa nani ka?* Tokyo: Fūtōsha.

Fukaya Masashi.

1969 *Gakureki-shugi no Keifu.* Tokyo: Reimei-shobō.

Hashizume Sadao, ed.

1976 *Gakureki Henchō to Sono Kōzai.* Tokyo: Daiichi Hōki.

Hazama Hiroshi, ed.

1977 *Nippon no Kigyo to Shakai.* Tokyo: Nippon Keizai Shinbunsha.

"Higatsuita Yobiko Gyokai Sensō."

1977 *Shukan Asahi.* Janaury 7, 1977, pp. 176–177.

Hyōgo-ken, Kikakubu.

1976 *Hyōgo-ken no Gakko.* Kobe: Kōyū Instasu K.K.

Hyōgo-ken Kōtō Gakkō Kyōshokuin Kumiai.

1971 *Kumiaiin no Shiori.* Kobe.

Ikutaro Kintaro.
1974 "Sengo no Kyōiku ni tsuite." *Chūō Kōron* 89:11:70–93.
Imada Takotoshi and Hara Junsuke.
1977 "Gendai Nippon no Kaisō-Kōzō: Chii no Ikkansei to Hiikkansei."
*Gendai Shakaigaku* 8:59–114.
Inamura Hiroshi.
1978 *Kodomo no Jisatsu.* Tokyo: Tokyo Daigaku Shuppankai.
Inazumi Kenjiro.
1974 *Hikisakareta Kyōiku.* Tokyo: Kyōiku Kaihatsu Kenkyūsho.
Jiyūminshutō Seisaku Chōsakai.
1977 *Wagatō no Kōyaku.* Tokyo: Jiyūminshutō/Kohō-iinkai Shuppan-
kyoku.
Kadowaki Atsushi.
1978 *Gendai no Shussekan.* Tokyo: Nippon Keizai Shinbunsha.
Kaigo Tokiomi, ed.
1975 *Kyōiku Kakumei.* Tokyo: Tokyo Diagaku Shuppankai.
Katsuyama Masami.
1974 *Nadakō no Moretsu Juken Seinen.* Tokyo: Kyōdō Shuppan.
Kawai Hayao.
1975 "Bosei Shikai Nihon no Eitoku no Shonen Tachi." *Chūo Kōron*
90:4:58–72.
Kobe-shi Kōtōgakkō Kyōshokunin Kumiai [Kobe High School Teachers
Union].
1973 *Kobe-shikōkō Hakusho.* Kobe: Kōtōgakkō Kyōshokunin Kumiai.
Kobe-shi Kyōiku Iinkai. [Kobe Board of Education].
1974a "Katei Gakushū no Jittai Chosa." *Kyōiku Kenkyū Tenbo.* No. 98.
1974b *Kobe-shi Kyōiku Nenpo, 1974.* Kobe: Kyōbunsha.
Kobe-shi Kyōiku-shi Henshū Iinkai [Kobe Education History Compilation
Committee].
1966 *Kobe-shi Kyōiku-shi.* Vol. 1. Kyoto: Nihon Shashin Insatsu K. K.
Konaka Yotaro.
1974 *Nadakō: Insaido Repōto.* Tokyo: Sankei Shimbunsha Shuppankai.
Kōseishō [Ministry of Welfare].
1974 *Kōsei Hakushō, 1974.* Tokyo: Okurashō Insatsu-Kyoku.
1978 *Kōsei Hakushō, 1977.* Tokyo: Okurashō Insatsu-Kyoku.
Kurowa Ryochi.
1978 *Nyūgaku Shiken.* Tokyo: Nihon Keizai Shinbunsha.
Kyōgakusha, ed.
1974 *Kobe Iidaigaku, '75: Mondai to Kaito.* Tokyo: Kyōgakusha.
Kyōiku Gyōsei Shiryō Chōsakai, ed.
1975 *Kyōiku Gyōsei no Genjo.* Tokyo: Gyōsei Shiryo Chōsai kai.
Mainichi Shimbunsha, ed.
1977 *Ima Gakkō de.* Vol. 6. Tokyo: Mainichi Shimbunsha.
Mainichi Shimbun Shakaibu.
1977 *Ranjuku Jidai: Gakushū Juku Repōto.* Tokyo: Simul Shuppankai.

Matsuoka Ei.
    1977  "Ranjuku Jidai to Kyōiku Tokkotai." *Sundei Mainichi.* April 3,
            1977.
Miura Shūmon.
    1982  "Daiseiko no Nihon Kyōiku." Chūō Kōron 4:72−79.
Mombushō [Ministry of Education].
    1976  *Waga Kuni no Kyōiku Suijun, 1975.* Tokyo: Okurashō Insatsu-
            Kyoku.
    1977  *Zenkoku Gakushū Juku no Toi no Jittai.* Tokyo: Mombudaijin,
            Tokei Kenkyūka.
    1981  *Waga Kuni no Kyōiku Suijun: 1980.* Tokyo: Okurashō Insatsu-
            Kyoku.
Naito Ryū.
    1974  "Gendai Kōkōsei no Seiishiki to Seitaiken." *Gendai Esupuri*
            86:169−179.
Nihon Hōsō Kyōkai.
    1975  *Nihonjin no Iishiki.* Tokyo: Shiseido.
Nihon Kyōsantō.
    1974  *Nihon Kyōsantō no Daigaku Seisaku.* Tokyo: Nihon Kyōsantō
            Chūōiinkai Shuppan-Kyoku.
    1977  *Kyōiku Kaikaku e no Teigon.* Tokyo: Akahata.
Oishi Yūji.
    1975  "Gakureki shakai." In *Gendai Kyōiku no Shindan,* ed. Kaoru
            Ohashi and Takeshi Yamamura, pp. 205−232. Tokyo: University of
            Tokyo Press.
Rōdoshō [Ministry of Labor].
    1978  *Rōdō Hakushō.* Tokyo: Okurashō Insatsu Kyoku.
Shimizu Kitaro
    1974  "Sengo no Kyōiku ni tsuite." *Chūō Kōron* 11:70−92.
Sōrifu, Seishonen Taisaku Honbu [Prime Minister's Office, Youth Policy
Office], ed.
    1977  *Showa 52 Seishonen Hakushō.* Tokyo: Okurashō Insatsu-Kyoku.
    1979  *Seishonen Hakushō: Showa 54.* Tokyo: Okurashō Insatsu-Kyoku.
Sōrifu, Tokeī Kyoku [Prime Minister's Office, Statistical Section].
    1974  *Nihon no Tokei.* Tokyo: Okurashō Insatsu-Kyoku.
Takasugi Shingo.
    1979  *Jukenkō Tsurareru Shindō.* Tokyo: Gakuyo Shobo.
Tamura Kenji.
    1974  "Teineijya no Kekkon." *Gendai Esupuri* 86:180−187.
Toita Tomoyoshi.
    1975  *Kyūsei Kōtōgakkō Kyōiku no Seiritsu.* Kyoto: Minerubia Shōbo.
Tominaga Kenichi and Ando Bunshiro.
    1977  "Kaisotekichii Keiseikatei no bunseki." *Gendai Shakaigaku*
            8:3−58.

Tsuda Masumi.
  1977  *Nippon-teki Keiei no Riron.* Tokyo: Chūokeizaisha.
Ushiogi Morikazu.
  1975  "Shinro kettei katei no path kaiseki." *Kyōikushakaigaku Kenkyū*
     30:75–86.
  1976a "Kōtōkyōiku no kaisoteki kaihōsei." *Daigaku Ronshū* 4:1–16.
  1976b "Keizaihendō, shokugyokōzō no hendō to kōtōkyōiku." *Shakai-
     gaku Hyōron* 26:4:40–59.
  1978  *Gakureki Shakai no Tenkan.* Tokyo: University of Tokyo Press.
Wagatsuma Hiroshi.
  1973  *Hikōshonen no Jirei Kenkyū.* Tokyo: Seishin Shōbo.
Zenkoku Shinro Shidō Kenkyūkai, ed.
  1973  *Nyūshiki Shiken: Nyūshiki Seido no Honshitsu to Kaikaku e no
     Torikumi.* Tokyo: Minshusha.

# Index

Designer: Eric Jungerman
Compositor: G & S Typesetters, Inc.
Printer: Vail-Ballou Press
Binder: Vail-Ballou Press
Text: 10/13 Trump Medieval
Display: Friz Quadrata Bold